To Richard,

Many thanks,

From,

Gary + Carol 2007

The Reign of
KING HENRY

The Reign of
KING HENRY

How Graham Henry transformed the All Blacks

GREGOR PAUL

EXISLE
PUBLISHING

First published 2007

Exisle Publishing Limited,
P.O. Box 60-490, Titirangi, Auckland 0642.
www.exislepublishing.com

National Library of New Zealand Cataloguing-in-Publication Data

Paul, Gregor, 1972-
The reign of King Henry : how Graham Henry transformed the
All Blacks / Gregor Paul. 1st ed.
ISBN 978-0-908988-77-8
1. Henry, Graham. 2. All Blacks (Rugby team) 3. Rugby football
coaches–New Zealand. 4. Rugby Union football–New Zealand.
I. Title.
796.333092—dc 22

Text design and production by *BookNZ*
Cover design by Nick Turzynski, redinc., Auckland
Printed in China through Colorcraft Limited, Hong Kong

Contents

Acknowledgements

AS ALWAYS, plenty of people have gone above and beyond the call of duty to make this book possible. Top of the list is Suburban Newspapers who generously supplied photographs and were a pleasure to deal with. Rob Nichol, the head of the New Zealand Rugby Players Association, gave generously of his time and was enormously helpful, as was John Mayhew, the former All Black doctor. Professor Will Hopkins at Auckland University of Technology and Ken Quarrie from the New Zealand Rugby Union were kind enough to let me read their superb research paper before it was published and for that I extend my sincere thanks.

There were plenty of others, too, who supplied insightful analysis but for various reasons wouldn't be keen to see their names appear in print.

And finally, thank you to Fiona, Mackenzie and Isla for your love, support and encouragement.

Introduction

THE ALL BLACKS did things a certain way for 100 years. Then Graham Henry came along and changed everything. As with all instigators of change, opinion is divided as to whether he is a revolutionary or a destroyer of traditions that should have been left alone. The All Blacks' achievements since his appointment in December 2003 point emphatically to the former – that he is a visionary who has created a new mould for his successors to follow. He has been bold where previous All Black coaches have been timid. He has been inclusive where some of his predecessors have been exclusive and he has been flexible where others have been rigid. As a consequence, his coaching record stands comparison with all those who have gone before and will almost certainly stand comparison with all those who succeed him.

But his reign has been about so much more than statistics. He has healed the chronic psychological frailty that had become endemic in New Zealand rugby since the All Blacks lost five consecutive games in 1998. He recognised that many young men who made it to the test arena were desperately lacking in the most basic leadership skills, which left them hopelessly equipped to make decisions under pressure. He recognised that the increased physicality and athleticism of the sport had shifted off the scale and the players were being pushed beyond breaking point by administrators hell-bent on stuffing more fixtures into an already bulging calendar. Coming to those realisations didn't mark Henry as extraordinary. Leadership and player burn-out had been prominent themes in New Zealand rugby for much of the modern era. Where Henry has differed from his peers has been in his determination and ability to find solutions to these problems.

At Ellis Park on 14 August 2004 he watched his All Black side capitulate when they were put under pressure. It left him with a choice; he could continue to do things the way they had always been done or he could follow a different path. The former held little appeal – his conclusion was that doing the same old things would lead to the same old results. So the decision was made to instigate dramatic changes.

Fortunately for Henry his time at the helm has coincided with that of another revolutionary – New Zealand Rugby Union chief executive Chris Moller. After a turbulent few years for the NZRU in which they lost the 2003 World Cup co-hosting rights and most of their board, Moller was appointed in December 2002 with a brief to transform the organisation into a sleeker, corporate entity. This has resulted in some major changes on the domestic scene, with Moller also a protagonist in driving change in the sport globally.

That executive support has been critical, for it has allowed Henry to become the first All Black coach in the modern era to devise a long-term strategy to win the World Cup. John Hart, Wayne Smith and John Mitchell before him all had to plan from campaign to campaign or at best they could plan an entire season. Henry, though, has been allowed to take one eye off the present and focus on the future. Since 2005, he has consistently argued that picking the best 22 players for each test was a recipe for long-term disaster. The injury toll would be horrific and New Zealand would never develop strength in depth. And without depth, the All Blacks would come unstuck at the 2007 World Cup as they had in 1991, 1995, 1999 and 2003. No other All Black coach has been indulged in this way. No other All Black coach has ever been granted permission to withdraw the bulk of his likely World Cup squad from the first seven rounds of the Super 14.

The NZRU have taken big risks, but Henry has provided them with big rewards. His selection policy put him on a collision course with the traditionalists who felt he turned the All Blacks into a finishing school for promising talent. Henry has dodged the bullets though, because the All Blacks kept winning. It became hard to criticise him for continually making experimental selections when the All Blacks, even with what most followers would view as a second-string side, were beating old foes rather handsomely.

And by November 2006, he'd won over even his most ardent critics. That's when his selection strategy came to fruition. When the All Blacks hammered France – the number two ranked side in the world – 47-3 in Lyon on 11 November, New Zealand's rugby public finally made sense of the last three years. That's when it became indisputable that the All Blacks had 30 genuine test players. They romped through Europe with the selectors able to mix and match their options as the fancy took them. It was rugby's equivalent of the 'shock and awe' tactics used by the Americans in Iraq. It was indisputable that the All Blacks were the best side in the world and few doubted the All Blacks were also the second best side in the world.

What unfolds in these pages is the story of how New Zealand rugby climbed out of the dark hole in which it found itself in the aftermath of the 2003 World Cup. This book is an attempt to piece together how Henry led the All Black cultural revolution and re-established an aura of invincibility that was in danger of being lost forever.

1   Dead man walking

AS THE ball soared through the Sydney sky, never once threatening to budge from its intended destination on account of the purity of the strike, rugby at last had a JFK moment. With an astonishing lack of concern for the occasion, England's Jonny Wilkinson dropped the mother of all goals to end 119 minutes of a titanic World Cup final. The wet leather glistened like a bloated fish under the floodlights as it bisected the posts and nudged England to an unassailable 20-17 lead.

The estimated 40,000 Englishmen at Telstra Stadium on 22 November 2003 brayed as one in a deafening roar that was emulated by their countrymen around the world. The pin-up boy of English rugby had forever established that he was more than just a pretty face. Not since Geoff Hurst hit an equally pure strike at Wembley 37 years earlier had England released their jubilation in such a spontaneous explosion.

The English had endured plenty of hardship in the intervening years. Not only had they been starved of glory, there had been spectacular failures on every front. The English cricket team had never strayed far from embarrassment. The odd snatched win could never make up for the ritual humiliation of the biennial Ashes series. The football team had, on occasion, shown promise. That only made things worse, for it had the effect of building hopes higher, making the inevitable tumble all the more painful. At the 1986 World Cup, England had to watch in disbelief as Argentina's Diego Maradona punched the ball into the net in an act that was seen by 4.9 billion people, but strangely, and indeed quite crucially, not by Ali Bennaceur, the man overseeing their quarter-final clash. In 1990 England encountered another old foe. This time, though, their dreams were crippled not by the industry and efficiency of the Germans, but by England's uncelebrated talent for finding the self-destruct button. A penalty shoot-out ended with Chris Waddle, one of the most talented players of his generation, ballooning the ball almost as high as Wilkinson did 13 years later.

There were plenty of other times, though, when England just fell over without ever managing to make any headway on the ascent. Things were so desperate in 1994 that manager Graham Taylor was portrayed as a turnip on the front page of *The Sun* – the paper of choice for the football yobbo.

More than warm beer or jellied eels, England wanted world champions. So when Wilkinson proved that his feet had been kissed by angels, he released the cork on 37 years of emotion. With one languid swing of his right leg, he sent a nation tumbling out of the boozer towards Trafalgar Square. It was there that every Rupert, Giles and Jamie, resplendent in their cream chinos and Hackett shirts – the regulation kit of England's rugby followers – could claim their stake in sporting history. It was at Trafalgar Square that they could dance in the shadow of their heroes and not care how silly they looked. It was there, breathing the same air as Wilkinson, Martin Johnson and Clive Woodward, that they could sing 'Rule Britannia' and really mean it. England had waited what seemed like forever for this moment. The team were supposedly too old. They were supposedly too slow and predictable. Wilkinson's genius said otherwise and there, in pride of place, safe in the giant mitts of Johnson, was the William Webb Ellis trophy to prove it.

Winning the World Cup meant so much to England. The night of 22 November 2003 was very special. And as the thousands of rugby disciples flooded into central London, already they were asking each other where they were when they saw the kick from heaven.

But while England rejoiced, a nation of four million souls felt as if their hearts were being danced on. England had invented the game but they had long ceased to be the custodians of it. New Zealand was the spiritual home of rugby. Pretty much as long as anyone could remember, the black shirt was the one every nation feared and respected. It was New Zealand that had been the standard-bearer ever since they had toured the UK in 1905. It was New Zealand that had won more tests than any other country. It was New Zealand that had won 17 tests between 1965 and 1969 and who then went undefeated for 25 tests between 1987 and 1990. It was New Zealand that had produced Colin Meads, Michael Jones, Christian Cullen and Jonah Lomu. It was New Zealand that had come up with the idea of having the World Cup. It was New Zealand that had won the first World Cup.

22 November 2003 was supposed to be an illustrious addition to the already bulging annals of New Zealand rugby. But just as they had in 1999, the All Blacks came into a World Cup as favourites, only to crumble in the semi-final. Wilkinson had not provided New Zealand's defining moment of the World Cup. That had come seven days earlier on the same ground against the same opponents when, almost as if in slow motion, Australia's Stirling Mortlock huffed and puffed his way up the deserted field. He had snaffled an interception and his try after eight minutes rocked the All Blacks so hard that they stopped believing in themselves. No one had the guile or standing to reassert the side's authority and they wilted as meekly as spinach against a side they had scored 50 points against only four months earlier.

The scars of 1999, when New Zealand had lost to a French side that had previously looked as if they couldn't beat an egg, had barely healed. After that event, Massey University had felt the need to offer students grief counselling. All Black halfback Justin Marshall returned home to find baggage handlers at Auckland Airport had scrawled 'loser' on his luggage. The nation was angry. How could people turn up to work on Monday and feel good about themselves after the All Blacks had been humiliated? The agony of defeat was never supposed to have been felt. Someone had to pay. That someone was coach John Hart. He was vilified beyond reason. Perspective went missing and an indecent number of people took the loss personally as if it in some way reflected badly on them. As thick as his skin had become, Hart couldn't block out the tidal wave of hatred and he feared he would drown in the volumes of poison. He fell on his sword almost immediately.

The capitulation on 15 November 2003 brought all the emotion of 1999 back to the surface. There were too many similarities. The All Blacks were favourites as they had been four years earlier. They were playing against a team that had folded like a bad poker hand in the two Bledisloe Cup encounters that year, just as France had been awful when they had come to New Zealand a few months before the 1999 event. What did it matter that Australia were the hosts? They had nothing beyond numerical support in the stadium with which to scare New Zealand. Complacency couldn't be a factor either because the All Blacks had learned the folly of underestimating opponents in semi-finals.

It was all too much, then, when Australia were the side showing the initiative and thinking their way through problems. They had sussed that New Zealand only had a couple of ball-carriers in the forwards and one real playmaker in the backs. Close them down and the Australians didn't reckon there was much else. They were right. New Zealand were exposed as lacking leadership on the field.

It proved to be every bit as painful as the crash at Twickenham four years earlier. The nation once again succumbed to that introspective theorising that wasn't looking for answers so much as hoping to find someone to blame. But by now, everyone knew that it would be easier to cut straight to the chase and get on with blaming the coach. Even the New Zealand Rugby Union saw it that way and they weren't prepared to wait and see if John Mitchell would fall on his sword. They thought it would be best to take no chances and give Mitchell a gentle shove.

Dressed in their black suits, NZRU chairman Jock Hobbs and chief executive Chris Moller looked like a couple of Mafia bosses as they fronted the media on 21 November in Sydney. They did nothing to change that impression when Hobbs announced that the post of All Black coach was going to be advertised. It was only six days after the loss to Australia – the corpse, so to speak, was still warm. It was a stunning vote of no confidence in a coach whose All Black side had only lost four games during his two-year watch. To the outside world, it looked as if New Zealand had gone stark raving mad. Here was Mitchell, a young, talented coach being given the boot because of one loss. It had to be a crazy move, a decision that had been made when emotions were still high. Maybe the NZRU needed to get some distance from events. No one heals like the hands of Father Time, and with space might have come perspective.

The union were closing their minds to the possibility that a chastening experience is often the necessary catalyst to spark a legendary coaching career. The essence of good coaching, after all, is to learn from one's mistakes. Look at Clive Woodward, the man under whom Mitchell served between 1997 and 2000 as England's forwards coach. Woodward had come into the job as young and as inexperienced as Mitchell. He made mistakes. England couldn't close the deal either – they became the ultimate tease, always threatening to go all the way but ultimately lacking the belief that they really felt comfortable doing it.

In 1999 only Wales stood between England and a treasured Grand Slam. With a few minutes left on the clock and a six-point lead, Woodward's boys thought the job was done. Until, that is, Welsh centre Scott Gibbs was somehow allowed to smash his way through a legion of white jerseys to pull off the unthinkable. In 2000 England came to Murrayfield to play a previously winless and hapless Scotland side. A win would secure the Grand Slam. The game was played in brutally cold rain that was being driven by one of Edinburgh's famous lazy winds – so called because they choose to go through you rather than round you. England couldn't adapt to the conditions and Scotland pulled off one of those rare Braveheart-style wins. A year later and England faced Ireland on the final day of the Six Nations with, for the third year in succession, the Grand Slam beckoning. Once again though, England couldn't nail the performance in the face of a feisty Irish pack. By 2001 it was apparent that England had a problem. They couldn't deliver on the big occasions.

Yet there was never any question that Woodward would survive. His employers were sure the stinging pain of those various defeats and the humiliation that came with them would make him a better coach. They felt that the greater his experience, the better his chances of one day getting it right. Woodward himself says that had it not been for the agony inflicted by Gibbs and the shame of Murrayfield and Lansdowne Road, both he and his troops might have lacked the mental fortitude to triumph in the World Cup final. Woodward had been given a long rope and although he had come damned near to hanging himself on several occasions, he survived to deliver the only trophy that mattered and earn himself a knighthood.

Such patience, however, was not going to be shown by the NZRU. The All Black legacy was far greater than England's. Crucial defeats couldn't be tolerated in New Zealand the way they were in England. There were almost 100 years of history serving as categorical evidence the All Blacks did not rate losing as a habit they fancied developing. The weight of expectation also prohibited leniency. New Zealand's continued failure to win the World Cup sat like the ugliest boil on rugby's prom queen and Mitchell was partly paying the price for the failures of those who had gone before. Modern rugby had drifted into a four-year cycle around the World Cup. The World Cup dictated the tenure of coaching appointments and players were picked with the World

Cup in mind. The World Cup was the only occasion when teams from both hemispheres peaked at the same time. It was nice to win the Six Nations or Tri Nations or come home undefeated from an end-of-season tour. But really, the World Cup was the only tournament that carried indisputable prestige.

That's why no one cared on 15 November 2003 that New Zealand had a few months earlier won the Tri Nations and the Bledisloe Cup. The only thing that New Zealanders really cared about was that the All Blacks had once again failed to capture the ultimate prize. They failed as they had in 1999, 1995 and 1991. By the time of the next tournament, it would be 20 years since the All Blacks had been able to call themselves world champions. That was a long time between drinks.

Such a weight of expectation was a heavy burden for Mitchell to bear, but that was the job. All Black coaches are hired to win and there was never any secret that Mitchell would be in the soup if he returned from Australia without the trophy in tow. It was a soup he could possibly have struggled out of if he could have convinced his bosses that he had nailed both his selections and strategy at the tournament. But the instant Tana Umaga collided with Carlos Spencer after 23 minutes of the All Blacks' first game against Italy, it was going to be a hard sell.

Umaga suffered a tear to his posterior cruciate. It was an unusual injury, the rupturing of the anterior cruciate being more common. Umaga's knee was swollen and painful but the prognosis was not as bleak as his grimacing face suggested as he was carried from the field. He wouldn't need surgery and he would be able to resume light training once the initial swelling came down. There was a chance he could regain full fitness before the knockout rounds, and as long as there was a chance, Mitchell wanted Umaga to stay in Australia. The 30-year-old was the best defensive centre in the business and a powerful presence in the midfield. The problem for Mitchell, though, was that he needed to find someone to hold the fort while Umaga was on the sidelines. And that turned out to be a tougher quest than anyone had ever imagined.

Ma'a Nonu had been taken to Australia as Umaga's understudy. Nonu was big, strong and powerful. He looked eerily like Umaga but the physical resemblance was where the similarities ended. Nonu just didn't have the same poise or instincts. That was understandable: he didn't have the same depth of experience. There was promise, for sure, but the diamond was just a little too rough. Nonu was the heir apparent coming into the tournament, but after a clumsy showing against

Canada in the All Blacks' second game where his defensive naivety was exposed, Mitchell decided someone else would be given the opportunity to stake a claim to Umaga's throne. Leon MacDonald, a regular fullback, was given a chance at centre and he pretty much took it, giving a gutsy display against Tonga and also kicking 12 out of 12 goals. MacDonald then got pass-marks in the crucial final pool game against Wales and was then rarely involved in a forward-dominated quarter-final against South Africa. Problem solved, then. MacDonald was the main man – a utility player capable of doing a job at No 13.

Australian coach Eddie Jones saw things a little differently. He saw MacDonald as a potential weakness and instructed the bruising Mortlock to hurtle into the All Black midfield. It was a smart ploy. The All Blacks creaked and leaked in that crucial channel and time and time again Mortlock made the big yards. It enabled the Wallabies to build momentum and suck the confidence out of a side that was suddenly realising the ante had been upped from the week before. Little blame could be heaped on MacDonald. He had simply done what he had been asked and had tried to do it as well as he could. But it was too big an ask. Centre is a tough defensive nut to crack. It took Umaga years to learn his craft. MacDonald had been given just a few tests before having to play in a World Cup semi-final.

If he chose to re-apply for his job, Mitchell would inevitably be quizzed on the lack of cover he had for Umaga. If there was not enough faith in Nonu to pick him, why was he at the World Cup? What was the rationale for choosing a utility back ahead of a specialist centre? These were legitimate questions as the selection of MacDonald had a critical bearing on the outcome of the semi-final. Perhaps the toughest challenge awaiting Mitchell though, was to explain why MacDonald was preferred not only ahead of Nonu, but also of Umaga, who had in fact been declared fit by team doctor John Mayhew.

Mayhew knew the reasons why Mitchell had shied away from selecting Umaga, but he always wondered whether there was more to it – whether there was a private view of Umaga that was not being shared with the wider management group. As Mayhew recalls: 'Tana had a scan within two hours of the game and we immediately knew what the injury was. Initially his knee was a bit sore and swollen and he was having physiotherapy. In the weeks leading up to the quarter-final he had been running for a couple of weeks, at pace and changing direction.

'The decision not to play him was on advice not so much from the medical team but from the trainer [Mike Anthony] saying, "I don't think he is quite sharp enough". My position was that we were in a situation that the only way to know whether he was any good was to go out there and see if he could do what he was expected to do. The concern with any player is that they lose a bit of their sharpness. But you have got to come back at some stage. We even thought about sending him home for an NPC game but the rules didn't allow us to do that. I believe that Tana should have been playing about quarter-final time, at least give him a chance – we had nothing to lose. Mike might have been right – I am not portraying Mike as a bad guy, he was an excellent trainer – but he was concerned whether Tana was sharp enough. That was always going to be the $64,000 question, we just never knew. But the bench was always going to be strong enough and we always had enough cover that we could put him on and if he was no good then we could take him off. They didn't want to risk that, though. By the time the semi-finals came around, they were not going to try him for the first time in that.'

There was justification for not selecting Umaga. Mitchell just couldn't be sure the player was going to be able to operate at full capacity. That was the advice from Anthony, an experienced and knowledgeable trainer, and Mayhew in essence agreed. The difference, though, was that Mayhew argued there were grounds to take the risk and find out for sure. What seems a little strange about Mitchell's reluctance is that he had not previously shown himself to be risk averse. He was brave enough to leave 21 senior players at home when the All Blacks toured England, France and Wales at the end of 2002. He backed promising talent such as Dan Carter, Mils Muliaina and Joe Rokocoko when others might have worried whether it was too soon to give them test jerseys. And, according to Mayhew, Mitchell made a big call in taking Ali Williams to the World Cup.

Williams had a stress fracture in his foot a couple of weeks out from the tournament. The injury was serious and prevented the big lock from training. The clock was ticking and Mitchell didn't want to go to Australia with a player he couldn't be sure was going to be fit. It would be best practice to make a call before the squad left New Zealand and that way, if Williams was ruled out, there would be less disruption and the replacement player would have longer to bed in. 'We got a screw put in Ali's foot and we were using new drugs – we really went to the nth degree,' says Mayhew. 'The physio was saying, "I don't think he is going to be right". After that, I can remember John saying to me, "I want a categorical decision whether Ali is going to be right before we go." When it came to the meeting the next week I said, "Yes, he's good to go." John asked if I wanted to discuss it, I said no. The physio said he was not sure and I said, "No, if you want an answer from me he's fit to go." That was a high-risk decision, much more high-risk than playing Tana.'

It didn't stack up. Umaga was perceived by most rugby aficionados as the glue that held the backline together. He was a class act, a player who during his 30 years had turned from finisher to creator. Capable of using his strength to bust holes and his guile to find them, Umaga was arguably the one player the whole country did not want to see injured. If anyone was worth a risk, it was Umaga. And it really wasn't that big a risk. Umaga was not in danger of inflicting long-term damage to his knee by playing. The only danger was that he would not feel quite right at top speed or changing direction. Anthony was right to air his concerns. Test football is not the place to field players who are not 100 percent. But, according to Mayhew, Umaga's work in training suggested any reduction in performance was only going to be minimal and might only be temporary as he felt his way back into test football. There was cover across the backline to start Umaga against Wales in the final pool game and stack the bench in case he was struggling. It was a classic case of a faint heart and all that. It surely had to be better not to die wondering what Umaga would have been able to do. Unless, that is, Mitchell and his selection team of Mark Shaw and Kieran Crowley were viewing the world through glasses that were not Tana-tinted.

'To this day I don't know whether they really didn't want to play him,' says Mayhew. 'About two or three years earlier Tana was going to pull out of the All Blacks. Mark Robinson was being selected ahead of him and he perceived Robbie Deans [All Black assistant coach] didn't rate him as a player. I can remember when we were in Hanmer Springs we had a training camp there in the middle of a Tri Nations. He came to me and I said, "Tana, if you want to get out, I'll pull an injury and you can have a couple of weeks out of the environment and do that rather than pull out."

'We talked it through and talked it through and he decided to carry on. I think he was a bit wary of Robbie. Maybe they wanted to have Leon there because of his goal-kicking. Mitch and Robbie were definitely worried about goal-kicking at the World Cup.'

Suspicion will always dog the 2003 World Cup campaign. There will always be theories, rumours and speculation as to what was really going on behind closed doors. But the evidence is strong that the only thing the All Blacks were struck down by was a dose of bad luck and a couple of judgement calls that didn't come off.

It was bad luck that Umaga picked up an injury and it was really bad luck that the supremely talented Daniel Carter was also hampered by a nagging knee complaint at the same time. If Carter had been fully fit for the knock-out rounds he might have found himself in the No 12 jersey with Umaga outside him in 13. Carter was a quality goal-kicker. Without Carter, the kicking duties would have to be handled by Spencer. For all his undoubted genius, Spencer never looked comfortable with the responsibility of goal-kicking, a point which Mayhew says the coaching team duly acknowledged.

The options, then, for the knock-out rounds were limited. Aaron Mauger only returned from injury to play his first game at second-five against Wales. To have brought Mauger, who was short of match fitness, and Umaga back together for that final pool game would have been high risk. It would have left the All Black midfield with two players short of sharpness and heaped the pressure on Spencer not only to orchestrate the offensive threat but also to handle the pressure of kicking for goal. When Mauger and MacDonald combined nicely against Wales and the latter kicked well enough, it's easy to see how Mitchell judged it best to stick with that pairing. The team needed consistency of personnel in the knock-out rounds.

MacDonald was being asked to play an alien role so the more confidence he could build the better. Then there was the risk/reward equation with Umaga. The reward of playing against South Africa was that Mitchell would find out for sure whether Umaga was fit, and if he was, then the All Blacks would have their defensive rock back in the midfield. On the risk side, though, was the fact he had not played for a few weeks so would have lost a yard of sharpness. The injury might have taken another yard off that too. He'd have to settle into his combination with Mauger, who himself was only just finding his feet again. Most crucially, the introduction of Umaga would put the goal-kicking burden back on Spencer. What if Umaga played the quarter-final and his knee packed up again? By the end of that calculation, there was a convincing case to be made for retaining MacDonald.

Mitchell made a judgement call. That is what coaches are paid to do and in professional sport the line between hero and villain is very fine. Who knows, Mitchell could have selected Umaga for the semi-final, endured the same outcome and then faced a barrage of questions as to why he'd fielded a player who was not quite 100 percent. Deans, who had no selection role with the All Blacks, has proven himself to be an outstanding coach, leading the Crusaders to three Super Ruby titles and two other final appearances. He hasn't made any decision on a whim and his reputation has been forged on his ability to make objective, non-emotional decisions. If he offered any advice, it would have been after careful assessment of all the possibilities.

Sometimes, though, life is just plain unfair. Up until the semi-final Mitchell had delivered astonishingly good results. He'd selected bravely and astutely for most of his tenure and there were times when his side played seriously good rugby. In July and August the All Blacks were on fire. The players were buzzing. They were in that perfect zone of being match-hardened, supremely fit and on top of their individual and collective skills. If the World Cup had been played then, the All Blacks probably would have won.

But it was played in October and by then they had crept to the edge of that zone. That made them vulnerable. Mitchell's bravery in selection came at a cost. His preference was for talent ahead of solidity. It was spectacular when it all clicked, but his team was full of young men who lacked experience and leadership. No one noticed in July when they put 50 points on the Boks and Wallabies in consecutive weeks. By November, though, when the pressure had been raised and some of the zip taken out of the All Blacks, the lack of seasoned war-horses became an issue.

When he had to explain to his employers why the side was short of leadership, he could argue that maybe he had underestimated the importance of experience in 2003, but if retained, he could eradicate the problem. Chris Jack, Richie McCaw, Mauger, Carter, Doug Howlett, Ali Williams, Jerry Collins, Joe Rokocoko and Mils Muliaina were all in their early 20s. These players were already world class and by 2007 they would be four years wiser. When they quizzed him about the perceived lack of depth in the squad, he could remind the review panel that he was unexpectedly appointed in September 2001. He had barely six weeks to pick his first squad and by the time he got back from his first All Black assignment, he had about 20 months before the World Cup. Then there was the fact he was contracted until December 2003. He had to win games to retain his job and he might suggest he had few opportunities to experiment with his selections. The pressure was always intense to focus on the now and never think ahead. And finally, if his assertion that the team were close to physical and mental burn-out was deemed his fault, he could remind the review panel he had actively tried to manage the workloads of his best players by resting the bulk of his World Cup squad for the 2002 end-of-year tour.

Yet when Hobbs and Moller sat down to announce that Mitchell's job would be up for grabs, there was no mention of the coach having not equipped himself on the field. It had been his work, or lack of it, off the field that had the Mafia bosses wearing their grim faces.

As Mitchell and Deans ran past the main lodge of the Terrace Downs Golf Resort near Methven in late September 2003, they were in full view of the assembled guests, who happened to be All Black sponsors and NZRU officials. The All Blacks were in the South Island for their last pre-World Cup camp. These camps had been held around the country and were the perfect opportunity to bring the team closer to their supporters and sponsors and generate that warm fuzzy feeling before they headed to Australia. But the sight of the All Black coach and his assistant pounding over the golf course probably brought a sour taste to the sherry.

Mitchell and Deans were very much invited to the gathering but according to Mayhew, had told All Black manager Tony Thorpe earlier that morning they would be unable to attend. The All Black coaches said they had another meeting. But that meeting appeared to be nothing more important than an early evening constitutional.

'We used to have a management meeting every morning. At that, Mitch and Robbie said to Tony Thorpe they couldn't make it to these drinks and dinner that had been planned with the board and sponsors,' says Mayhew. 'We were in Methven and we thought what could they be doing – you can't ski in the dark. We thought it might have been something important that we didn't know about. We were all on the balcony having a beer and there were Mitch and Robbie running round the golf course. Everyone saw it.'

Mitchell and Deans did show up later, but the fact they had earlier sauntered past the assembled guests could have been interpreted as a direct snub to the NZRU and their various sponsors. It appeared to some as if Mitchell was saying he wouldn't be told what to do. He would follow his own agenda and turn up at a time that was convenient to him. It was as if he was operating outside the jurisdiction of the board or was at least unafraid of any recriminations. Or possibly the late arrival was symptomatic of what had become a strained relationship between the All Black coach and the NZRU board.

Moller, as a man immersed in the corporate entity, spoke in terms that suggested he wanted the All Black coach to think of himself as the chief executive of the playing division. Obviously that meant the coach would be responsible for team selection and performance. But the team didn't exist in isolation. There was a massive support network providing for the All Blacks' every whim. There were external backers who had made serious investments in the brand and who were looking to get value for money. There were hundreds and thousands of fans backing the team too, reliant on various media to keep them informed of All Black developments. The All Blacks were about a lot more than just the 22 players selected for match day.

The All Black coach couldn't be oblivious to these connecting threads. The whole network had to be acknowledged and the various relationships that underpinned the fabric of the national team had to be worked at. The flesh had to be pressed. The All Black coach needed to front the brand. There was an expectation he would show for a few corporate dinners, sling out a few pithy anecdotes, pose for a few photos and offer just the faintest insight into the team. The expectations were not onerous – they were in line with the demands placed on senior managers in other, similar-sized organisations.

The media too, in all its various guises, had to be adequately serviced. Television, radio and newspapers were, after all, the conduit to the public. The people who put their hands in their pockets to buy merchandise and match tickets had a right to be informed. They were doing their bit in oiling the wheels of the All Black machinery and deserved to know a little bit about selections and the personalities in the team. Moller and the rest of the NZRU board respected that Mitchell's main priority was to deliver results on the field. The peripheral duties, however, couldn't be ignored. They were part of the gig and it was vital the All Black coach gave the appearance of being accessible and committed to the external relationships.

But since taking the job in 2001, Mitchell's relationship with the media had been curious. A bright and normally articulate individual, Mitchell took to talking in jargon for much of his tenure. What appeared to be straightforward questions at the various pre- and post-match press conferences would often be answered in a manner that left no one particularly sure what had been said. There were also numerous occasions where Mitchell would use his stock response of, 'I'm not ready to share that,' when he was asked something he felt he didn't want to get into. Every international coach has the right to keep information on tactics and strategy out of the public domain, but Mitchell's threshold seemed to be set unusually low in that even the most innocuous probing had him unwilling to share an answer. That attitude wasn't letting the media down – it was failing the good people who supported the team. Ultimately it was those paying fans who were being snubbed and left none the wiser about life inside the camp. That Mitchell was often late for press conferences and inconvenienced reporters was not a major failing, but it was discourteous and hinted at a lack of respect for the fourth estate. It also created the suspicion that Mitchell had become a super-powerful figure who had burst his own management shackles.

Mitchell's first taste of international coaching came with England where he was the forwards coach working under Clive Woodward. Mitchell liked the fact that Woodward reported directly to the RFU chief executive, Francis Baron. Mitchell was keen to install a similar structure when he took the All Black job. But he inherited Andrew Martin, the former SAS Colonel who had been appointed All Black manager in 2000. Martin was seen as slightly unorthodox but no one doubted his work ethic, honesty and integrity. He earned a significant public profile as All Black manager during Wayne Smith's reign largely because Smith was happy for Martin to front the media and share that load. When Smith was ousted, the NZRU's chief executive at that time, David Rutherford, was keen to retain Martin. Mitchell was still young and relatively inexperienced and Martin, a seasoned campaigner, could be a useful sounding-board and sage influence.

But there was uneasiness on the part of Mitchell. He preferred the manager to be an organisational supremo who made the travel arrangements and catered for the various needs of the team. Tension between Mitchell and Martin was apparent from the earliest days. In Anton Oliver's autobiography, *Anton Oliver: Inside*, the All Black hooker reveals how on the end of season tour to Ireland, Scotland and Argentina in November 2001, the relationship between Mitchell and Martin was obviously not working well. At a team court session – an All Black ritual that required players to be administered drinking forfeits – Martin was singled out for some heavy booze intake. According to Oliver: 'He [Martin] was asked to consume a lot of beer, rapidly, and was soon in serious difficulty. I hated what was happening. Unbeknown to me, Martin had been sick, vomiting the night before, and suffering from diarrhoea as well. Everyone was being asked to drink far too much. Lots of boys were off their faces, but Mitchell and Deans did not move to intervene to prevent Martin's humiliation.'

Martin's report from that tour is understood to have contained some pointed criticism of the coaches. It was clearly a divided All Black management team, and when the NZRU board was broken up as a consequence of the Eichelbaum Report into the loss of the 2003 World Cup co-hosting rights, Mitchell saw his chance to strike. The All Black coach approached acting chief executive Steve Tew and detailed his concerns. The board were informed of these issues and on 12 October 2002 Martin's departure was announced. The official press release portrayed the departure as a consequence of the job description being changed. But Hobbs later said the decision had been forced on the board. 'We were effectively in a situation where we could make no other decision,' he said. 'The board was put into a position where it could make no other decision to have a functional All Black management team.' Under the new structure, Mitchell would report directly to the chief executive, and by January 2003 that was going to be Moller, a former Fonterra director, who had been appointed to replace Rutherford.

By January 2003, the key men who had put Mitchell at the helm of the All Blacks had all gone. There was no one fighting his corner in the board room. Rugby, just like every other corporate beast, is riddled with politics. Those in power need allies, not enemies, and by the start of the World Cup, Mitchell was in a precarious position. To be sure of keeping his job he really needed to win the World Cup and even then, Mayhew is not sure he would have been retained. Mayhew felt the relationship between Mitchell and Moller had disintegrated to the point where it was unsalvageable. He couldn't see how the two could ever resolve their issues because in his view, there was no mutual respect to form the basis of reconciliation.

'I could have seen a situation where the All Black coach won the World Cup and lost the job,' says Mayhew. 'You had the feeling the executive were waiting for him to fail. The issues were apparent 12 months out from the World Cup. Moller wasn't respected by the players and I don't think he was respected by John and Robbie. He was seen as ineffectual. At the World Cup after the first game, he had obviously had a bit to drink and he came into the changing room and one of the senior players said, "If that fuckwit is going to come in here at least he can come in here sober". The message got back.

'I don't think the executive ever liked Mitch. He got there by default. It was a huge mistake to get rid of Wayne Smith. I was having dinner with John Graham [NZRU president] a few months after and John said that Wayne's interview was the best he had ever heard in his life. Then in the afternoon he had some self-doubt and when John saw that, Wayne was out of there.'

On the day Hobbs and Moller announced that Mitchell would have to re-apply for his job, it certainly appeared as if the executive were out for the All Black coach's blood. Mitchell had been told about the plans after the All Blacks had beaten France on 20 November in the third/fourth place play-off game and, by all accounts, took the news pretty well. But the next day, he had just cause to feel more than a little dismayed and betrayed.

He possibly had the right to feel aggrieved that the board had acted before they had fully reviewed his performance. He definitely had the right to believe the announcement would be played straight, that Hobbs and Moller would simply let it be known that applications would be taken for the post and the position was contestable. Hobbs pretty much did just that when he said: 'If we had won the World Cup a review would have been undertaken which may have led to a contestable process but not necessarily so. We're not happy that we haven't won the World Cup and nor is John Mitchell. We're very disappointed. It was our number one priority for the year. The board made the decision that we would have a contestable process and provide John Mitchell, should he apply, with the opportunity to prove that he's the best person for the job.'

But then Moller waded in with the claim that Mitchell needed to 'lift the bar' in a number of areas. 'There is concern around areas of the media, the interface with the Rugby Union and some sponsor activity as well,' he said, adding that the off-field performance of a coach had grown in importance in recent years. 'Clearly there has to be an appropriate balance. It can't be one way to the exclusion of the other. But at the end of the day, the on-field performance is the crucial key performance indicator.'

On the basis of Moller's comments, Mitchell appeared to be a condemned man. And there was an unshakeable sense of injustice about that. There was also a whiff of amateurism about the way Mitchell was being treated.

If the board had been harbouring concerns about his activities, had they ever let him know prior to the public announcement? Mitchell was reporting directly to Moller. Presumably there had been opportunities for those issues to have been dealt with as they arose? The corporate world has an unwritten rule that the dirty washing never gets hung in public. If the market senses there is trouble at mill, share prices go tumbling. Personality clashes get dealt with behind closed doors. If an executive is failing to deliver, he's told over a decent lunch that things have to improve.

There was a sense from Moller's comments that the board had allowed Mitchell to take the rope almost in the hope he would hang himself. Sometimes relationships strain to the point where they can never be fixed. Sometimes it is better for everyone if there is a clean break and an organisation starts afresh with someone else. But whatever the board was thinking, Mitchell was entitled to a fair and transparent process. John Haigh, QC, an expert in employment law, is not sure that right was extended to the incumbent All Black coach.

'As I recollect, one of the main criticisms of Mitchell was his PR skills, that there was a lot of subterfuge and that he was secret in the way he operated,' remembers Haigh. 'The issue I became involved in was that his job was up for renewal and he had to re-apply. My concerns were that the NZRU's public statements appeared to destabilise the process. They were releasing information that indicated a preconceived view that he would not be reappointed. I thought in terms of employment law this was an error and unfair. This is a process that has developed over the last two years – requiring people to re-apply for their jobs. But to be fair to the NZRU this was a fixed contract and there was no undertaking that he would be re-employed. But there is still an obligation to maintain fairness. You have an existing employee, who may not have an absolute entitlement to a position, but the fact is he or she is entitled to a fair hearing dealt with on its merits. My initial view was that there were public statements that were being released to gear a situation where the prospects of him being reappointed were negligible.

'I had two phone calls with Mr Mitchell, but I was never formally briefed and I want to make that clear. There were a lot of people advising him but I don't think any of them were lawyers. I said if I could provide some left-of-field advice I would be happy to do it. It was never on a paying basis. There were intermediaries who were outraged at the way he was being treated. It seemed as if there was a systematic attempt by a variety of people to ensure he wasn't reselected. There was a strong feeling out there that he wasn't the right man for the future. In going into the selection process he was really behind the eight-ball. The prospects of him being reappointed were limited.

'I do a lot of this sort of stuff because I often advise employers. You go through the process, wink, wink, nod, nod, be objective on the face of it, but as often happens with a senior manager you get a scenario where it is not working and the company wants to get rid of them. You go about trying to get rid of them by getting legal advice, you try to make it look fair and the person is out of there. I am not saying that is what happened but the statements coming out made me think there was a lack of procedural fairness.'

Mitchell had not been at the press conference on 21 November. If he had been there, it would have been interesting to see whether anyone would have actually shouted 'dead man walking' when he entered the room.

2   The coronation

MAYBE JOHN MITCHELL knew it was futile, but within days of returning to New Zealand he made it apparent he was going to fight for his job. His employers had shown their hand. They had said the All Black coach had to have a friendlier face. They said the Cold War had to end. That was fine with Mitchell – he was going to start a new era of *glasnost*.

He wanted to keep his job. It was the biggest in world rugby and one bad night aside, he'd handled things pretty well. His record was excellent, and maybe if he showed some humility, displayed a willingness to conform, he could mount a compelling defence. He seemed genuinely surprised that his off-field work had been questioned. The media portrayal of him as arrogant and aloof was at odds with his self-image. He had been engrossed in the coaching side, and in launching a charm offensive at the end of November, perhaps he realised, too late, the importance of his peripheral responsibilities.

Mayhew feels that Mitchell was more naive than calculating in his thinking. The former All Black doctor believes that Mitchell, probably through a lack of experience, simply didn't realise the importance of fronting sponsors and media and maintaining a strong working relationship with the NZRU executive. As an example of Mitchell's naivety, Mayhew can recall a meeting he had in Wellington in early 2003 with Mitchell and team manager Tony Thorpe. 'We were having a meal together that night' says Mayhew. 'Tony went to bed early – about 10 p.m. Then John's PA Bridget [Hickman] came with her sister. She said, "Why don't we go down to Courtney Place to get a drink?" We were going to get in a taxi and I said to Mitch, "Do you think this is a good look for you? You are the All Black coach, getting into a taxi with two younger women." He said, "There is nothing going on." All it would need was the paparazzi there.'

Mayhew had been around the team for a few years and had some friends in the media. He was aware there were all sorts of rumours circulating about Mitchell. When Hickman was sent home from the World Cup after the pool stages, the fires were fuelled. But Mayhew is convinced there was no fire and the smoke was being created by others. 'It was quite simple. She [Hickman] was quite useful when we were in New Zealand, but when we were at the World Cup everything was organised for us and she didn't have a job to do. Basically she was at her wits' end as she had nothing to do. She was staying in the apartment next door to me at the World Cup. She got sent home as if there had been some sort of impropriety. I can categorically say nothing was going on. About a third of the nights she went out I went out, and if she was having an affair with anyone I don't know where she was doing it.'

There was clearly a huge amount of ground for Mitchell to make up on the public relations front, which is probably why he turned to his life coach, Tony Winn, to help him formulate strategies to reverse the tide. His first significant appearance came on 30 November when he let a camera crew from TV One's *Sunday* programme into his Hamilton house. They posed a number of thorny questions and Mitchell didn't flinch. Asked if he was arrogant, he suggested he was merely passionate about his job and apologised if anyone had mistaken him for being rude. The toughest ball to defend came when he was asked if it had been a kick in the teeth to hear Moller and Hobbs go public on his perceived failings. 'It was like my employer did not support me,' replied Mitchell. 'You have to take those kinds of things. Now I'm in a contestable process I have to prove to the panel I want to continue to coach the All Blacks.' It was an answer that was both honest and lined with humility. He'd revealed the hurt but also a readiness to put it behind him.

He would have tugged at a few more heartstrings when he then revealed that both his father-in-law and his wife had received anonymous phone calls claiming his marriage was over. At last we were getting a glimpse of the softer side of Mitchell – proof that he wasn't as aloof and detached as he was portrayed. He was a committed family man, loyal to his wife and devoted to his kids. If he had made a mistake at the World Cup, was it so hard to forgive him? The All Black job came with intolerable pressure. He had handled things his way. He had done what he thought was best for the team and there was no arguing with an 83 percent success rate.

If his way was at odds with his employers, he was showing a willingness to change, to bring himself back into line. There was a danger the NZRU were going to throw the baby out with the bath water. Mitchell was getting the hard bit right – he was building an enterprising and successful All Black team. There was a lot to be said for keeping him as coach with personnel around him to reduce his overall control and off-field duties.

To help make that point, Mitchell and Deans circulated a four-page press release on 1 December through the Christchurch-based PR company Word of Mouth Media NZ. The release listed the All Blacks' achievements in 2003 and statistics on the average age of English and Australian players in the 1999 and 2003 World Cups. It also detailed how many survived from 1999 and compared Mitchell's test record with Australia's Eddie Jones and Rod Macqueen and England's Clive Woodward. It was an attempt to win media coverage urging the NZRU to be patient. History had shown there was mileage to be gained by retaining coaches who had shown promise but made mistakes. Clearly the NZRU cared what the media thought, so if Mitchell could win the battle for hearts and minds and get column inches espousing the logic in reappointing him, it would add some real strength to his case.

But there isn't a lot of sympathy in the business of professional sport. Mitchell could be reappointed with stricter management controls. But probably the board wondered if that would really work. How long before they ran into the same old problems? Mitchell had made it clear he wanted to answer only to the top. Would he accept the arrival of a chaperone in the guise of a manager? To reappoint him on those terms was risky and the last thing New Zealand rugby needed was more turbulence.

The rot had to stop. The All Blacks had become a massive brand and they couldn't afford to be giving off any whiff of amateurism. They needed to be winning. They needed to be presenting a big smiley front to media, sponsors and fans. There needed to be unity throughout the organisation – from the coach down to the baggage handler and then beyond into the wider stratosphere of the Rugby Union. The team had to accept its wider responsibilities. The coach had to accept that his job extended beyond the white lines. He had to be accountable to the board, respect the hierarchy and conform.

There were obviously doubts about Mitchell's ability to come into line in that wider capacity, as expressed by Moller and Hobbs. That, as Haigh said, didn't bode well for Mitchell and nor did the fact there was a rival candidate waiting in the wings who was in possession of a mighty fine set of credentials.

'This opportunity has got me excited,' was Graham Henry's response to the *New Zealand Herald* when he was asked on 21 November about his interest in applying for the All Black job. 'I've just got to get the job now. It's something I've held dear for a long, long time and I'd love to do it.'

Henry probably didn't need to say he would love to do it. Every man and his dog knew this was the job 57-year-old Henry had coveted his entire coaching career. It was the one that had always got away though. Just as there were golfers who picked up the dreaded tag of being the best player never to win a major, Henry was arguably the best New Zealander never to coach the All Blacks.

In the 1990s he coached Auckland to four NPC titles and earned the top seat with the Auckland Blues franchise in 1996. His success continued and the Blues won the inaugural Super 12 and defended their crown in 1997, when they didn't drop a game. They made it through to the final in 1998 but lost to the Crusaders. Shortly after, Henry abruptly terminated his contract with the NZRU and took a job as head coach of Wales. He'd left primarily because he was desperate to coach at international level and couldn't see that his chance would come with the All Blacks.

When the NZRU extended John Hart's contract at the end of 1998 through to the next World Cup, Henry felt that was it. That was his window of opportunity lost. The Blues and Auckland were playing some of the best provincial football ever seen. Henry's star was shining brighter than it ever had. Maybe if he hung around until after the World Cup in 1999 his chance to coach the All Blacks would come up then. Few coaches had managed more than four years in charge of an international side. Surely, regardless of what happened in 1999, Hart would step aside or be pushed aside. The job would come up for grabs and Henry could mount his challenge. That was a big risk though. The Blues were an ageing side. They had already lost former All Black skipper Sean Fitzpatrick in the 1998 season and incumbent captain Zinzan Brooke was quitting too at the end of the year. Without those two leaders, both hugely experienced players, the Blues faced an uncertain future.

If Henry had stayed in New Zealand, his reputation might have taken a hit so he took the offer from Wales. It wasn't the All Black job, the job he really wanted. But he was going to take charge of an international team.

Within a year of arriving it appeared an inspired move. Henry led Wales on an unbeaten 10-game streak. The Welsh had no hesitation in bestowing him with the title of Great Redeemer. Then the Lions appointed Henry – the first foreigner – to coach them on their 2001 tour of Australia. Everything had been going swimmingly for Henry until that Lions tour. So what that he wasn't wanted by the All Blacks? He was wanted elsewhere and he was working with some of the best players in the world. But the Lions tour, initially so sweet, turned decidedly sour.

The test series was lost 2-1, and as the tour progressed voices of dissent began to be heard. England halfback Matt Dawson used his column in the *Daily Telegraph* to blast Henry's methods on the eve of the first test. Dawson's England team-mate Austin Healey was just as effusive in his criticism. It was unprecedented for players to be so public with their gripes.

Worse was to come for Henry when he returned to Wales. His side was trounced 54-10 by Ireland in February 2002. Only a few months earlier, in October 2001, Wales had been hammered 36-6 by the Irish in a Six Nations match (rearranged after being postponed in March due to the spread of foot-and-mouth disease). The Welsh fans all too cruelly suggested some of their players must have been infected back in October, so bad was their performance on 3 February 2002. It was enough for Henry to call it quits and admit he had lost the changing room. The players were no longer responding to him and he felt he had to leave. It was an inglorious ending to what was essentially a respectable tenure.

But rather than signal the end of a coaching career, in many ways it heralded the beginning. Henry had emerged from the Lions saga wiser and more flexible. The abrupt ending in Wales had made him aware of his own limitations. In a sense he had undergone the same chastening experience as Mitchell, but Henry had fallen from grace while an employee of the Welsh Rugby Union. It was better to learn from mistakes made in charge of someone else's international side rather than while doing it on All Black duty. All that experience and that ability to learn from his mistakes marked Henry out as an outstanding candidate to challenge for the All Black job.

And yes, he still very much wanted it. Coaching Wales and the Lions had not eased the itch. It had satisfied him to a point. He had played with the big toys and as much as he had enjoyed it, there still burned an ambition to coach the All Blacks. He couldn't pretend for one second that he could sidle into retirement satisfied his life ambition had gone unfulfilled. After quitting his job in Wales, he returned home to New Zealand and slipped under the radar when he was offered a position at Auckland as technical adviser to Wayne Pivac and Grant Fox. It was a post he also held with the Blues, who went on to win the Super 12 in 2003. That not only fulfilled eligibility criteria for the All Black job – applicants had to be working in New Zealand in either the Super 12 or NPC immediately prior to the post being advertised – but it also won him more accolades.

From head coach of Wales and the Lions to technical adviser with Auckland – it was a bit of a comedown, but Henry's ego coped. When Pivac and Fox opted to move on after the 2003 NPC and Henry was appointed coach of Auckland, it showed he was ready to put more back. He'd been there and done that and although he himself would never say it, the job was beneath him, which is why his lawyer David Jones made sure there was an escape clause in the contract, which was signed on 14 November. Henry would be allowed out of the deal if the All Black job became available – which it did just one week later. When Henry's application dropped on the desk of the NZRU bigwigs, it was going to be one that demanded serious attention. Not just because it was a bit special, but also because, other than Mitchell, there was not much in the way of competition.

Hurricanes coach Colin Cooper shied away from making a bid. He'd done well with the Hurricanes but felt his depth of experience and level of achievement were not sufficient to push for the top honour. Long-term Maori coach Matt Te Pou was a great motivator, but he too lacked the test experience or range of roles that Henry could boast. It was too soon for rookie Super 12 coaches Greg Cooper and Ian Foster to mount a challenge. Deans opted not to run, preferring to back Mitchell's campaign and take a role as assistant, while a number of overseas-based Kiwis such as Warren Gatland, Wayne Smith and Steve Hansen were ineligible for the post.

Henry stood out like the proverbial sore thumb as the most likely challenger to Mitchell, and no matter how hard the NZRU denied it, New Zealand knew it was a two-horse race.

The New Zealand Rugby Union was determined to make the right appointment. Putting in place the best available management team was critical. New Zealand arguably had the most talented team at the 1995, 1999 and 2003 World Cups but they had come home empty-handed. Talent alone was not enough. The talent needed to be managed and directed, moulded into a team that could deliver the ultimate prize.

A three-man panel was put in place to conduct the interviews and make a recommendation to the full NZRU board. On that panel were former All Black captain and NZRU president John Graham, NZRU director Mike Eagle and NZRU chief executive Chris Moller. They were going to put their shortlist contenders through a tough process. That's the way it had to be. And by 15 December when the interviews began, it had become public knowledge there were only two short-list contenders – Mitchell and Henry. It was a straight shoot-out, with the challenger afforded the honour of striking the first blow.

For four hours Henry was grilled by the panel at the NZRU's headquarters in Wellington. They fired 50 questions at him. Mitchell had to endure the same session the next day, but he would first have to finish his season review in front of the same panel. It was normal practice for the All Black coaches to give a thorough debrief of their work and Mitchell only managed to get through half the season in the three hours allotted to him on the morning of the 15th. The panel had to cut him off so they could interview his rival for the job. It made for two intriguing situations. The first was that it left Henry and Mitchell in the same building, as Mitchell stayed on after the first part of his review to conduct some individual player reviews. The NZRU had the good sense to keep them on separate floors. The second point of intrigue was that Mitchell would have to come back the next day, finish his season review, take an hour's break and then be confronted by the same panel who would interview him for the job he already held.

It would be a tough day for Mitchell, but when he emerged late in the afternoon of 15 December, he wore a broad smile and seemed at ease with the world. 'It's still ongoing, but it was good,' he told reporters. 'It was an opportunity to talk about the season, not just the one loss [to Australia at the World Cup]. It was an opportunity to talk about a very exciting season and a young All Black team. We got an opportunity to table a few issues. It's really important we go through this process and there is an enormous amount of learning. It's beneficial for myself, but what's more important is that it's beneficial for the All Blacks going forward.'

After Mitchell's grilling on 16 December, Graham, Moller and Eagle met the next day to compile reports on both candidates that would be presented to the board. Once the board had the reports and the panel's recommendation, they would interview both Henry and Mitchell on 18 December. Both men would give a presentation of about 45 minutes and then field questions. If all went to plan, the board would possibly make a decision later that night. Both candidates had already agreed contractual terms should they be successful, eliminating the possibility of the announcement being delayed.

It wasn't going to be an easy choice for the board. Both men had their merits. Mitchell had clearly fallen down on some areas of his work, but no one could argue with his overall record. He won the job in 2001 on the strength of his vision, attention to detail and emphasis on planning. These were skills he had not lost. His side had crucially lost one game against Australia. But it was just one game, and to discard his abilities on the basis of just one game would be doing a major injustice to the 39-year-old. On the other hand, there was an opportunity to bring in one of the world's most respected coaches, an older man who carried more scars and was much the wiser for them. Henry had done the business on the test scene. He was an innovative thinker, someone always capable of keeping one step ahead of the opposition.

And that ultimately is what the NZRU wanted from the All Black coach. The All Blacks had to be the world's leading rugby side. It was not up for negotiation. That was number one bullet point in the mission statement. By 2007 it would be 20 years since the All Blacks had won the inaugural World Cup. The next man put in charge of the All Blacks absolutely had to be capable of ending that drought, which is why at midday on 19 December, NZRU chairman Jock Hobbs informed the world that Graham Henry would be the next All Black coach.

It was the hammer blow that Mitchell had spent the last month desperately trying to avoid. It was, however, a hammer blow he possibly knew in his heart was coming. Mayhew recalled that Mitchell had given an eloquent and moving speech to the players in the changing room before the All Blacks played France in the third/fourth place play-off game at the World Cup. According to Mayhew: 'John conducted himself with real dignity and humility and told the players that this might be the last time they were all together as a team. It was a moving speech and I think even then he knew that he was going to lose his job.'

Maybe he did, but it didn't soften the blow when the call came from Hobbs.

The chairman rated that call as one of the toughest he had made and was pleased Mitchell agreed to take an as yet unspecified coaching role with the NZRU. Mitchell would, of course, have much preferred to have been taking on the highly specified position as coach of the All Blacks, but the board had been impressed with all facets of Henry's application.

Henry's final speech to the NZRU board was about his undiminished passion for coaching. Even after almost 30 years, he was able to claim truthfully to still hurt when his teams lost and to reiterate that winning games still gave him a huge buzz. He made reference to his maturity, experience and desire to keep learning and honing his craft. Perhaps poignantly, given Mitchell's shortcomings, Henry talked about the need to create the appropriate team management and of adopting an inclusive policy that would embrace the entire rugby family of fans, sponsors, media and broadcasters. It was a speech that connected with the board and it meant that Henry could spend the afternoon and evening of 19 December attending NZRU Christmas functions and conducting media interviews in his new capacity as head coach of the All Blacks.

By the time Henry appeared live on TV3 news to be interviewed by John Campbell later that night, he was still beaming. He was, after all, the cat who had got the cream – and the fish and the ball of wool. It was a smile that said 25 December 2003 had come six days early for him. Henry had landed a job that he always hoped would be the pinnacle of his 30-year coaching career. And it was a job that five years earlier he had been barred from ever holding.

The NZRU had not been impressed by Henry's defection to Wales. There had been some legal haggling over the terms of his Auckland, Blues and NZRU contracts once he revealed he was in talks with the Welsh Rugby Union. As is often the way when lawyers are thrust into proceedings, the whole business turned rather sour. The Auckland Rugby Union took on the role of jilted lover – a wronged wife looking for some financial payback in an acrimonious divorce settlement. Henry ended up having to pay back $150,000, while his two life tickets and car park at Eden Park were withdrawn. The messiness of the split partly explains why Henry ended up calling a press conference on the day of his departure and announced: 'I'm going to Wales and I'm going tonight.' It was an ugly business, no way for such a loyal and successful servant of the union to end his time.

The NZRU were having similar issues coping with the loss and their reaction, although not punitive financially, still had the appearance of being driven by spite. The board reacted by changing the union's legislation to state that no one who had coached another international side could return to New Zealand and coach the All Blacks.

It was an extraordinary reaction. Rugby was a professional game and New Zealanders were going to be in demand in markets that could recompense them handsomely for their knowledge and expertise. This was the inevitable consequence of opening Pandora's Box in 1995 and decreeing the game professional. This was why the old boy brigade had preached about the perils of knocking through the amateur walls. Loyalties would be tested once money could legally and openly change hands. Henry couldn't get the job he wanted in New Zealand so Wales saw their opportunity. They made him an offer, upped the cash to the point where it became too hard to turn down and, hey presto, market forces had done their bit. That was the business of professional sport – it was clinical and both blind and deaf to the sensibilities of individuals who thought a chap was duty bound to do the right thing by Queen and country.

Henry was gone, and to make a ruling that would prevent him from coaching the All Blacks if he ever came back appeared the most futile protectionist measure in a market that was never going to show respect for trade barriers.

The reality for New Zealand was that the Super 12 had been an instant, phenomenal success. The quality of rugby had been breathtaking from the first game, as had many of the Tri Nations tests in those early years. It was exactly what media tycoon Rupert Murdoch had wanted to see when he bought the television rights for both. His customers in Europe could get hooked on this thrilling new world of bonus point football as images beamed into their front rooms through their satellites. This was rugby's great awakening – players in New Zealand, South Africa and Australia could become instant global superstars. Children in the UK could get up early on Saturdays and be mesmerised by the dazzling feet of Christian Cullen or the genius of Zinzan Brooke.

No longer were the great players of New Zealand merely creatures of myth until they appeared on the doorstep touring the UK with the All Blacks. With satellite TV came knowledge and familiarity, and inevitably the sugar daddies who were ploughing their fortunes into English clubs wanted a piece of the southern hemisphere's action.

The game in the UK had bumbled out of the shadow of amateurism into an era of infighting and confusion. The volunteers who had poured their heart and soul into running Britain's famous old clubs were not relinquishing power to the new breed of professional sports administrators wanted by the money men now at the helm of their vanity purchases. There was money swilling around but it was not necessarily putting bums on seats the way everyone had hoped. There was something missing. The new game lacked glamour. There was none of the exotic football on show in the Super 12. It was still the same old faces following the same old game plans. That blood-and-snotters theme had gripped the old guard, but if rugby was ever going to become the game for the masses, if it was ever going to convert paying fans from the round ball code, it would need to do things a little differently. Games would have to be sexier, faster, less gritty and stoical. And more importantly, new heroes would have to be found.

To achieve that aim in the long term, money was ploughed into academy programmes. Centres of excellence were springing up all over the country in the hope that further down the track, rugby clubs would start spitting out superstars. That was the long term, though. There needed to be plans in place to achieve those aims in the immediate future. There was only ever going to be one solution – the new faces would have to be bought.

The South African Rand was so weak that luring them out of the Republic was going to be a doddle. The Australians would add competitive steel and instil a bloody-minded will to win in any team. But while players from those two nations had their attractions, it was New Zealand that held the rugby world's respect. It was the Blues and Crusaders who dominated those early years of Super 12, and it was the All Blacks who went through the 1996 and 1997 seasons losing only one game. New Zealand was rugby's centre of excellence. It was the nation that held most of the sport's intellectual capital. Some big investments had been made in European rugby, and those men who had tipped much of their life savings into their local club were going to be picky about making sure they were hiring the best. As to who were the best, there was no debate. New Zealand was going to be the chosen recruiting ground of every major European rugby club and rugby union.

And it wasn't just going to be the players in demand. Henry was not going to be the only New Zealand coach to be offered a major overseas opportunity. NZRU independent board member at that time, Kevin Roberts, remembers having a number of discussions in those first years on the subject of talent retention. 'We felt we had to put in place some rules to help us keep the players from the Japanese, from the French and especially from Super League, which we saw as the biggest threat. So we said you can only play for the All Blacks if you are contracted to the NZRU and playing in New Zealand. We felt the aura of the All Blacks was always going to keep players in New Zealand. We said we would also be very flexible and when these guys reached an age where they were slowing down, we would help them get out of their contracts so they could go to Japan and earn $300,000 or $400,000 a season.

'When the coaching issue came up in the late 1990s we were bereft of experienced coaches. John Hart was retained in the job after losing five consecutive games in 1998. The thing is, no one was ready to take over at that point and we were very worried that we did not have the quality. Graham Henry was always going to be on the shortlist to take over from Hart and he was always destined to coach the All Blacks. I can remember having a conversation with him in Christchurch where he asked me if he was going to be the next All Black coach. He was very honest and said he had an offer to go to Wales but he wanted to know where he stood with the All Blacks.

'I told him that he would have to apply and go through an interview process. He was worried about that because he was concerned he would not have the full support of the board, that there might be some anti-Auckland sentiment. He had some infallible statistics to support his application and I would have backed him but I would have been just one of eight votes. If we had been able to offer him the All Black job I have no doubt he would have taken it and not gone to Wales. But that didn't happen and he really liked the idea of coaching in Wales to broaden his experience. The money was very good and he and Raewyn [Henry's wife] wanted that overseas opportunity.

'After Graham left we felt that a whole lot more coaches would go too and we felt we needed to buy ourselves some time. So we put in place the same rules we had for the players. We needed to get the next wave of coaches up to speed. We couldn't afford to lose any more and it was a defensive measure, one that we thought would be revisited in three years.'

It was a defensive measure and it was of course revoked within three years. Henry has frequently said he always thought the decision would be overturned. But the smile on his face on 19 December was partly driven by relief. It was relief that not only had he reached the destination of his dreams but that the game in New Zealand had an opportunity to step into a brave new world.

Henry's departure to Wales had been messy. Mitchell's removal from office had been messy. But the NZRU had learned from the Henry clause and had been big enough to revoke it. The great hope was that they would learn just as much from the fall-out with Mitchell. The relationship between the All Black coach and the executive could not be allowed to disintegrate. If there were issues developing, they couldn't be allowed to fester. To succeed there had to be an era of honesty, respect and openness. Those values had to be carried into dealings with the wider professional rugby fraternity, sponsors, broadcasters and media.

Both Henry and the NZRU board had served their apprenticeship. They had made mistakes and learned from them along the way. But Henry's smile was not driven just by relief. It contained an element of pure joy at the thought of what lay ahead. But you could be sure that when he woke up on 20 December, in his first full day in the job, he was already thinking about who he wanted next to him as he embarked on the next leg of his incredible journey.

3   Friends reunited

BY JANUARY 2004, the tragedy of the World Cup had slipped a few rungs in the public consciousness. Time, of course, was renowned for being a great healer and that little bit of distance had helped the nation put events at Sydney's Telstra Stadium into perspective. The worry beads were being put away as there was something else to focus on.

The appointment of Henry had provided the ideal distraction. There was no need to fret endlessly about what might have been. With a new man at the helm there was an opportunity to take the eyes off the rear-view mirror and actually scan what lay ahead. There was reason enough for optimism.

Henry came into the job saying all the right things. He saw the immediate need to connect the team with its public. Even in the professional age, the All Blacks remain the people's team. The history, the heritage, what it means to wear the black jersey – they would mean nothing were it not for the way the New Zealand public clutches the team so close to its heart. Mitchell had delivered some memorable football and a decent haul of results. But there was always a feeling that the paying spectators, the very people he needed to have on his side, were being kept at arm's length.

When you trace the money that pays for the All Blacks' five-star hotels, six-figure salaries and sponsored vehicles, you find at the end of the chain Mr and Mrs Joe Public. It is always Mr Joe Public emptying his pockets for the cause. The broadcasters recoup their investment from selling satellite packages. And to whom do they sell them? Mr Joe Public. When adidas tipped an obscene amount of cash into the NZRU's coffers, it was in the expectation that Mr J. Public would buy any number of leisure-wear items adorned with the three stripes to pay for the German firm's involvement. And of course there is the simple transaction at the turnstile that sees hard-earned money disappear out of the wallet of Mr Public, straight into the pocket of Mr Next Big Thing.

From Invercargill to Kaitaia, there are four million New Zealanders with ownership rights in the All Blacks. Those rights have to be respected and Henry essentially did just that when he came into the job, promising to restore some traditional values. 'We were flaky at set-piece and especially the lineouts, our general kicking is not strong and defence as a unit needs to be addressed,' he told the *New Zealand Herald*.

It was the bit about the set-piece that had salt-of-the-earth, heartland men nodding sagely. The All Black scrum had once been a fearsome machine – a late version of the Sherman Tank which, just like the original model, didn't pay too much attention to anything daft enough to get in its way. By 2004 though, it was getting hard to remember that the scrum was once something of which New Zealanders could be proud. The last time anyone could remember the All Black scrum being any good was when Sean Fitzpatrick, Craig Dowd and Olo Brown packed down together in the early to mid 1990s. By 2003, it had become so lacking in grunt that opposition teams were publicly questioning the All Blacks' authority. No one was scared of the All Black forwards any more. The likes of England, France and Australia knew the All Black forwards had a wider range of skills. They knew most of the All Black forwards could run, pass and kick just like backs. But more crucially, they knew the All Black forwards also scrummaged and rucked just like backs.

Henry's initial declaration, then, that he was going to put the emphasis back on the set-piece was long overdue. The All Blacks had to send out a message that the scrum was not just a mechanism to start the game. The same was true of the lineout, while the tackled ball area was going to become the critical battleground for Henry's All Black side. When Mitchell arrived in Australia before the 2003 World Cup, the coach instructed his players not to ruck. His reasoning was valid: the law book (and so what that the law was an ass?) does not allow players to ruck. Mitchell was smart enough to know that with TV audiences in the billions, any careless footwork would be heavily penalised. His thinking was sound enough, but it was naive to believe he could publicly state that his players had been banned from rucking and not incense the rugby public. If Mitchell really meant he had warned his players about being careless with their feet and had laid down the law about the penalties awaiting anyone found guilty of stomping, then that is what he should have said. He needed to make it plain to Mr J. Public that the All Blacks would be rugged and aggressive, but also disciplined. None of the four million stakeholders in the All Blacks want to believe there is anything soft about their team. They want the coach to reiterate that point in all his public utterances. So, it was possibly with Mitchell's rucking faux pas in mind that Henry tried to restore confidence in the early weeks of his reign.

Having already set out his stall to improve the possession-winning aspects of the All Blacks' work, Henry crept further up the popularity stakes when he didn't shy away from having a pop at the pat-a-cake nature of Super 12. As someone who had coached the Blues for three years, Henry was a big admirer of the tournament. The pace, vision and skill of the athletes were light years ahead of the dirge being played on muddy fields in Bath and Newcastle. But the exaggerated focus on offence and the pursuit of bonus points had reduced the importance and expertise of some of the darker elements of the game. The laissez-faire refereeing had not helped encourage a contest at the breakdown either.

The consequence of these factors, according to Henry, was to create two distinct brands of rugby – Super 12 rugby and test rugby. The former was no longer adequately preparing individuals to excel at the latter. Some bad habits were being picked up in the Super 12 that, if applied at test level, would only end in tears before bed. Henry wasn't over the top in his criticism of the competition. He gave an honest view with which it was hard to disagree. There needed to be some adjustments if New Zealand was going to succeed. For the All Blacks to fulfil their potential, they would need to borrow a little from the world champion England team and be more confrontational. There would be no harm in emulating the Poms' dedication to both scrums and lineouts either. But attacking flair and inherent natural ability were not going to be sacrificed on the altar of drudgery.

Henry's plan was to maintain much of what was already in place. It would be madness to stifle the running talents of Joe Rokocoko or Doug Howlett and Henry wasn't mad. He was going to combine the best of England with the best of New Zealand. And to help him create this hybrid style, there would be a specialist forwards coach and a specialist backs coach. A new game-plan required a new coaching structure. There would be a three-man panel, with Henry at the head. By the end of January 2004, it was little wonder no one was thinking about the last World Cup. All the nation wanted to talk about was the identity of Henry's lieutenants.

Steve Hansen, or Shag to those who know him, is a gruff sort of bloke who can be a little intimidating. But once you crack through that outer, protective shell there is a soft yolky centre that harbours a dry wit and a warm personality. A fine rugby brain also lies in there. It was a brain and personality that Henry was fond of. The long and the short of it is that Henry rated Hansen as a coach and he liked the guy, felt they could work well together. He must have, for when Hansen was officially announced as the All Black assistant coach on 16 February, it was the second time Henry had asked Hansen to be his sidekick.

When Henry was head coach of Wales, he hired Hansen as his assistant in June 2001. Hansen was coaching Canterbury and assisting the Crusaders at the time, and a bit like Henry in 1998, was beginning to wonder whether New Zealand could offer him the next step in his career. Robbie Deans was doing a rather fine job with the Crusaders, leading Hansen to believe that it would be some time before that particular hot seat would be vacated. Wayne Smith and Tony Gilbert were winning plaudits for their work with the All Blacks and the remaining Super 12 posts had all been filled when the Welsh Rugby Union came calling in May 2001. What was a man to do?

Hansen was ambitious and wanted a crack at the next level. By then the Henry clause had been revoked, so he could head to Cardiff without killing off his All Black aspirations. He was being offered the chance to work with a guy he trusted and respected and hey, the money was good. Hansen signed a deal that would see him honour his contract to coach Canterbury through the 2001 NPC and then head to Wales in January 2002. When he signed the contract, the future looked very rosy for the former policeman who had played for the red and blacks as a centre. But in the interim, the Great Redeemer suffered an alarmingly quick fall from grace and quit a week after Hansen had arrived. Hansen had barely unpacked and was just learning the names of his players when he was left to fend for himself. He was Henry's man and there was a fair chance the new coach, whoever that might be, would arrive with broom in hand, happy to sweep away all remnants of the Henry regime. That was the way of the world. Coaches wanted to work with their own people. There had to be trust. There had to be rapport and compatibility. Fortunately for Hansen, the Welsh Rugby Union decided he should step up and be the new man. The job was Hansen's through to the end of the Six Nations in April and then the board would review the best course of action.

It looked as if Hansen had been handed the most poisonous chalice in world rugby. Morale was low, fitness levels were still questionable and Welsh club rugby was in a financial mess that left players embroiled in permanently draining contract negotiations. There was also the fact that Hansen had only been there for five minutes. And yet, despite all this, the public's expectations remained ludicrously high.

Bearing in mind he was effectively driving a Hyundai and expected to make it race like a Ferrari, it was hard not to be impressed by the way Hansen bunkered down and got on with the job. Performances were not brilliant but they were improved, and on 6 April the Welsh Rugby Union announced that Hansen would be retained through to the end of the Six Nations in April 2004.

He continued to make the most of what was at times an impossible job. Welsh rugby went through the biggest upheaval of its proud history when it transformed the previously privately owned clubs into regional franchises. There was bitter in-fighting and constant distractions that partly explained why Wales didn't win a single Six Nations fixture in 2003. Hansen's plight was best demonstrated when the Welsh team missed their flight for a three-match tour of Australia and New Zealand in June 2003 because pay negotiations with union bosses dragged on too long. The team bus was on its way to Heathrow when the players called an impromptu stop on the M4 to nut out a pay deal they had supposedly settled a few weeks earlier. The talks dragged on, traffic was heavy and the team missed their flight. Against that backdrop, Wales were predictably hammered twice by Australia and then 55-3 by the All Blacks in Hamilton.

It seemed a lost cause, and Hansen would have found a number of sympathisers if he had given up the ghost right there in Waikato Stadium. That wasn't his way though. He stood by his beliefs and four months later, when Wales met the All Blacks in their Pool D clash at the World Cup, they frightened the life out of John Mitchell's team. From somewhere, the players found a belief no one thought they possessed. Where they had been tentative and risk averse in the previous games, they were suddenly playing some of the most enterprising rugby seen in the last decade. It was breathtaking and they had the All Blacks rattled. They couldn't clinch the deal, eventually losing 53-37, but for 60 minutes they had the world watching. And that was enough for Henry to confirm what he already knew – that Hansen was made from good stuff and the right sort of man to have in the trenches with him.

Hansen had certainly never hidden his intention to come back to New Zealand once he had seen out his commitment to Wales. He spoke to Radio Sport on 25 November 2003 from Cardiff and said. 'Yes, I'll be looking for a job at home when I get back. The circumstances for me wanting to go home haven't changed. From the outset I made the comment I'd be coming for two and a half years and the whole objective would be to try to improve the team and other things within Welsh rugby that I've got some control over.'

Both Henry and Hansen felt a little unresolved about the way things had panned out in Wales. There was a genuine desire on both sides to work with each other and see how effective their partnership could be. When Hansen spoke to Radio Sport on 25 November he already knew there was a chance he could be coming back to New Zealand as assistant coach of the All Blacks. Henry had already sounded him out and by 23 December, after Henry had secured the job, it had become an open secret that Hansen was on the radar. When confirmation of Hansen's appointment came on 16 February, it not only (finally!) secured their previously aborted alliance, it also allowed Hansen to play with the toys he had jealously admired from afar.

After Wales were hammered in Hamilton in June 2003, Hansen spoke with a curious mix of exasperation and veneration. It was as if he had just seen someone nick off with his girlfriend, yet he couldn't help respecting both the audacity and aplomb with which they had conducted the manoeuvre.

'We couldn't get our hands on the ball and they got a roll on,' Hansen said. 'People like Kees Meeuws, they just keep running and running and then Ali Williams decided he had had enough and they throw on a bloke like Brad Thorn. There is no respite – that is what makes them such a great side. What happened tonight was one group of people getting the right coaching and environment and support from about the age of 14. Now that is not happening in our place.'

As he sat underneath the stand in Hamilton on 21 June 2003, Hansen's mood might have been considerably lightened if he had known that 12 months later he would be back at the same ground once again, proclaiming a solid All

Black performance, except this time it would be one that he had played no small part in delivering.

The phone message Graham Henry left on Wayne Smith's answering machine didn't make instant sense to him. Henry said to ring back 'for the obvious reasons'. The obvious reasons, as far as Smith could tell, would be to offer Henry some advice about his pitch for the vacant All Black job.

Smith knew Henry was in the running and, having done the job himself, thought he was going to be a sounding-board for his old adversary. Instead, when Smith got back in touch, he learned that Henry, if he were to get the job, wanted Smith to coach the All Black backs. Now that was unexpected. Really unexpected. 'He got a hell of a shock when I said I would like him to be with me if I was chosen as All Black coach,' Henry revealed after Smith was officially announced as assistant coach. 'He knew I was going to have a crack for coach but no idea I wanted him involved.'

This would complete the dream team Henry had envisioned when he pitched for the job. He knew he wanted a three-man coaching structure that would see him as the boss with two assistants respectively in charge of the forwards and backs. Yet it wasn't going to be a hierarchical structure in the traditional sense. The two assistants would be selectors and would have considerable input into strategy. This was a very new concept, and to make it work, it was vital both assistants had experience as head coaches and that both assistants were strong enough to air their views, hold robust debate, yet also be prepared to compromise and co-operate.

When Henry sold Smith his vision he had already won him over. But it wasn't quite that simple. Smith was settled in Northampton, the English club that had hired him in December 2001 when they found themselves slipping uncomfortably close to the relegation zone. There was that, and also the fact Smith already had the T-shirt when it came to the All Blacks. His stint as head coach between 2000 and October 2001 was emotionally demanding. Smith had wrestled with self-doubt after the All Blacks lost a Bledisloe Cup on 3 September 2001 that probably even the Wallabies would agree was a trifle careless on New Zealand's part. Smith expressed his doubt and ignited a tender process for his job. The honesty of his self-evaluation was a little too much for some on the NZRU board. As he recalled in November 2005 in the foyer of the hotel where the All Blacks were staying before their Twickenham clash with England: 'I was being accountable. We were under pressure. We lost a game against Australia we should've won. I put myself under pressure. I was questioning whether I was the right person for the job and I guess I wanted confirmation of that. I raised questions and other people answered them and I ended up coaching at Northampton.'

As Smith reminisced, it became apparent that while he had valued the review process and respected its outcome, it had still been a traumatic period. He had wanted his job back, hoping his high review mark would seal the deal. But his honesty was perceived as weakness and he was bundled out the door. The dismissal hurt. He'd opened his soul in the belief it was the right thing to do but, as he said four years later in the Royal Kensington Garden Hotel, he was perhaps misunderstood. Given his time again he'd make the same point, but express it in a different way. So when Henry made his offer, Smith had to be sure he would not be returning with unwanted emotional baggage.

What Smith also needed to assess was whether he could live with himself if he walked out on Northampton before he had achieved all he wanted. His time at Franklin's Gardens had been cathartic, an opportunity to rediscover his faith and confidence. It's an ugly town with few charms, but Smith fell in love with the place and built a special bond with the players, supporters and club owner, local businessman Keith Barwell. It wasn't unrequited love. Smith put the Saints back into the territory they believed it was their right to occupy.

Having inherited a side in turmoil, sitting second to last in the English Premiership, Smith quietly went about restoring confidence in a club that had won the biggest prize in European rugby – the Heineken Cup – in 2000. The Saints finished fifth in 2002 and then enjoyed consecutive third places in 2003 and 2004. The erudite Smith was hailed a hero, the brains behind the revolution, and with the Saints once again marching, there was a reluctance to leave, even if it was the All Blacks who had come calling. Northampton's director of rugby at the time, John Steele, can remember how difficult Smith found leaving the club. 'Wayne spoke to me and chairman Keith Barwell quite early when it became a possibility that he might be involved with the All Blacks. He didn't want to be talking covertly and he knew we didn't want to get to May and find out that he was leaving as that would leave us with little time to appoint a replacement. What I saw was a man torn between a club where he was doing a very good job and what was almost a calling for him. He had a torn loyalty: to the Saints where he felt his work was not finished and to the All

Black jersey that he felt so passionately about. We took the view he had been a great coach and we really didn't want to lose him.

'He'd done a great job in changing the way we did things, in improving performance and getting results. I think he felt his work wasn't done and I know he had a few sleepless nights tossing up what he was going to do. It wasn't a move where he would necessarily be better off financially and he had already ticked the box, having been head coach of the All Blacks. He didn't seem to have any problem with the way he had left the All Blacks. I don't think that process had been handled very well. He had asked for criticism if there was any to give and he got it. But it was typical of him not to bear any grudge and be prepared to go back. In the end he went with his heart and I think one of the key factors was he felt he could make a difference.'

Like Hansen, Smith agreed to come home after he had taken Northampton through to the end of their season in May 2004. That was going to be a potential problem as Henry would be the only New Zealand-based selector until his lieutenants returned. Smith and Hansen could do video analysis and air their thoughts from afar, but the preference would have been to have them at Super 12 games.

Henry was sure it wasn't going to be a big deal, and anyway, he had another solution up his sleeve. Having won kudos with the old school for his straight-talking promises to restore traditional values, Henry went to the top of the class when he announced on 3 March 2004 that former All Black captain and coach, Sir Brian Lochore, would be coming on board as a selector. Sir Brian was the only New Zealander to coach the All Blacks through a successful World Cup campaign and remained an astute judge of players and their capabilities. A man of the land and a man of dignity and honour, the quietly spoken farmer from Wairarapa Bush was a universally approved choice as fourth selector.

A few weeks later, the competent and likeable Darren Shand was named as All Black manager. Optimism peaked. Henry had assembled his dream team. There was experience and ability in every corner, except one – the new management team had to find a field general.

Not that it necessarily made John Mitchell feel any better, but there was one man just as vilified as him in the aftermath of the semi-final loss to Australia: the All Black captain Reuben Thorne. A genuinely nice bloke, honest, reliable and committed, Thorne was everything you would want in an All Black captain.

Yet somehow he never really won the whole country over. His reliability was portrayed not so much as a quality but as a necessity, given his lack of flair and ability. His commitment was more regularly referred to as graft, on the basis that he wasn't delivering comic book feats of heroism, just toil.

It's a funny old business working out why some leaders carry an enormous popularity rating while others don't. Look at Bill Clinton – he lied to the nation that he was having a bit of extramarital slap and tickle. But the fact he was both a liar and a cheat didn't really shoot down the Clinton star. It merely said he was human, a likeable philanderer bristling with charm and personality. His successor, George W. Bush, on the other hand, just doesn't make people feel the same way. He choked on a pretzel and blacked out. There was no well of sympathy, just a flood of Internet jokes reaffirming the perception of the spoilt daddy's boy too dumb to remember to chew. Thorne probably fell into the same camp as Bush, except the mystery of his perennial unpopularity was easier to fathom.

New Zealanders are by and large a forgiving bunch. A man can file a dodgy tax return and people will understand. He can cheat at golf, which is obviously more serious, but forgivable all the same. But what he mustn't do, under any circumstances, is lead both Canterbury and the Crusaders on an unprecedented run of success. That is heinous as far as everyone who lives outside the Garden City is concerned. That was Thorne's big failing – he was consistently and at times aggressively Cantabrian, with the crime made much worse by the fact he actually grew up in Taranaki. That made too many people instantly suspicious of him, and whenever he played there was no shortage of detractors to pounce on his failings. Unfortunately for Thorne, there were times when they didn't have to look too hard.

Against England in 2003 he had his big opportunity to prove to those who reckoned he was Captain Invisible that he was in fact Captain Invincible. In the first test of the year in Wellington, England were reduced to 13 men with both Lawrence Dallaglio and Neil Back receiving yellow cards. The English captain Martin Johnson had been incensed by the dismissals and was visibly raging. Everyone got barked at and somehow Johnson inspired his team to lift their efforts and dig that bit deeper. As for the All Blacks, they couldn't push the six-man English pack over from a five-metre scrum. They huffed and puffed, won a few penalties, one of which No 8 Rodney So'oialo tapped on his own and blew the chance. The English were giving classic bulldog spirit while the

All Blacks were timid, unsure how to deal with their numerical advantage. No one looked more unsure than Thorne, who was rendered mute on the side of the scrum, unable or uncertain how to impose himself on proceedings. That wasn't a great look for an All Black skipper, and a few months later when that semi-final started sliding away, there was no discernable evidence that Thorne was scurrying round the decks imploring his men to try something different. He seemed to go down with the ship all too easily.

In the aftermath of that defeat all the players got behind their skipper. There was no question that within the squad Thorne's authority went unchallenged. He had earned the respect of his team with his high workrate and grafting persistence. His leadership style was understood: no one minded that he was quiet – they knew what he wanted.

But the problem for Thorne came once he lost the man in whose mould many felt he was created. Mitchell, himself a limited but dogged player, was in the market for a leader who could cruelly be termed an honest toiler. Henry wasn't. Henry and his new panel wanted someone who was guaranteed selection. That wasn't going to be Thorne. While Thorne was captain there was debate about whether he should even have been in the team. Throughout Mitchell's time, Jerry Collins had a major support group arguing that his explosive ball-carrying and fearsome defence should have seen him play in his preferred blindside berth instead of No 8. Auckland's Justin Collins also won plenty of admirers in 2003 with a storming Super 12 season with the Blues. Not only did Henry want someone guaranteed of selection, he wanted someone who was respected around the world. Again, Thorne was going to struggle as it was apparent from the derogatory tone of the UK papers that the Brits were a little perplexed as to what the All Blacks saw in Thorne.

There was also the other problem that Thorne was very much Mitchell's appointment. The broom had been swept pretty hard by Henry – new assistants and a new manager had been appointed, while a new doctor, new fitness trainer and new physio were all on the way too. The future didn't look terribly bright for Thorne and it got a whole lot bleaker on 24 May 2004 when Tana Umaga was announced as the new All Black captain.

When Henry, Smith and Hansen met in March to discuss the captaincy, they had been unanimous – they wanted Umaga. He ticked all the boxes, he was world class and a natural leader. His style was different from Thorne's. He was more demonstrative, his heart being that bit closer to his sleeve. His blood ran hotter and he had become a skilled communicator as his career had developed. With 53 test caps under his belt there was plenty of experience to take into the role and perhaps most importantly, Umaga was not a Cantabrian. He was a staunch Wellingtonian with proud Polynesian roots, but somehow that didn't matter with Umaga. He didn't provoke regional bias the way Thorne did. He was first and foremost a New Zealander. The nation was not polarised by Umaga and Henry needed the nation behind his team. The All Blacks had been estranged, or at least not on speaking terms with the supporting public for too long. As Henry had said in his final pitch to the board – the whole rugby family had to be working together. For that to happen there couldn't be widespread dislike of the chosen skipper. There couldn't be debate and as far as Henry could see, Umaga was the only man capable of healing the cracks in a divided nation.

The announcement was made a few days before Umaga's 31st birthday, but Henry had offered him the job several weeks earlier. 'I didn't believe it was Graham so it was a bit of a shock when he told me the news,' Umaga told the press just after the announcement was made. 'I had to talk it over with my wife, she plays a big part in my life. You're under the spotlight and the demands of being the captain are more than if you're just playing. She was happy with that.'

It had been an agonising couple of months keeping the whole business secret. It's not the kind of news you can take on board and not want to tell everyone about. But Umaga kept his inner circle to just his wife, Rochelle, and big brother Mike. He kept the circle tight, partly out of necessity, or the beans would be spilled, but also because his wife and brother had been his two closest confidants throughout his career and there was no way he could keep them in the dark about news so big it would blow their socks off.

The disappointment of his non-selection at the World Cup and the manner in which New Zealand crashed out had been like a knife through the heart for Umaga. Having come over the crest of the hill in terms of his age, 2003 was probably going to be his last chance at the big one. For it to end in such rank bitterness was not good. But Umaga, as he had done throughout his career, stayed loyal to New Zealand. He never once spoke poorly of Mitchell or Deans. He never lost his passion for the jersey or forgot what it meant, which is why he turned down several enormous offers to play overseas after the World Cup. He was off contract and the French and Poms reckoned he was worth a bomb. But Umaga didn't have his price. He was a devoted family man, and New Zealand was for him. He'd laid his body down for the cause, and to have that commitment recognised by being awarded the captaincy made all the emotional suffering worthwhile. The night before the official announcement, Umaga was finally allowed to tell his extended family the big news. They learned that Umaga was the new All Black captain over a home-made broth. It was an emotional night and tears were shed. The great hope for New Zealand was that 23 May would be the only time the new All Black skipper would feel the need to cry into a bowl of soup.

4   Coming off the rails

SIR CLIVE WOODWARD fell back into his seat. He would have loved nothing more than to have shut his eyes and made his jet-lag go away. But that was not an option. He was on a mission – a fact-finding mission ahead of the British Lions tour to New Zealand later that year. It was only 13 January 2005, but that in itself summed up Sir Clive. He was nothing if not meticulous. Coming to New Zealand six months early, he would be checking the hotels where his team would be staying, the places they would be training and most important of all, the venues in which they would be playing their three tests. As much as he wanted to sleep, he knew he couldn't.

The other part of his mission was to win the public relations battle. He wanted the Lions to be liked by their hosts in a way they never were when they toured Australia four years earlier. He was flying to Christchurch from Auckland with a New Zealand reporter riding shotgun. It was a golden opportunity for Woodward to establish that the Lions were going to be accessible, embrace the people of New Zealand and win friends as well as tests.

Coming six months early to check the pillows were all fluffed-up in the various hotels and to try and win a few positive column inches ahead of the real war seemed a bit over the top. But Sir Clive, the man who had coached England to World Cup glory in 2003, talked of how professional sport was about inches. A test was 80 minutes. However, in the usual run of things the team would gather a full week beforehand. Do the math, he reckoned, and it was obvious the preparation was the most important part of the process. A test win was just the by-product of the earlier hard work.

With Auckland fading into the distance, he talked of how the famous black jersey had always been the one to strike fear in the northern hemisphere. He talked about famous New Zealand players down the years. He remembered coming to New Zealand with the Lions as a player in 1983. His abiding memory was that if you weren't ready for the All Blacks, they would show themselves to be a merciless, ruthless bunch. They could smell fear, hunt it out and then take pride in the kill. But as he continued to talk, without ever saying it, he hinted that he felt the All Blacks had lost their way in recent years. He recalled that back in 1999 he'd been torn between celebrating and commiserating the resignation of All Black coach John Hart. Woodward admired Hart, had met him a few times and walked away impressed with his vision and understanding of professional rugby.

Woodward had been in the England job for two years before the 1999 World Cup. He'd begged the press and his employers to put off making judgement on his ability until the World Cup. When the jury finally made their verdict, it wasn't pretty. England had slumped in the quarter-finals in a weak effort against South Africa. Woodward somehow survived and when he heard Hart had been hoofed, he could barely believe his luck. 'I was a young coach,' he recalled as flight NZ0531 got its first glimpse of the South Island. 'I was under a lot of pressure and I couldn't believe it when New Zealand got rid of Hart. I thought he was a great coach and getting rid of him was mad. I saw that as a really lucky break for me. I felt if New Zealand had stuck with Hart it would have made my life really difficult. There would have been these experienced, skilled rugby coaches like Hart and Nick Mallet in South Africa putting out outstanding teams. But when Hart left and then Mallet, I really sensed that was a big opportunity for me and for England.'

Woodward was right and it was an opportunity that he and England grasped. By April 2003, England were the team the rugby world was chasing. They had finally secured a Six Nations Grand Slam, and in November 2002 they achieved the equally significant goal of defeating New Zealand, Australia and South Africa in consecutive weeks at Twickenham. England were building up steam. 'John Mitchell made a huge mistake,' reckoned Woodward. 'He came to Twickenham a year before the World Cup and left some of his main players behind. I think full strength they would have beaten us and that would have given the All Blacks a huge boost. But they lost and we came to New Zealand a few months later and all of a sudden we had won twice in a row and the momentum was with us.'

It was momentum that had been deservedly built. Rugby is a cyclical business and the seat of power tends to be transferred every few years or so. First the Scots and English had the power because they had the rules. Then the New Zealanders wrested it away with their pioneering lifestyle ideally suited to the physical demands of the game. Then the Boks ruled the turf, for similar reasons, with the Welsh desperately trying to stake a claim. Throughout most of the 1990s it was Australia who came up with all the innovation. By the start of professionalism, New Zealand were miles ahead in their thinking. They were turning out athletes who could do anything and everything. But by 1998, the power of the All Blacks was fading and there were more pretenders to the throne than there had ever been.

Australia's constant exposure to New Zealand through the Super 12 and Tri Nations, combined with their Institute of Sport, was making them an awfully tough nut to crack. They were smart, streetwise and very tricky in the way they borrowed ideas from other professional codes. The premeditated, sequenced rugby mastered by the Brumbies was all the rage by the turn of the millennium and Australia, who took on the same game-plan, were arguably the most consistently successful team from the southern hemisphere. As more and more money flowed into the English game and Woodward reverted to an old-fashioned ploy of forward-dominated rugby with a big-kicking No 10, it was England who were leading the way in the northern hemisphere. All the good ideas, all the workable game-plans that actually led to the winning of big tests were coming out of England and Australia. As much as New Zealanders protested to the contrary, the evidence was irrefutable: England and Australia clashed in the 2003 World Cup final. Sir Clive had never been in any doubt that the embedded superiority of England and Australia would shine through. He had predicted an Australia versus England final six months before it happened.

Woodward had identified, perhaps inadvertently, what had really got the New Zealand rugby public's goat. Not winning the World Cup had hurt. But what hurt more was the painful realisation that New Zealand was no longer the trendsetter in world rugby. After the 1987 World Cup, kids in France didn't want to be Jean-Pierre Rives, they wanted to be Michael Jones. In 1995 you could walk into a bar in any soccer-mad British town and hear the locals talking about Jonah Lomu. Schools throughout the UK had their First XVs watching videos of the All Blacks. Clubs across the country had moves named after All Blacks. By

1999 no one in the UK knew who Taine Randell was. In 2005 Sir Clive couldn't even remember Reuben Thorne's name. Jonny Wilkinson was the poster on every wall. It was Woodward who was the guru. He had the answers on how to get success. His was the seat that apprentices came to kneel before.

Graham Henry's mission was not only to deliver results, it was to put the All Blacks back on the map. It was to get the rest of the world to follow his lead. For too long the All Blacks had not been the real power-brokers. At the start of Henry's tenure that honour belonged to England, which was handy, because the Poms, as fate would have it, were heading to New Zealand for a two-test series in June. It was a glorious chance to make an early statement of intent.

The names on the team sheet said it all. Henry was serious in his mission to restore set-piece dominance. He was also serious about stacking the team with leaders. The day he had been anointed, he told the *New Zealand Herald*: 'We have got to produce a rugby-smart culture because at the end of the day brains beats talent. We have to be rugby smart. We can't be inhibited [by the World Cup loss]. We have to take the initiative. The only way you are going to achieve that is to produce leaders and decision-makers on the field, so we make the right decisions when the heat is on. We had talent in 1999, we had talent in 2003 and we didn't do the job.'

In his first test side were Chiefs duo Keith Robinson and Jono Gibbes, as well as Blues No 8 Xavier Rush. Robinson was an out-and-out hard nut. Gibbes and Rush were possibly not quite All Black material but they were the captains of their respective Super 12 sides. They were natural leaders, players who will run all day, put their body on the line and die for the cause without asking any questions. That is exactly what Henry wanted. There were plenty of younger, more athletic legs around Gibbes and Rush to give the side an intriguing balance of intuition, explosive power and experience.

The accusation in Sydney seven months earlier had been that there were too many Indians and not a single chief. Henry had gone some way towards upping the quota of chiefs and it was a formula that delivered instant success. Success not purely because the All Blacks dominated the scoreboard in their two tests against England, but success in that some of the swagger of old had returned. The English side, even shorn of many of their World Cup stars, still fancied a bit of rough and tumble. They were still a tight unit that reckoned the game was as much about bottle as it was ability. The All Blacks tested that bottle.

Robinson was the agitator supreme, brazenly waltzing into lineouts from the wrong side and then happily throwing out a few jabs in the direction of anyone saying 'cor blimey guvnor'. It was classic enforcer stuff – the kind of rugged, testy approach that the great Colin Meads thoroughly approved of. In the front-row, the oversized Carl Hayman was putting his not inconsiderable frame to good use, and with his Grizzly Adams beard, he looked as if he had just wandered off the mountains in the hope he would stumble across some extreme physical contact. The All Black pack looked like tough men and they played like tough men.

After 80 minutes at Carisbrook and 80 minutes at Eden Park, there was no question the All Blacks had restored some pride. The English couldn't cope with the ferocity of the All Black forwards, and the backs had little hope of stopping an in-form Carlos Spencer who had the backline flowing like good claret. In two tests the All Blacks racked up eight tries.

Henry had won early plaudits for hiring Smith and Hansen. Recalling Brian Lochore had been a very smart move, as had the re-introduction of the All Black trial. The media had been treated with respect and Henry was appearing all over the country at coaching clinics and sponsors' functions. The All Blacks were back in the bosom of the people. The corporate world had a champion they could trust to front the All Black brand and the relationship with the executive was underpinned by respect and open lines of communication. Before a ball had been kicked or thrown in earnest, Henry had the nation very much behind him. But as always, that support would have evaporated if the All Blacks hadn't delivered on the pitch. To smash England 36-3, then 36-12, on consecutive weekends was impressive – well ahead of expectation. But to have done it with a very deliberate combination of rapier and bludgeon – that had everyone believing New Zealand really could climb back into pole position and make the rest of the world wonder how they would ever close the gap.

Well, not everyone. One man was resolute he was witnessing a false dawn. Sir Clive just couldn't lose with dignity. In almost three hours of rugby his side couldn't muster a single try, yet he insisted England had been the better team. In Auckland he raged about a refereeing decision that saw English lock Simon Shaw sent off after 15 minutes. He was probably right to rage as, seen in slow motion, the big lock appeared to do nothing more than carefully lower his knee and push it unconvincingly into the back of Robinson. According to Woodward, the red card had denied England a meaningful opportunity to win the game. With a full complement, the red rose of England would have levelled the series. It sounded like utter nonsense to those assembled under the South Stand at Eden Park. It had to be the deluded ravings of a bitter loser, a man used to winning and now under pressure. The gulf in class had been apparent – eight tries to nil is as convincing as it gets.

Woodward was a pantomime villain, the Lex Luthor of the rugby world, so by prophesying doomed portents for the All Blacks he was just playing the role he had been assigned. However, as much as New Zealand booed and hissed, Woodward's assertion that the All Blacks had not yet turned a corner began to look a little less like crazy talk in the weeks to come.

Argentina were put away comfortably enough the week after England had been hammered in Auckland. The selectors took the opportunity to make 10 changes for a fixture against a Pumas side that were battling jet-lag, inadequate recovery time and a chronic lack of funding. The new personnel inevitably took time to gel, so there was an element of understanding that the performance was scratchy.

On 10 July the All Blacks were made to sweat hard for a 41-26 victory against the combined Pacific Island team in Albany. The first rumblings of discontent surfaced after that game. The forwards hadn't imposed themselves the same way they had against the English. They had been sucked into playing the Island way, which was loose and fast and opened the game up. That was a worry. That was like the bad old days when All Black forwards were powerless to shape an alternative destiny. If they had been in control, they would have tightened proceedings. As the game wore on it became apparent that the Islanders were relishing the freedom they were being given to run. The All Blacks needed to roll up their sleeves and wrap a big arm round the throat of proceedings. The team had leaders, they needed to lead. The big squeeze never came though, and the Pacific Islanders were allowed to get uncomfortably close.

Some of those fears that surfaced in Albany were alleviated in Wellington a week later when the All Blacks were in control for the full 80 minutes against Australia in filthy conditions. The swagger from the first two games was back. The forwards obviously had a rocket put up them and they bumped and burled, scrummed and jumped all night. There was a touch more mongrel too, but still, the words of Woodward must have jabbed into Henry's heart. While the forwards had lifted their game in Wellington, the backs were still in a muddle.

Wayne Smith had them aligned closer to the traffic and flatter in relation to each other. The premise was that it would better fix opposition defenders and stop them automatically drifting to the outside men. The All Blacks needed to pose more of a threat by carrying the perception of being able to strike close to the ruck, in the middle or down the flanks. The theory stacked up, but the application was proving a different matter. The fluency that had marked Mitchell's reign had disappeared. The backs were now tentative and unable to pull off those sweeping movements that had seen them put the ball from touchline to touchline the year before.

By the time they played South Africa a week later in Christchurch, the only threat the backs were posing was to their own careers. The South Africans employed a rush defence that put the inside backs in a bigger tizz than a nun in a nudist colony. Spencer, an instinctive genius, looked troubled. He needed a little more time to pull the strings, and standing so flat was not his bag. The ball would arrive pretty much in the same package as a green shirt and that combination sucked the creativity right out of him. The backs were a bumbling shadow of the division that had cut such a dashing swathe the year before, scoring 17 Tri Nations tries. The flat backline left everyone flat and from looking a million dollars for most of 2003 – one unfortunate intercept pass aside – Spencer was starting to look like a player you could pick up in the two-dollar shop.

The All Blacks won though, thanks to a Doug Howlett try in the dying seconds. They scarcely deserved it. It wasn't just the backs who would be looking at their shoes come the debriefing on Monday morning. The old failings in the pack were very much back. The scrum was only steady and the lineout was not delivering much in the way of quality. The forwards only had Keven Mealamu and Jerry Collins who could carry the ball with any real purpose, and as the Boks knew there was no other dynamic threat in the pack, they double-teamed those two on defence. As a consequence of having so little firepower, the pack couldn't build momentum or work out how to create space for the backs. The Boks were practising organised chaos and it worked all too easily. The All Black leaders had crept way back into their shell. If there was a small mercy for Henry, it was that his side remained unbeaten. But everyone knew it was only a matter of time before that changed.

When defeat came in Sydney on 7 August and then again in Johannesburg on 14 August, there was nothing protecting Henry from a snarling public. The early promise had evaporated. The memory of Robinson plugging Lawrence Dallaglio square on the snoz seemed a lifetime ago. Maybe the fact Robinson had succumbed to a serious back injury before the start of the Tri Nations was linked with the decline in form. So too the loss of Richie McCaw, after the brilliant openside had taken a massive head knock in the first test against England and was forced to sit out the Tri Nations. Certainly the All Blacks lacked aggressive edge without him and Robinson. Maybe those promising beginnings had only been possible because England were simply no good. The Poms couldn't mount any sustained pressure to test the mental fortitude of the All Blacks under Henry. No one cracked under pressure because they were never put under any pressure.

It was a different story against the Boks and Wallabies. They had the firepower to ask questions, and the horrid news for Henry was that his side had not managed to come up with any of the answers. More than eight months after crashing at Telstra Stadium in Sydney, the All Blacks went back there under Henry and it looked as if not a single thing had changed. It was as if all the ghosts of games past had risen out of the ground and infiltrated the souls of those trying to exorcise them. Just as they had in the World Cup, the All Blacks had bashed away aimlessly with no real idea of how to break the defence or turn the Wallabies. Just as they had eight months earlier, the All Blacks showed no understanding of deviating from the plan. The story in Johannesburg was exactly the same. The pressure came on and no one in the All Black camp wanted to know. Or if they had wanted to know, there was no real knowledge of how one went about standing up to be counted. The All Blacks were some way, a very long way in fact, from becoming rugby's great innovators.

It was a sobering thought for Henry and his panel, that for all the window-dressing of the earlier games, the All Blacks had in fact progressed by a factor of exactly zero. By some calculations, they might even have regressed under Henry. After all, the flat backline had shone in the classroom but failed miserably in its practical assignments. The All Blacks finished the Tri Nations with a try tally of five. It was pretty depressing and spirits would have been almost crushed had it not been for the fact that at least Henry and his assistants had a clear idea of where they had gone wrong.

When the All Blacks trudged off Telstra Stadium having lost 23-18, the coaches had their suspicions. When the All Blacks retired to the changing sheds at Ellis

Park after losing 40-26 a week later, they knew for sure. The players were physically and mentally drained for both of those tests.

The bulk of Henry's test squad had begun pre-season training with their respective Super 12 squads on 5 January. For those who had been at the World Cup, that was only a month off. The first Super 12 match had kicked off on 20 February and most of Henry's squad had played between nine and 13 games in that competition. It was a big ask. The Super 12 is deceptively physical and the schedule is intense. It's non-stop, with teams only afforded one bye week. Some weeks there are short turnarounds – a game on Saturday followed by a game on Friday. There is also a hefty travel burden. By the last weekend in May, the winning team is usually elated not only because they have been crowned champions, but also because they are at last going to get a mini-break from rugby.

But in 2004, with Henry having re-introduced the All Black trial and the Crusaders reaching the final, that mini-break was not on offer to the likes of McCaw, Daniel Carter, Justin Marshall, Aaron Mauger and Chris Jack. The Probables and Possibles assembled for a week in Palmerston North from the end of May. It was an opportunity for Henry, Hansen and Smith to do for the first time what they were being paid to do: actually coach the players. It was a week of hard work for the players followed by an uncompromising trial match at Eden Park on 3 June. Those selected in the All Black squad of 26 then had to get through some more hard work in training before playing England at Carisbrook on 12 June. Then there was England again on 19 June, followed by Argentina on 26 June. A few days with the family were scheduled before the players reconvened in Auckland on 5 July to play the Pacific Islanders on 10 July. After that there were consecutive tests against Australia on 17 July and South Africa on 24 July. The squad arrived in Australia on 3 August to play the Wallabies on 7 August and then had to fly to South Africa the day after a bruising test to play the Springboks at altitude on 14 August. It had been a murderous schedule – eight tests in 10 weeks. And it was a schedule that came after an intense Super 12 season.

By mid-August most of the All Black squad had been assembled in one rugby team or another for eight months solid with no significant break. Henry and his coaching team admit they underestimated both the physical and mental drain so much time in the environment causes. The actual games were only one factor. Sure, they took a lot out of individuals, but the real drain on energy was training and being mentally and spiritually locked into the confines of the team environment.

The preparation required to play even at Super Rugby level is quite staggering. The normal training week starts on a Monday, usually with conditioning games such as touch and soccer that get the heart-rate going and ease out the stiffness. Tuesdays and Wednesdays are usually set aside for more technical and physical work such as scrummaging, lineouts and defensive drills where there is a high aerobic demand as well as a contact load. The players also fit in weights sessions around team training. Thursday would be a day off for a Saturday game with Friday hosting the traditional captain's run. The All Black training week is fairly similar, maybe a little more intense as it is another level up. And it's the training that players will tell you is the grind.

Test rugby is a glamorous business. But the glamour is largely restricted to the 80 minutes viewed by the world. The rest of it is not anywhere near the life of beer and skittles some would have you believe. As with any job, there is a sense of being stuck on the hamster wheel. Wake up, go training, have lunch, train some more, eat again, study the opposition, watch crappy movie, go to bed. Repeat five times a week. The life of a rugby player is every bit as mundane as that of us mere mortals. In fact, it is probably more so. Adding to their mental anguish is the constant living out of a suitcase. Once you have seen one five-star hotel you have seen them all. There is so much time away from home. So much time in the pockets of team-mates. So much time devoted to the repetitive chores of training and recovering. So much time required to attend team meetings and analysis – and so little time left for horizon-broadening activities.

No All Black would seriously expect to sit down with a random group of data processors, bakers, delivery men and accountants and be treated to a chorus of sympathetic 'ahs' if he banged on about how much his job sucked. There is a recognition within every individual privileged to wear the black jersey that they have an opportunity others would remove limbs for. The players simply respond to the demands of the job and when it comes to the All Blacks, it is the coaching panel that sets those demands.

By the time the All Blacks got to South Africa, Henry and his team knew they were making too many demands of the players, and the realisation was growing that they were perhaps overworking them. There was also a failure to realise how mentally stale the players could become. Asked to do the same-old, same-old, week-in, week-out, many of the squad were in dire need of a holiday by the time they embarked on that final leg of the Tri Nations. A sharp, enthused mind is just as vital in the test match arena as fresh legs. There was no one really showing the required mental energy in those two away Tri Nations games.

There were other problems too. The initial team Henry selected had contained an abundance of natural leaders: McCaw, Robinson, Gibbes and Rush. With those four in the pack, there was no shortage of advice flying around. There was a pleasing directness about much of the All Blacks' work. The English got antsy and Gibbes and Robinson met fire with fire. The All Blacks, in those first two games, were no longer a soft touch. Nor were they a rudderless side – it wasn't a case of all being individually superb at their craft but with no one on the field to conduct them into some sort of meaningful collective.

But once McCaw and Robinson were lost to injury, that edge was blunted. Their respective absences also robbed the team of the best operator in world rugby at the breakdown and probably their best lineout forward. Simon Maling came in to replace Robinson at lock, and while he gave dutiful and honest service, he just didn't carry the same presence as the Waikato man. Marty Holah would make the test side of any country other than New Zealand. He's unfortunate his time has overlapped that of McCaw, possibly the greatest No 7 ever to play the game. And as gallantly as Holah battled at the bottom of rucks, he was never going to be able to fully replace McCaw. Without McCaw, the All Blacks were missing that special something, that critical, undefinable X-factor that often makes the difference between winning and losing. McCaw is one of those 'follow-me' leaders, his work ethic an inspiration and his passion infectious.

Compounding these problems was the realisation that Rush was not really a test No 8 and that a loose forward trio containing both Rush and Gibbes lacked the necessary pace and ball-carrying power. Rush had stormed into the team after a solid trial. Henry knew him well from his time with Auckland and the Blues, and he liked the leadership value Rush could bring. Yet by the latter half of the season it was apparent that Rush's leadership value was being offset by his lack of genuine pace and ability to smash the hard yards. Gibbes was cut from similar cloth and was winning time in the No 6 jersey partly as a result of his leadership and partly as a result of his aerial work at the back of the lineout.

Henry and Hansen liked having an athletic blindside to increase the options at the lineout. But like Rush, Gibbes was fractionally short of pace and impact. If McCaw had been fit and if the All Blacks had a world class, bruising No 8, Gibbes would have been offering a complementary skill-set. The balance of the back row would have been good and the few weaknesses in Gibbes's game would have gone undetected. As it was, the mix just wasn't right and Gibbes and Rush were left exposed, their faults exaggerated.

By the away leg of the campaign, both men were short of confidence, leaving the All Blacks light on leaders. Other than Umaga, there was only one other senior figure who was still fizzing and making himself heard: halfback Justin Marshall. The Cantabrian was the most experienced player in the side and in possession of a seriously tenacious character. Back in 1997 he'd enjoyed a short stint as All Black captain when Sean Fitzpatrick had picked up a knee injury on the end-of-season tour to the UK. Marshall didn't lack confidence and was one of those rare players with the courage to speak his mind. He was a go-to guy for many young All Blacks who were seeking advice. He was the voice that could be heard snapping away at the back of every ruck, cajoling, demanding and directing.

Yet, strangely, the coaches were keen to hear less of Marshall's voice. There was a feeling his shining light was casting a shadow over other potential leaders in the team. The strength and force of his personality was such that others were standing back and looking to Marshall to lead them. Test football was a jungle and without light, certain species would never grow. It wasn't that Marshall needed to be cut down; the coaches just wanted to trim his canopy, as it were, so there was more opportunity for others to flourish.

There was, of course, another major problem. The so called flat backline had proven more trouble than it was worth. The All Blacks were not generating width. They wanted to pose a threat tight to the ruck, through the middle and out wide. They were failing on all three fronts and the deadliest backline in world rugby no longer had a single weapon at its disposal. The system didn't suit Spencer. It restricted his natural game, which was instinctive. The selectors had a choice; they could either pick Spencer and allow him a free hand to run the game as he saw it; or they could persevere with the flat backline but try another first five-eighths who was more suited to the demands of the strategy. After a difficult night in Sydney, the coaches opted to change the personnel. They were convinced the tactic was good. It just needed the right man to lead it and for the forwards to get on the front foot. Spencer was dropped and in came Andrew Mehrtens.

It was perhaps a sign of how low morale had sunk that Spencer gave the impression of almost being relieved to be part of the team no longer. The enjoyment had disappeared for Spencer. He was being charged with orchestrating a system that appeared flawed and copping heaps for not being able to make it work. He never played for the All Blacks again, and the following June he moved to the UK. It wasn't his way to leave the scene kicking and screaming. He took his medicine quietly and didn't have a bad word to say once he returned from South Africa. But a year later, sitting in the lounge of his new home in Northampton, he opened up a little bit. 'I knew what the problem was,' he said of the All Blacks' woes in 2004. 'Players always know where the problems are but we don't say that. I have accepted it. It doesn't bother me. I always knew that deep down I could achieve and that was all that mattered to me.'

When Mehrtens didn't fare any better, it was obvious the problem was not Spencer – it was the strategy. Mehrtens was more comfortable on the gain line. He was more of a distributor and facilitator, unlike Spencer, who was more of a runner and a creator. The fact Mehrtens couldn't really make it work either suggested the perseverance with the flat backline had been misplaced. The coaches needed to be bold enough to accept that some of their ideas were not working. And more importantly, they needed to accept that test football was a more physically demanding business than they had initially imagined.

5   Super size rugby

IT WAS little wonder the All Blacks were fatigued by the second half of 2004. Rugby was suffering from the most extreme growing pains. The professional player of 2004 was a staggeringly different beast from his amateur predecessor. So different as to be considered an entirely different species. The last decade had seen the amateur player evolve into a professional athlete.

Back in the old days, amateur players had the mighty inconvenience of holding down a day job, which had restricted the potential hours a player could spend training. Sports science had not really bothered too much with amateur rugby either. Few coaches put it top of their agenda and there was no cash to encourage impoverished academics to delve into the code. And besides, most academics were smart enough to know that any advice they offered, based on valid research, would simply drift in one ear and out the other of most players and coaches.

Rugby was not such a serious business in the era before money worked its way into players' bank accounts. Even the world's best players were playing for the love of the game. Sure, there were perks to be had. Jobs with friendly, empathetic employers could be found. Travel expenses could be imaginative. New boots could appear in a locker with no questions asked, while any All Black invited to spend an off-season in France or Italy might find himself exceptionally well looked after – picked up at the airport, put up in flash digs with a shoebox full of cash sitting unobtrusively at the bottom of the wardrobe. But no one got rich. And because no one got rich, everyone had to hold down some other form of employment. And because they were holding down some other form of employment, even if that employment was with an understanding and empathetic employer, there was a massive restriction on the number of hours the players could train. That restriction prevented the players from exploiting their full athletic potential.

Time, or lack of it, was their greatest enemy. Only so much strength work could be done and as a consequence the elite rugby player didn't differ massively in size from the general population. Only so much speed work could be done so even rugby's fastest players would have been left for dead by any full-time track sprinter.

The world's best players did what they could. They squeezed in gym sessions around work and family life. The off-season would be spent pounding the roads and pumping iron whenever possible, but there needed to be balance. Rugby, prior to 1995, was essentially a lovable distraction for even the very best All Blacks. The mighty Colin Meads had his farm, Earle Kirton had his dentistry practice, Chris Laidlaw his legal and political work, David Kirk his medical studies, Olo Brown his accountancy firm. They loved their rugby, and while they took it deadly seriously, they were driven by Corinthian motivations.

Making friends for life was a good reason to play. Just being part of something, that feeling of belonging – that was reward enough for even the best players. Which is why, come Saturday night after they had dragged their weary limbs off the paddock, even the very best players wanted to sink a few cold ones as was their right. No sports scientist on earth would have a hope in hell of persuading bruised and victorious amateur All Blacks that a heavy booze intake after playing was going to delay their recovery time. If they could chase the beer down with a good feed, so much the better. They deserved it. If Sunday was a write-off, so what? Training could wait until later in the week. Rugby, after all, was not their job. It was their hobby and if they weren't getting paid, they had to make sure they actually enjoyed being part of the sport. That was the amateur way.

By 2004 the sport bore no similarity to that bygone era. The single greatest difference was time. The professional player had oodles of the stuff. Now there was no restriction, other than the limitations of the human body, on how much training could be crammed into the week. Every player had the opportunity to fulfil his athletic potential. There was time to push the body to its limits and beyond. There was time to get through the necessary strength and conditioning work. There was time to devote to speed and speed endurance work. And not only was there time, there was also knowledge. Now the game was professional there was opportunity for experienced fitness trainers and conditioning coaches to get involved. Knowledge and understanding of how to prepare professional athletes were being stolen from other codes and all of a sudden rugby was inundated with the latest thinking from the sports science world. Rugby had embarked on one of the steepest evolutionary curves ever seen in professional sport.

Since 1995 the professional rugby player had become bigger, faster and stronger. The new species of super-athlete bulged where the old had sagged. The new players rippled. The old lot had wobbled. The change in size, power and athleticism had been dramatic. Exactly how dramatic became apparent when the Lions toured New Zealand in 2005.

The All Blacks named to play the Lions in the first test in Christchurch were on average 10 kg per man heavier than the All Black test team that had last played the Lions in 1993. Where the 1993 All Blacks had averaged 93 kg, the 2005 All Blacks were boasting an average weight of 103 kg. In what seemed like the blink of an eye, players had added an extra 10 percent to their frames. No one had really noticed, or at least not fully appreciated the new scale. Sean Fitzpatrick, for example, considered a bulky scrummaging hooker in his day, was 93 kg in 1993, heavier than only one All Black who started in 2005. That All Black was Daniel Carter, the pin-up boy of New Zealand rugby. And even then, Fitzpatrick was only just heavier. Va'aiga Tuigamala, universally recognised as a scarily big wing in 1993, was the same weight as All Black halfback Justin Marshall. This was a mind-blowing realisation. Rugby was supposed to be a game for all shapes and sizes, and halfback had traditionally been the berth for the little man, the nuggety bloke who was a bit lippy and definitely undersized. And first-fives had forever and a day been weedy sorts who never fancied the rough and tumble but carried themselves with elegance on slight, graceful frames.

But in 2005, at 94 kg, Marshall was heavier than every single All Black back of 1993 except Tuigamala, who was the same weight. And at 91 kg, Carter was heavier than every back bar Tuigamala and the same weight as the legendary openside flanker Michael Jones. Rugby had followed the lead of fast-food chains and super-sized itself. Rugby had learned the art of turning a simple hamburger into a Big Mac and the sport's ability to build a super-athlete was quite remarkable. In 2003 a tall, skinny kid emerged from the gloom of club rugby to fill in for Wellington during the NPC when they had an injury crisis at centre. It turned out that the kid in question, Conrad Smith, was rather good. The following year he was offered a Super 12 contract and when he followed that with another very encouraging NPC campaign, Smith was elevated to the All Blacks. He had come into the professional ranks at 85 kg. When he played in the final test against the Lions in 2005, he ran on to Eden Park at 95 kg. In the space of 18 months, Smith had gained 10 kg.

The population as a whole has grown both in height and weight since 1995. But professional rugby players have grown disproportionately quickly. They have also grown disproportionately powerful. Smith might have become 10 percent heavier, but most reliable estimates suggest he would be about 30 percent more powerful than he was when he weighed 85 kg. He is faster too. Since 1995 the fastest players in the game have seen their times for 40 m come down from five seconds to about 4.75 seconds. Such improvements in speed have been emulated by players in every position. The effects of power-based training have not just added bulk, they have added strength and incredible raw power. And with the players capable of running faster, hitting harder and operating at maximum capacity for longer, it was inevitable that the type of game coaches wanted to play was going to change as well.

In 1963 Scotland played Wales in Edinburgh in a Five Nations game that became memorable solely for the fact it contained 111 lineouts. That's one lineout every 45 seconds. In an 80-minute game of rugby, it doesn't leave much time for anything else. That game at Murrayfield was extreme, but in the pre-professional days it wasn't uncommon to have close to 100 lineouts in a match. It meant there were quite often backs who played an entire game without touching the ball or making a tackle.

But that was the nature of rugby for much of the amateur period, and even as the game moved closer to its modern format in the 1980s and 1990s, it was still very much a stop-start affair with higher quantities of passive content.

The arrival of the 2005 Lions provided another reminder of how much rugby had changed in the last decade. In the build-up to the second test, a big screen was erected on Wellington's waterfront showing historic footage of Lions versus All Black tests. The games from the 1970s and 1980s, even the three-test series in 1993, bore little resemblance to the test football of the last five years. There were the obvious differences in the size and shape of the players. Those players in the old footage were noticeably smaller and less athletic, even allowing for the fact that their lack of tone and bulk was exacerbated by the billowy cotton shirts they wore, as opposed to the body-hugging lycra we have now come to accept. Then there was the appearance of skinny white guys throughout both teams' backlines. New Zealand especially just didn't pick skinny white guys any more. Terry Wright was the last of that breed and it seemed almost comical watching such slight, non-confrontational athletes in operation at the highest level. But what was most noticeable were the endless lineouts, the constant scrummaging, the scragging tackles and the emphasis on kicking as opposed to running. In the old footage, both teams committed numbers to the ruck and maul. It was a totally different game – a fact that has been borne out by research.

Professor Will Hopkins of Auckland University of Technology and Ken Quarrie, the New Zealand Rugby Union's injury prevention officer, have analysed the opening Bledisloe Cup games of each year between 1972 and 2004. The purpose of their research was to illustrate the changes in elite rugby during the last three decades. Essentially they ran the state-of-the-art analysis programmes used by the All Black coaches today through video footage of all 26 tests. What they found provides possibly the most compelling evidence to date as to the enormous physical demands being placed on the modern rugby player.

Hopkins and Quarrie found that between 1995 and 2004, the time the ball was in play increased by five minutes and 54 seconds. That increase has an obvious impact – it places a higher aerobic burden on the players, and all research shows that players are more likely to be injured when they are fatigued. The real burden on the players, though, is that in those extra six minutes of action, they have managed to squeeze in an extraordinary amount of physical contact.

After the 1990 series, the leather ball was ditched in favour of a synthetic product that made it easier for players to grip. The improvement in the ball combined with the improvement in ground conditions and the increased time available to hone individual skills, meant the game became much faster and more accurate in the professional era. Hopkins and Quarrie noted there was a slight decrease in the frequency of scrums in the professional era, while lineouts have been cut dramatically. Between 1972 and 1974 there were more than 60 lineouts per match. By 1995 that number had dropped to 39 and by 2004 there were only 28. There was also a 30 percent reduction in the number of kicks per match during the professional era. The big increases in activity came in two areas – tackling and rucking. The research shows the number of rucks in the professional age has increased fourfold. Hopkins and Quarrie put the increase down to the introduction of the use-it-or-lose-it law in 1994. Bored rigid by watching teams like England set up rolling mauls that could begin in London and end in Newcastle, the International Rugby Board sanctioned a law change that meant if a team started a maul and then couldn't generate any forward momentum or was unable to release the ball, a scrum would be called, with the opposition awarded the put-in. That encouraged professional teams to ruck rather than maul and to seek contact to try and commit opposition defenders to the breakdown. This was very different from what had gone before.

Hitting rucks was high impact for both attacker and defender. The toll on the body was massive. Shoulders were taking huge punishment. The upper body was being pounded again and again by the constant collisions. The collective tackle counts also went through the roof after 1995. A lot of the extra tackling was a direct result of the greater rucking activity. The pattern of play became almost formulaic. The attacking team would look to set up a ruck, while the defence would look to tackle the ball-carrier aggressively to try to turn the ball over. The attacking team would hope to suck significant numbers of defenders into the ruck and, once the ball was released, go through the whole procedure again, hopefully to generate momentum and commit the opposition defence to the point where space is created further out from the breakdown. All that activity close to the breakdown was built around explosive leg work, with the attackers trying to drive through tackles and defenders trying to land the king hit to wrap up man and ball.

That change in tackling technique was crucial. Not only are players now making a greater number of tackles per game, but they are far more explosive, higher in the target area and therefore placing a massive physical strain on the body. In the amateur days, players were coached to tackle an opponent round the legs and slide down. The idea was to stop the attacker from running. There was no concept of driving the man back or dislodging the ball with the aggression of the initial hit. Nor was any team consistently looking to wrap up the ball-carrier to ensure the ball couldn't be transferred to a team-mate. By the turn of the millennium it was commonplace to see every player target his opponent's midriff or chest. Nor was it uncommon to see sides double-team, with two defenders hitting one runner. There was no room in the game any more for passive tackling – locking the legs of an opponent and then relying on their momentum to bring them to ground. Defenders were looking to launch into the hit to make a high-impact connection.

As a consequence of these high-impact strategies, certain positions have changed dramatically in terms of the key skill and athletic requirements. The Lions series once again provided evidence of that. In 1993 the All Black midfield of Grant Fox, Walter Little and Frank Bunce had a combined weight of 236 kg. In 2005, Daniel Carter, Aaron Mauger and Tana Umaga were 16 kg a man heavier. The midfield was still a place for creative sorts, but they had to be big, bruising creative sorts. It is the same with the front-row. Carl Hayman, Keven Mealamu and Tony Woodcock were collectively 31 kg heavier than their 1993 counterparts Olo Brown, Fitzpatrick and Craig Dowd. Scrummaging technique had changed. To be destructive in the modern game, props and hookers have to engage with an explosive hit. They also have to be able to carry the ball in short, powerful, bursts as well as make aggressive and effective tackles. No wonder the attrition rate in the front-row is so high. These players pound into almost 20 scrums a game, hit 40-odd rucks, make at least five tackles and can sometimes carry the ball for more than 100 m a game.

As All Black conditioning coach Graham Lowe said in the build-up to that first Lions test in Christchurch: 'The game is physically more demanding. The whole goal is bigger, stronger, faster. But, if you have both groups trying to put bigger, stronger, faster people on the field, the end result is we have bigger impact happening all over. At the very least, I would want my players to be playing no more than week-by-week. When they play a test they get bashed. It takes them two to three days to recover and our training has to reflect that. There is so much damage, they build up a lot of waste product in their bodies. They need to get rid of that and then gradually build the training week back up.'

That training build-up really does have to be gradual. When Lowe says the players get bashed when they play a test, it's at the *Once Were Warriors* end of the scale.

Chris Jack hobbled down the corridor of Dublin's Castleknock Hotel and then curled his giant frame into one of the easy chairs in the lobby. What an irony

– an easy chair. The All Black lock was not finding anything easy about getting comfortable on this particular piece of furniture. Mind you, he wasn't finding anything particularly easy after a physical encounter a few days earlier against Wales in Cardiff. Wales might have been fairly ordinary but they were still a side loaded with big units who needed to be subdued. It was Wednesday, almost four full days since the test in Cardiff, and still Jack was moving a touch too gingerly for everyone's liking. 'I'm still stiff as hell,' he said when he eventually got settled. 'I have been training these last couple of days but I'm still not moving as freely as I would like. It was a physical game against Wales. It takes time to recover. I'll be feeling better by the end of the week.'

Jack wasn't alone in looking as though he had stumbled out of a casualty ward. Most of the forwards who had packed down alongside him in Cardiff were still feeling the effects. Those soft-tissue areas were still tender and the legs were still heavy despite the best efforts of sports science to reduce the length of recovery times. Players no longer come off the pitch to a shed full of beer and a long night on the town. The first hour after a test is deemed the crucial time to replace those lost fluids. That doesn't mean alcohol. Gallons of sports drinks and protein shakes go down the hatch. After a night game, most players are in need of sustenance, having restricted their food intake to a decidedly bland bowl of plain spaghetti and grilled chicken or fish four hours before kick-off. Most players will eat and then have a massage and/or a swim if there is a pool in the changing rooms. There is rarely a night on the tiles to be had after that, and usually the players are back in the team hotel some time after midnight and into bed between 2 a.m. and 3 a.m. A lot of the forwards climb into the scratcher wearing 'skins' – waist-to-toe tights that aid muscle recovery. It's back in the pool first thing in the morning, maybe even a light jog with stretching and massage to get the stiffness and bruising out.

Even after all that, most players are still incapable of anything more than a light run on the Monday after a test. And on the Monday after the All Blacks played England at Twickenham on 19 November 2005, even the light run around was beyond most of the players who had been involved in that brutal encounter. In the history of rugby, there has probably never been a game as physical as that match in London where the All Blacks clung on to win 23-19. The impact of some of the collisions could be felt in the highest reaches of Twickenham's steepling stands.

On the tighthead of the All Black scrum was Hayman, a 1.95 m, 115 kg beast. On the loosehead of the English scrum was Andrew Sheridan, a 1.95 m, 120 kg beast. When the first scrum went down, 80,000 people winced at the ferocity of the clash. All across the park there were big, powerful men determined to smash the living daylights out of other big, powerful men. When the players came out to meet the press after the game, there were plenty who looked as if they were in considerable distress. There were bruised and cut faces, gammy legs dragging behind sore players, ice packs being pressed everywhere and there was even one ear clinging gamely to the side of England captain Martin Corry's head. The rugby hadn't been brilliant through the 80 minutes, but it sure as hell had been physical. The English are a giant side and try to make their presence felt. They had succeeded on that front at least. The All Blacks knew they had been in a game – a game that had moved off the scale in terms of physicality and brutality.

The sport was moving so fast, the players changing in shape and capability almost by the week, it was easy to underestimate the demands of test football. It was easy to forget the players were being pushed beyond breaking-point. When the games were consecutive, the problems were most severe. On the Monday after a test, the coaches were focusing on the next assignment and were anxious to get working on the game-plan and any improvements they felt had to be made. But the players were not able to keep up. They were still struggling to deal with the effects of the previous Saturday night.

Former All Black conditioning coach Mike Anthony recalls from his time under John Mitchell how the training week had to be structured. 'It was frustrating because the ideal scenario was to front-load the work at the start of the week so the players were fresh by the time you came to play on Saturday. But it couldn't work like that because the players were still feeling the knocks on the Monday. We ended up having what we called a "flush" on Mondays, which was a conditioning game session that got the players running around and easing the stiffness out. We wouldn't do any contact work until a Tuesday or more usually a Wednesday and there would be some players who just weren't able to take any contact at all before they played again on the Saturday. None of the forwards could really do any heavy weights and we tended to restrict the contact work to hitting pads.

'The impact when these guys were hitting each other was huge. They were about 10 kg heavier per man than they were 10 years ago and we noted from our data that the backs were comparable in weight to most of the forwards that played in the 1960s and 1970s. Midfield backs were 100 kg, which was about the weight of most locks 30 years ago, and they could still run under 5 seconds for 40 metres.'

Henry and his team were managing the training load in largely the same way as Mitchell and Deans had before them. The difference in 2004, though, was that the game had taken another step up in physicality. The momentum was now irreversible.

The increase in size, power and speed was accelerating. The main driver of that was the improved knowledge and understanding of the players' capabilities and the best way to train them. Training methods were being constantly refined. The traditional four-mile plod that would have been the staple of most amateur players' pre-season work was booted out. In the first few years of professionalism the focus moved to building conditioning work around blocks of 40-minute endurance runs and strength work in the gym. As the season came closer, the emphasis would shift to speed that was honed by short sprint repetitions in straight lines. But by 2004 even that approach was being thought of as outdated.

Rugby was an explosive game where athletes were required to burst into life for short periods. Lowe began pushing new ideas into the All Black camp when he was appointed. On the eve of the Lions tour, he was happy to explain how training methods were evolving. 'In our conditioning work we may look at getting players to run five times 1000 m, getting down to 50 m sprints with short recoveries. And we might do a lot of work on hills. The early stuff that came out in New Zealand was that we would do three times 40 minutes of running. That was in the pre-season programme but we were just running at the same speed. A lot of rugby is obviously short, sharp bursts.'

The training was evolving because Henry wanted to build a new type of rugby player. He wanted top quality athletes who could also handle the demands of the breakdown and set-piece. The emphasis was more firmly on explosive power – creating athletes who could accelerate over much shorter distances of 10 m, 20 m and 30 m. The concept of being able to do it in straight lines was also looking as if it came in with the ark. The statistics were adamant that players, even outside backs, rarely ran flat out for 40 m in a straight line. Yet the 40 m sprint had been the traditional measurement of speed in the professional era. That was mainly because NFL scouts had used that as the speed test at pre-season camps and it had been adopted by other contact sports across the world.

To thrive in the new regime, players would have to become even faster, at least over shorter distances, and even more powerful.

There was another significant factor that was super-sizing rugby. By 2004, rugby was in its tenth year of professionalism. In the first year of professional football, all the players came into the game on a level playing field in that no one, bar the odd player who might have returned having spent some time in League, had any experience as a professional athlete. Plenty of players had trained hard in the amateur era but not to the same extent as they would be required to do once they were being paid. That meant most players came into the competition with what the conditioning coaches would call a training age of zero. When players retired or moved overseas in the early years of Super 12 they were generally replaced with players who had emerged through the NPC. These new players tended to have a lower training age because anyone just playing NPC would only have been semi-professional. There was a lag period, then, as it took time for the new players to build their strength and speed to the level required, which diluted the impact and physicality of the Super 12 and also test football.

But as the sport advanced and the organisation improved, better development programmes were put in place. Unions began to develop Academy systems that identified the area's best players. The top schools too, were becoming more serious and professional in their outlook and pumping money into new facilities and specialised staff. The upshot was that once elite players hit 17 or 18 they were being put through the same sort of training programmes as the full-time professionals. Take the kids going through the Auckland Rugby Union Academy system as an example of what was being replicated around the country. Under the direction of elite performance director Mike Wallace, the athletes in the programme are expected to train twice a day four times a week between September and March. Depending on their size and position their programme is split between conditioning sessions and weight sessions. A slightly built outside back may split his sessions so the emphasis is on building strength, which would see him working five times in the gym with three sessions of exhaustive aerobic work. A heavier, stronger athlete hoping to play in the front row would possibly split his work the other way – completing five conditioning sessions and three weights sessions.

The conditioning work is punishing. Players are expected to complete pyramid sessions that require them to run 400 m, rest, 800 m, rest, 1200 m, rest, 1600 m, rest, and then work back down through 1200 m, 800 m and 400 m. There are other killer sessions to be had, like running up Mount Eden. In the gym the players are taught how to lift heavy weights correctly. They learn good technique and the concept of power. By the time your typical Academy player graduates into the professional ranks, he will most likely be anything from 10 kg to 15 kg heavier than when he was first picked up by the programme. His training age will be between three years and five years depending on his age when he signs a professional contract.

The consequences of having the game repopulated by such fit, strong athletes are significant. There is no drop-off in power when a rookie player makes a professional squad. There is no lag. The new player comes in at a level equal to, and in terms of athletic capability, sometimes higher than that of the players already on the books. A player with a training age of four, say, at the age of 21 will also be able to make accelerated increases in size, strength and speed once he moves full-time into the professional set-up.

The success of the Academy systems can be seen in the products they produce. Isaia Toeava made his debut for Auckland in 2005 as a 95 kg 19-year-old inside back. He is a creative player, blessed with blistering pace and even at that age he was already heavier than incumbent All Black second five-eighths Aaron Mauger. Halfback Taniela Moa was another who pushed his way into the Auckland squad in 2005, tipping the scales at 97 kg. Again, at just 20, he was already on a physical par with the likes of Byron Kelleher, Piri Weepu and Jimmy Cowan.

These players weren't being churned out at that size for the sake of it. The system had not set itself the goal of building bigger athletes just to see if it was possible. The purpose of the Academy system is pragmatic – it is simply giving young athletes a chance to survive in professional football. As Wallace says: 'They are not there to build their beach muscles. It is vital they build strength around the vital joints, in the muscles and ligaments around the knee, ankles and shoulders. Rugby is such a high impact sport that these young athletes have to be prepared physically to be able to cope with that.'

Going professional had opened Pandora's box. It had set in motion an evolutionary process that no one had really seen coming. The athletes were obviously bigger than the general population in a way they hadn't been during the amateur days. The game itself was played in a style that exposed the players to more contact and an intensity of contact that was significantly greater than it had been 10 years earlier. There was no going back. The wheels had been set in motion and the players were going to get bigger, stronger and faster every year. The impacts were only going to increase in frequency and intensity. Throughout Henry's first season in charge there had been a consistency to the All Black selections. The strongest side had been identified and, barring injury, that was the side the selectors picked. By the final two tests, they were fully aware that if they persevered with the same players every week they were going to burn them out. There was going to be blood on their hands as players became more exposed to injury.

But the picture was clouded by a dangerous paradox. The players had made these dramatic advances in athleticism and test rugby had evolved into a gladiatorial contest that sucked every last molecule of energy out of every participant. It left bodies ravaged and only ready to perform again after several days' recuperation. And yet, in direct contrast was the policy pervading the administrative ranks.

Rugby's executives had been charged with bringing the necessary cash into the game to make sure the players could exist as professionals, so that they didn't have to hold down alternative employment. The biggest benefactor in the southern hemisphere had been media mogul Rupert Murdoch, who had pumped US$555 million into the game in 1995 when he bought the broadcast rights for both Super 12 and Tri Nations. That 10-year deal was almost up. In August 2004, just as Henry and his assistants were starting to think the super-size nature of rugby was demanding that individuals play less rather than more, New Zealand Rugby Union chief executive Chris Moller was in a locked room with his counterparts from South Africa and Australia pushing for the exact opposite.

6   Grabbing Murdoch's millions

THERE ARE some scientists who believe in chaos theory. It's one of those constructs that has a butterfly flapping its wings in one part of the world, eventually setting off a tornado on the opposite side of the world. The Sanzar alliance, in a way, was feeling the effects of chaos theory in September 2004.

The respective heads of the New Zealand, Australian and South African Rugby Unions were locked in negotiations with executives from News Limited, the arm of Rupert Murdoch's media empire charged with securing the broadcast rights for both the Super 12 and Tri Nations. In 1995 News had paid US$555 million to secure the exclusive 10-year rights. It was an extraordinarily good deal for the three individual countries. It was particularly sweet for New Zealand, given their relatively small population and limited means to raise the necessary cash to fund a professional sport. News left it to the three countries to split the money as they saw fit and New Zealand came out all right, taking roughly 34 percent of the pot with South Africa about 37 percent and Australia 29 percent.

The TV money was essentially used by the NZRU to pay the players and to meet the travel and operational costs of the five Super 12 franchises. That guaranteed revenue was critical in allowing the NZRU to plan ahead knowing they had the financial means to keep all five franchises in the competition for the full 10 years of the contract. With that box ticked, they could divert funds generated from other sources into the development of the game and ensure they had all the structures and systems in place to keep a constant flow of talented players.

By 2004, Murdoch's millions accounted for almost half of the NZRU's total revenue. That was partly because the contract was tiered to pay out more in the final years, but it was also because someone within the NZRU had made the smart move of striking a currency hedging deal a few years previously. With the News contract paid quarterly in US dollars, the value of each payment depended on the exchange rate. The fluctuations in the currency market were extreme and if the money was repatriated every quarter, the difference in value throughout the year would be significant. Being at the mercy of currency traders had little appeal to the NZRU, so they bought a number of contracts that fixed their quarterly payments at around US 42 cents. Regardless of how strong the Kiwi dollar became against the greenback, therefore, the News money would be paid out at US 42 cents. By 2004, when the Kiwi dollar was trading at well above 60 cents for most of the year, those futures contracts looked a very smart move indeed. Without them, the NZRU would have been staring at a $6.5 million financial loss in 2004 rather than the $20.5 million profit it posted.

The futures contracts were, however, all due to expire at the end of 2005, as was the deal with News Limited. The broadcast money was absolutely vital to the NZRU. The entire professional structure was underpinned by Murdoch's cash. Without it, the salaries on offer to New Zealand's best players would have nosedived. The market would have become unsustainable and every decent player in the land would have headed north to see if he could fill his pockets with the loot being flung around by the sugar daddies who had bought European rugby. The very future of the All Blacks was at stake and the renegotiation of the broadcast deal was, in a sense, the tornado that had the potential to crash into New Zealand rugby and cause serious damage. It was a wind that had been created 14 years earlier by what appeared to be a fairly innocuous merger of two struggling broadcast companies.

In early 1988, the fledgling British Satellite Broadcasting (BSB) consortium was awarded a licence to operate three channels by the Independent Broadcasting Authority. It had been anticipated that BSB would be the UK's only satellite service but in July 1988, Rupert Murdoch announced that having failed to gain regulatory approval for his pan-European satellite service, he was going to launch a four-channel UK-based service called Sky Television. The race was on. As in all new fields, the competitive advantages for the first company to get operational are usually massive and fatal for competitors.

BSB was the hot favourite until it ran into technical difficulties with its more expensive technology and had to watch Sky successfully launch in February 1989. BSB didn't get on air until March 1990 and because its satellite dishes were incompatible with Sky's there was a consumer stand-off. People didn't want to commit to one system or the other until there was a clear winner. By November that year, both firms were struggling. They had been hit with massive financial losses and BSB had no choice but to wave the white flag. The two firms merged, or rather, Sky effectively took over BSB and created the new company, British Sky Broadcasting that would be known as BSkyB. The new firm would be headquartered in a shabby-looking warehouse in Isleworth, West London. The butterfly had flapped its wings and it was from those humble roots that one of the largest and most successful media brands would be grown. BSkyB inherited BSB's powerful satellites and with the market clear, it could build without fear of competition. Consumers were ready to commit too, now that they knew who had won the duel. BSkyB had everything it needed to grow except one thing – it needed more content on its channels. And more specifically, it needed sport.

Sport was the modern-day opiate for the masses. If Murdoch could secure exclusive rights to broadcast the biggest sporting events, his business was going to boom. It was a simple idea – buy the rights and then show them on an extra-terrestrial service that consumers could only watch if they bought satellite dishes and then monthly subscriptions. It was going to be a win-win scenario for everyone. As BSkyB came into existence the broadcast market for sports in the UK, or more specifically soccer, was a pretty unimaginative business. The two key terrestrial players, BBC and ITV, bought highlights packages and the rights to show the odd game live. The sums paid were modest and the fans were left with one regular outlet: BBC's *Match of The Day*.

Murdoch was going to shake things up big style when he bid for and successfully secured the broadcast rights for the newly formed Premiership in 1992. The leading clubs had split from the Football Association to form a new top division. The BBC and ITV couldn't put up anything like the £191 million BSkyB offered to buy the five-year rights to show 66 games a season live. This was a very new concept for the fans. Previously, live league football was a rarity. The FA had never previously allowed it because it feared if one game was shown live it would affect attendances at games that were being played concurrently. But BSkyB was not confined by the programming restraints of the BBC. It had a dedicated sports channel which meant there was programming space to allow some games to be played outside the traditional Saturday afternoon 3 p.m. window. The fans loved it – they could get a fix of live football in the comfort of their own home. The clubs loved it too, because all of a sudden they had spare cash thanks to Murdoch's bid.

But Murdoch wasn't content with just soccer. BSkyB successfully chased the rights for everything. Murdoch could use the profits from the other parts of his media empire to fund the acquisitions. He had newspapers, broadcast networks and publishing houses to make sure BSkyB could outbid the competition. By 2004, BSkyB was a critical part of the Murdoch empire. It had extended its tentacles into a number of other satellite companies around the globe – it bought a significant stake in News Limited – and had become a major revenue generator.

BSkyB became involved with rugby when it bought the rights for the English Premiership in 1994. But Murdoch got really serious about the sport the following year when he saw Jonah Lomu at the World Cup. Legend has it that when he saw Lomu destroy England in Cape Town, Murdoch turned to his executive team and said 'get me that man'. They duly did get that man and the contract signed in 1995 gave News the first option to renewal. As the deal had been a massive success for both the Sanzar nations and the media conglomerate, News was absolutely going to invoke its right to renegotiate. The big question, however, was at what price was it going to re-commit? The world of broadcast rights had changed dramatically since 1995. Back then, Murdoch was in expansion mode. He needed to keep winning the rights for the biggest events so that he could corner the market and be the leading satellite broadcaster. Once he had secured the rights on medium- to long-term deals it became almost impossible for competitors to enter the market. And once he had the rights and had built relationships with the various sports he was broadcasting, it was going to be easier to renew contracts rather than win them. It had been an astonishing decade of growth for the satellite division, and by 2004 there was a belief the market was ready for a sustained period of consolidation. From a standing start, BSkyB won its five millionth subscriber in 2001, and two years later it had seven and a half million subscribers. But the sales curve had to flatten, and because everyone understood that cool-off was inevitable, the analysts employed to monitor the value of broadcast rights were all agreed the boom years were over.

There were big-picture factors that fuelled the perception broadcast rights were not worth what they once were. In 2000, when BSkyB renewed its contract with the English Premiership, the UK's major stock index, the FTSE 100, was trading well above 6000 points. The dot.com boom was in full flight, property values were soaring, confidence in the City was at an all-time high, as was consumer confidence. Everyone was thinking positively, and with so many paper millionaires about and pretty much everyone believing they had discretionary cash to spend how they liked, satellite TV was a must-have product. But the technology bubble burst as fast as it had appeared and all the paper millionaires vanished overnight. Then the Twin Towers of New York were hit on 11 September 2001 and stock markets around the world plummeted, economies faltered and the confidence was sucked out of every individual who witnessed those atrocities. By November 2001 the FTSE 100 was trading at just 3200 points. In the space of 18 months it had lost almost half its value.

Against such a backdrop, the omens looked particularly bleak for Sanzar. They were even bleaker when you examined the specifics of the market they were dealing in. Both Super 12 and Tri Nations had grown TV audiences in New Zealand, South Africa and Australia. But New Zealand was considered a saturated market with little room for growth. Australia was a worry too, with the sport still struggling to win the ratings of more popular codes such as NRL and AFL. In February 2004 Australia's Channel Seven dropped its free-to-air coverage of the Super 12. Fox Sports owned the subscriber rights and Channel Seven could only show the games after a delay of at least 90 minutes. It was an uninspiring package for viewers and uneconomic for the broadcaster. There was not a stampede to try and secure Channel Seven's forfeited package.

And then there was South Africa. Potentially, with its bigger population, South Africa was the most lucrative market. It was still largely untapped too. But both the country and the rugby administration were riddled with politics that made everyone uneasy. It was all a bit too volatile and it was to no one's great surprise that Murdoch himself dropped a public hint that Sanzar had better get ready to see a drop in the value of its broadcast contract.

Maybe that was an obvious negotiating stance, but even if it was, it was not a comment the Sanzar team could brush off without their respective hearts skipping a beat. By 2004 Murdoch was really the only player in the global market. If Sanzar didn't like what News Limited offered there was no alternative broadcaster waiting in the wings with a shoulder to cry on. As much as the

Sanzar executives tried to suggest otherwise, their negotiating position was not as strong as they would have liked. To improve it, they were going to have to come up with some stunning new innovations to the existing product.

In February 2000 the various heads of Sanzar met in Dublin. They were all in Ireland for an International Rugby Board get-together so it seemed a good idea to catch up. The basis of the meeting was to discuss further Australia and South Africa's request that each be granted another team in the Super 12. Australian Rugby Union chief executive John O'Neill firmly believed that to grow the sport, Australia needed to be granted a licence to operate four rather than three teams. Both Perth and Melbourne were crying out for representation and the expansion, O'Neill was sure, would be to the long-term betterment of the product Sanzar was offering News Limited. Such was the way of the alliance, South Africa argued that if Australia was to be granted another team, then it was only right that they too should be allowed to increase their number. The South Africans had four teams and had the player base to sustain a fifth, which would bring them in line with New Zealand.

The proposal was to introduce the new teams in 2003, two years before the existing broadcast deal with News Limited expired. There was no suggestion of renegotiating an increased fee to pay for the expansion. The same pot would have to be split among more teams, but there was a belief among all three partners that it was right to take a short-term financial hit if it meant reaping the rewards in the long run by creating an improved competition that was more appealing to fans, sponsors and broadcasters.

Yet while the NZRU was amenable to the concept of expansion, it didn't want to do so in an ad hoc, piecemeal format. It wanted to set down a long-term vision for Sanzar and both the Super 12 and Tri Nations. Negotiations for a new broadcast contract were likely to begin in 2003 to make sure they were completed in advance of the expiry of the current deal, and the NZRU felt it would be appropriate to have a clear idea about the type of competitions it wanted to sell to News. So an agreement was reached in principle to back the Australian and South African expansion in 2003, on the condition that consulting firm Accenture was commissioned to examine the way forward for the Sanzar alliance.

When Accenture reported back in July 2001, it presented a 500-page document that contained some innovative plans for advancement. The document envisioned massive expansion of the Super Rugby format, taking it far beyond its current geographic frontiers. It proposed the competition become global, operating in geographic conferences that would lead to end-of-season play-offs between regional winners. New teams would be introduced, based in Japan and Argentina, and to help make them instantly successful, they should be filled with players from around the world. Accenture had reasoned that for the product to capture the rugby world it needed to contain the best players regardless of nationality. The professional game couldn't be halted by parochial loyalties – the new Super Rugby competition had to have the best players and it had to move into new countries and win support in new markets to keep the broadcasting money rolling in.

It was a radical document. The possibilities were exciting, the growth potential of the sport huge. The report also helped the NZRU see that allowing Australian and South African expansion in 2003 was a smart move. It would not prevent the implementation of any of the other visionary suggestions proposed for further down the track. So the NZRU agreed, but only if certain other conditions were met. The NZRU approached its partners in December 2001 and said it wanted all future Sanzar broadcast revenue to be split on an equal basis. It also wanted support for its proposal that test revenues should be shared equally. The traditional model of the home side pocketing the gate receipts had become a bugbear for the NZRU. The All Black brand was easily the biggest in world rugby and whenever the All Blacks played away from home, they sold out. The biggest grounds in the world – Twickenham, Millennium Stadium, Stade Français – could all be sure of a full house when the All Blacks came to town. That led to a big pay day. A sell out at Twickenham was worth about £3 million (NZ$9 million). The NZRU felt it was only fair that their premium brand got a slice of that action. The frustration was intensified by New Zealand's relatively small stadiums, which meant the NZRU's home receipts were minuscule in comparison.

Those were the terms attached to expansion, but O'Neill found them totally unacceptable. On 17 February 2002 he accused the NZRU of an act of treachery. 'The NZRU was happy for us to support those elements of the Accenture Report which suited them, and we gave that support without conditions. But the one element which was important to SARFU and the ARU, the expansion of Super 12, belatedly had quite unreasonable conditions attached to it,' he fumed. 'In effect, the NZRU has abused its position in Sanzar to block the development of the game of rugby union in Australia. It is an act of treachery. A joint venture involves give and take, and the NZRU has done all the taking and at the end of the day has given nothing. The whole Accenture process has been an expensive waste of time and money as a consequence of the actions of the NZRU. What goes around, comes around, and down the track the marketplace will determine the underlying factors of any renegotiated broadcast rights deal, which is what Sanzar exists for.'

Mr O'Neill was not a happy bunny and he was right about the Accenture Report essentially being an expensive waste of time. The collapse of the proposed expansion agreement didn't quite put the Sanzar partners at war but there was clearly some major bridge-building to be done. It was the relationship between New Zealand and Australia that was particularly damaged as it was O'Neill who had been leading the drive to grow Super 12.

The Accenture Report didn't stand a chance of having any of its findings implemented after 17 February. All the innovative thinking produced by the consultants would have to wait until things were patched up between the ARU and NZRU. And patching things up was going to become a whole lot harder after New Zealand lost its World Cup co-hosting rights a couple of months later.

New Zealand and Australia had been granted the right to co-host the 2003 World Cup, but when the NZRU refused to sign the agreement, arguing it could not agree to deliver stadiums free of advertising for the event, the IRB awarded the sole rights to Australia in mid April 2002. O'Neill, a smart and seasoned businessman who had earned his corporate spurs in the banking world, had played a canny hand. He was by no means the architect of New Zealand's downfall, nor was he the villainous schemer he was portrayed as by some in New Zealand. But, unquestionably, tension between the NZRU and ARU increased as a consequence of the World Cup fall-out. That whole saga also meant the Accenture Report was pretty much chucked in the back of the filing cabinet and forgotten about.

By the second half of 2002, both New Zealand and Australia had plenty of other things on which to focus. The Australians had to rework their World Cup logistics to host the 23 games that were originally scheduled to be played in New Zealand, while the NZRU had to investigate just how it was they lost those co-rights. Chief Justice Sir Thomas Eichelbaum was tasked with coming up with answers and on 27 July, after his report was released, both chairman

Murray McCaw and chief executive David Rutherford resigned from their posts. There was also a major clear-out on the NZRU board, leaving the union in what coaches would describe as a rebuilding phase.

It took until 16 December 2002 for Chris Moller to be appointed as the new man at the helm. Re-negotiating the TV deal was obviously going to be a major task for Moller but it was not an immediate priority. He was asked to restructure the organisation first – to make it a more streamlined, responsive, corporate vehicle, better equipped to administer both the professional and amateur components of the game. It was going to take Moller time to get round to strategising how best to grab a slice of Murdoch's millions. Not only was there the re-organisation of the NZRU's structure to be pushed through, but there was also the need to complete the Competitions Review, an in-depth document analysing the best format for domestic rugby tournaments. In addition, by July 2003 there was the distraction of lengthy negotiations with the players about World Cup bonuses, and then after the tournament in November there was the whole process of assessing who should coach the All Blacks. By January 2004, when Moller finally had a bit of breathing space to devote some time to the News Limited renegotiation, there was executive turmoil within the unions of the Sanzar partners.

On 5 December 2003 South African rugby managing director Rian Oberholzer stepped down. His resignation came after South Africa endured a woeful season and were also torn apart by their infamous pre-World Cup training week at Kamp Staaldraad. At about the same time, O'Neill was stabbed in the back by his own people and left to take up a post as chief executive of Soccer Australia. In the 12 months since the NZRU quashed the proposed expansion of Super 12, all three countries had seen plenty of blood let in their respective boardrooms. All three Sanzar partners wanted to sign off on a new TV deal at least a year before the current contract expired at the end of 2005. The clock was ticking, and because of all the new faces round the table when Sanzar officials met in Wellington on 6 February 2004, there was a rising sense of panic. The organisation had been robbed of nearly all its intellectual capital. There was barely an official in the room who knew that, in the back of a filing cabinet somewhere, there was a 500-page document offering them a range of ideas to pursue before they kick-started negotiations with News Limited.

In the room were Moller and NZRU chairman Jock Hobbs, new South African Rugby Football Union president Brian van Rooyen, acting general manager of SA Rugby Ltd Songezo Nayo, ARU chairman Bob Tuckey and ARU commercial boss Brian Thorburn. No one was thinking about a brave new world where Super Rugby would be played in geographic conferences. The tone was far more rudimentary. What everyone wanted to know was whether there was still unanimous commitment to the Sanzar concept. There was a vote of confidence and when every hand went up in favour of persevering with the partnership, the suits emerged four hours later knowing their mission was not to advance their position, but to consolidate it.

Around the same time as the Sanzar chiefs were meeting in Wellington, the respective domestic owners of the pay TV broadcast rights were meeting in Johannesburg. Sky TV was there from New Zealand, Fox Sports from Australia and Super Sport from South Africa. It was normal for all three to meet annually and plan both at a micro and macro level. This meeting was a bit different though, as Ian Frykberg, the former News Limited executive who had been the lead player in the initial broadcast deal with Sanzar, was also in attendance. Frykberg, now running his own business, had been hired by Sanzar to help with the re-negotiations. No one knew the market better than the South African-born Frykberg, who had emigrated to New Zealand and played prop for Northcote before pursuing a career in journalism in Australia. Sanzar executives wanted to know what the three domestic broadcasters were hoping would come out of the new deal in terms of the formatting of the two competitions. Sanzar would sell the rights to News Limited, then News would recoup its money by selling individual packages to broadcasters in the three countries. News said it was up to Sanzar to decide how it wanted to run its competitions. News didn't want to dictate how the sport should be set up, so it would simply attach a value to the proposal Sanzar put forward. But Sanzar wanted to have some idea what would work and what wouldn't for the domestic broadcasters.

Sky TV and Super Sport where closely aligned when they got their chance to speak. Rugby was the main sport and the main driver of business for both companies. Sky TV had research which showed that 86 percent of its subscribers had bought in purely to watch live rugby. The situation was similar in South Africa and there was another critical link – both Sky TV and Super Sport had a significant commitment to the NPC and Currie Cup respectively. Rugby – be it Super 12, tests or provincial – ran from February through to the end of November in both New Zealand and South Africa. Neither broadcaster expressed a desire for more content – they already had a massive logistical job dealing with what they had. It wasn't quantity that Sky TV and Super Sport were after, it was quality, and both New Zealand and South Africa wanted tests to be kept sacred. Anticipation was critical in building viewer interest, and that heightened expectation would be lost if meaningless tests were crammed into the calendar.

Australia's Fox Sports wasn't quite so vocal, probably because they held a different view. Rugby was still only the third most popular football code in Australia behind rugby league and Australian Rules. If the gap was going to be closed, then two things needed to happen. First, Australia needed more teams so the sport could make a footprint in areas where it was barely played, most obviously Melbourne and Perth. It also needed to develop its own provincial competition to unearth more talent and add another pathway for emerging players. The problem with building a domestic competition was that it would only involve Queensland, New South Wales and Australian Capital Territory until Western Australia, Victoria and South Australia got up to speed, and there was no guarantee those three states would ever do so. For the short to medium term at least, it would be far better from a broadcasting and player development point of view to use the Super Rugby competition as the vehicle to build more content and depth. Why go to the trouble and expense of funding a domestic competition when it could be done far more effectively by expanding the number of teams in Super 12?

Matt Carroll, who briefly replaced O'Neill as chief executive of the ARU, was in the Sanzar engine room until a couple of months before the News deal was re-signed. He remembers that period like this: 'It was critical for the game in Australia that we got another team. The market in New Zealand was more mature and close to its capacity. South Africa definitely had room to grow but there were social and political factors that put a different pressure on. Australia still remained the biggest opportunity and the only way to grow that market was to give more content and try to build critical mass. We looked at a whole number of options from staying at Super 12 to going Super 14, Super 16, the number of rounds, what to do with the Tri Nations and in-bound tours. In 1995 there had been an alignment of certain things. The biggest one was that News Limited was expanding and in Australia, pay TV was taking off. We had come close to getting another team in 2002, but our dear brothers in New

Zealand were not all that keen. And to be fair, South Africa didn't exactly go out on a limb for us.

'The question of whether the market had cooled was fairly critical. The number of games players should play and the length of the rest they should have has always been fairly high on the agenda since rugby turned professional. But that has to be balanced against the commercial imperatives. If the players wanted to command major salaries then we had to sell broadcast rights to pay for it, and broadcasters will only pay if the quality of the product is A1. Our aim was to do better than or as well as we had in 1995, but at the end of the day the critical thing for Australia was that we wanted another team.'

That need to keep Australia happy – to put the betrayal of 17 February 2002 firmly in the past – meant Australia was always going to get the fourth team they coveted. There was, of course, a strong economic rationale for expansion in Australia and a genuine desire held by Fox Sports to see more cross-border content.

The case got more compelling when no financial argument could be made for expanding into new geographic frontiers. Research was conducted into whether it was feasible to create a Super franchise in Japan and/or the Pacific Islands or whether Argentina could be introduced to the international competition. But when Frykberg crunched the numbers he concluded there was little appetite within the Japanese broadcast market for the inclusion of a Tokyo-based franchise, while the introduction of a Pacific Islands team, even if it was based in Auckland, stacked as a heavy loss-maker.

The Pumas had shown at the last three World Cups that they were a handful, certainly capable of beating the likes of Wales and Ireland, and in 2001 they came dangerously close to popping the All Blacks' scalp in their goody bag. The problem, though, was that there was no professional domestic competition in Argentina, so all their test players were based in Europe. With the Tri Nations played in July, August and September, the Pumas would not be able to get their best players released. And without their best players, they would be forced to select a side from the locally based amateurs who, with the best will in the world, were not going to be a match for the All Blacks, Wallabies and Springboks. While the combined Pacific Islands team had proven in June and July of 2004 that they were more than capable of surviving against the Tri Nations big guns, they would have had the same player release issues as Argentina, and Japan just weren't good enough to add value.

There had been sporadic attempts to interest the northern hemisphere in some form of regular tournament, but the logistics were never going to work until there was a total restructuring of the global calendar to align the two hemispheres' seasons. So on the international front, there was no realistic option in terms of injecting new blood. Despite the reservations of both Sky TV and Super Sport, there was a belief among the Sanzar executives that they could command a greater price with News Limited if they offered more of the same content. Frykberg agreed. 'There was real concern about the market,' he said. 'But I felt there was reason to believe we could get parity with the existing deal and with some careful negotiation we could improve it.'

While both Sky TV and Super Sport had issues about expansion, they did still have a number of non-rugby weekends during the season where they could shoehorn in more content. Both broadcasters could live with more content as long as it was premium quality. The concept of re-introducing old-fashioned tours where a team would visit for a three-test series and play a number of provincial games was discussed. But the broadcasters feared that tours would only command interest in the host countries, creating dead zones in global markets. New geographic markets were out, traditional tours were out, so the Sanzar officials agreed that the best proposal to put forward to News was an extended Tri Nations format where New Zealand, Australia and South Africa would play each other three times a season rather than just twice.

Similar changes were agreed for the Super Rugby format. They would propose the creation of a fourth Australian franchise as well as a new team in South Africa. If the proposed fifth team in the Republic had been offered in 2001 just to prevent the Boks from feeling they were missing out, it was offered under very different circumstances in 2004. South African teams had always had their gripes about the Super 12. The competition was not set up well for them as their travel burden was greater than that of either the Australian or New Zealand teams. The South African franchises had to play four consecutive overseas games every season. It was murder for them, and to no one's great surprise South African teams rarely won in New Zealand or Australia, and in nine years of competition had not produced a winner. The coaches and players gave the impression their hearts were never really in it.

That underlying discontent had kept South African executives alert to alternative opportunities. Geographically, it made far more sense for South Africa to be in partnership with Europe where they shared a time zone. That was critical. Europe was still a 10-hour flight away but there was no jet-lag to be incurred in the travel. The common time zone also appealed to broadcasters, as competitions could be structured so that games were always played in prime viewing slots. The time differences between South Africa and New Zealand and Australia were rotten for broadcasters. As negotiations moved towards a conclusion in 2004, press reports continued to leak out of the Republic that there was a desire to break away from Sanzar. Frykberg said it got to the stage where News Limited had to confront the issue. 'South Africa said they had been in discussion with some English clubs about a provincial competition that would run alongside the Sanzar set-up. But they confirmed they were still committed to the Sanzar partnership.'

That was what News and the Sanzar partners needed to hear. South Africa would no doubt continue to explore the possibilities with the Europeans. Internationally, while there had been rumblings about the Six Nations being keen to invite South Africa to join them, the Boks had a passion for regular clashes with the All Blacks. They weren't keen to give that up and they gave News strong reassurances that the Tri Nations was a competition they greatly valued. But on a provincial level there was a desire to see if a regular competition could be built around their existing commitments. In May 2005 an agreement in principle was reached to launch what would be called the Rainbow Cup – an early-season tournament that would include Scottish, Welsh, Irish, Italian and South African provincial teams. South Africa's revelation that they were actively looking at opportunities outside the Sanzar partnership was a sharp reminder to Australia and New Zealand that they had to keep their partner sweet as the threat from the north was very real. Hence the decision to award South Africa a fifth franchise.

Frykberg worked out what the proposal would be worth and when Sanzar saw the predicted value, they agreed to put the document in front of News. On 22 December 2004 it was announced that News had bought the five-year rights for Super 14, as it was to become, and the extended Tri Nations for US$323 million, with the prospect of another $20 to $30 million to flow into Sanzar's coffers when they sold the European, Asian and American rights.

In pure financial terms, it was an extraordinarily good deal for New Zealand – a 16 percent annual increase in funding. Frykberg had proposed a new model on how the pie should be divided and Sanzar agreed, with New Zealand's slice dropping slightly to about 33 percent, South Africa earning the right to claim 38 percent and Australia 29 percent. In the 2003 NZRU annual report Moller had said he was happy to support expansion, 'provided New Zealand's revenue base is directly or indirectly enhanced.' On that front it was mission accomplished. The fact that the real value of the new deal would most likely be worth significantly less to the NZRU because of the high Kiwi dollar and the end of the hedging contracts, was beyond Moller's control.

But while it was a great deal for the three Sanzar partners, it wasn't necessarily a great deal for rugby. It lacked imagination and could probably best be described as a holding deal. The Pacific Islanders, Japan and Argentina had all been shunned. The sport would not be embracing new markets and finding new heroes. Instead, it would be shovelling out more of the same-old, same-old. There would now be 94 instead of 69 Super Rugby games. There would now be nine rather than six Tri Nations games. A few weeks after the Sanzar broadcast deal was announced, All Black halfback Justin Marshall revealed he was going to play for Leeds in July 2005. He'd been offered a top contract and at 31 he knew he would be daft not to take it. But he didn't feel he was just being pulled. For Marshall, the Sanzar deal was a major push factor. 'To be honest, the Super 12 and Tri Nations does not enthuse me,' he said on 8 January 2005. 'I have been playing against the same teams since 1996. I would have liked to have seen something different. I would have liked to see things go a bit more global. The idea of taking the All Blacks to places like Canada and the US, even Japan, would have been a new and different experience.'

The players were already struggling to cope with their existing workload. As of 2006, they were going to be asked to front for two more tests and play two more weeks of Super Rugby. The physical toll would be obvious, but more travel to South Africa, more time in Australia and more time on the field against the same players were going to add a huge mental burden too. Henry and his fellow coaches knew they couldn't carry on the way they were. The players were going to have to be given new skills to cope with the physical and mental demands of a sport that was being governed by administrators who always had to think about the bottom line first, player welfare second. If they carried on doing the same old things they would get the same old results. And that was not Henry's way.

7   Old dogs learn new tricks

NELSON MANDELA walked onto the field at Ellis Park, the crowd went berserk and at that instant the All Black management group had an epiphany. They looked around the packed stadium and realised everyone there knew what it meant to be South African. They realised the Springboks had a clear sense of what and whom they were representing on 14 August 2004. Most importantly of all, perhaps, Graham Henry and his colleagues knew they needed to spark a cultural revolution within the All Blacks if they were ever going to conquer the rugby world.

The Springboks played with unity and passion, having sensed the need to rise to the occasion. The All Blacks couldn't match them for intensity and the faultlines in their fragile psyches were once again exposed, with predictable consequences. The decision-making went to custard that day at Ellis Park the way it had so many times before when the pressure was cranked. The All Black defence creaked and then cracked, with even the ultra-reliable Tana Umaga and Justin Marshall dropping off simple tackles. Fatigue was a factor, but it didn't explain why the side had capitulated under pressure.

The sad truth was that despite being the only globally recognised rugby brand, despite being the most revered test side on the planet and despite having produced a disproportionate number of the world's best players, there was a flaw in the All Black culture that was preventing the side from winning games when they were put under intense pressure. There was plenty of evidence to support this – the 1999 World Cup semi-final, the last-minute Bledisloe Cup losses in 2000, 2001 and 2002, the opening test of 2003 against England and, of course, the 2003 World Cup semi-final later that same year. That pattern had continued in 2004 both at Ellis Park and a week earlier in Sydney.

The All Blacks' psychological frailty was hard to understand. If an independent panel of rugby experts had been asked to score every All Black, Wallaby and Springbok player out of 10 on various categories such as speed, agility, vision, flair and decision-making, New Zealand would unquestionably have come out with the highest points total. Yet, at the end of an 80-minute test match, it was the Springboks and Wallabies who crucially came out with a higher points total on the only scoreboard that really mattered. Something was being lost in the All Black machinery, preventing the team from adding to the sum of its parts.

Not since 1987 had New Zealand held the World Cup, and it was apparent that whatever the problem was, it was deeply ingrained. Henry has never really been into losing, but he has always acknowledged that defeat is often a more powerful learning tool than victory. What he and his fellow coaches learned in August 2004 was that they needed to rethink how they went about their business. In fact, everyone connected with the All Blacks had to rethink how they were going about their business. There needed to be a serious and honest evaluation of the team culture. Everyone needed to air their feelings on where things could be improved. It was time to open up, to ask searching questions of the players, of the coaches, of the support crew. They were all going to be in the trenches together, so they needed to know the men they were fighting alongside. They needed to know where their team-mates were strong and where they were weak. They needed to have trust, support networks that could empathise and sympathise, and most importantly they needed to know what they all stood for. That was arguably the key – knowing what values they wanted to uphold. It was time to discover what boundaries they must operate within, what code they must abide by and what was the essence of being a New Zealander.

For too long the All Black ethos had gone unchallenged. Everyone who was granted membership of this very special club had to learn from history and their current peer group what it meant to be an All Black. There wasn't a leaflet handed out with the jerseys explaining what it all meant, how one should behave and what standards needed to be upheld. That was all assumed, and the culture evolved as players came and went. But by 2004, Henry and his cohorts felt all that needed to change. The players needed to take control of the culture within the team. They had to dictate the boundaries. They had to set the standards. They had to define what it meant to wear the black jersey, what values they believed in, what they were trying to achieve as a group.

It wasn't a case of being disrespectful to the 101 years of All Black history that had gone before, but of simply adapting to what was a significantly different environment so that a proud history could be honoured and maintained. If the players owned their team and, therefore, their own destiny, they were always going to work that bit harder to protect it. As All Black manager Darren Shand said a couple of years later: 'The initial driver was looking at teams prior to our tenure and seeing poor decisions being made under pressure and people not being able to react under pressure. Probably in our first campaign, including that Tri Nations in 2004, we didn't really see any shift in that area. I think it really came home to roost in that Johannesburg test that we lost. We saw the sense of nationalism the Springboks had that really galvanised them and we didn't feel that we had. It was a combination of getting that leadership right and us understanding ourselves as New Zealanders.

'The legacy they inherited was a burden for them. It was kind of a negative burden in that the expectation was presented in quite a negative way – "don't let the jersey down ... this guy has gone before you," and that kind of stuff. We wanted to flip that on its head. We were proud to wear the All Black jersey but let's put a positive slant to that. "Kapa o Pango" was born out of that, of us understanding ourselves and us putting some concrete blocks in the ground and saying this is our team and our legacy and what we are all about. That was the most obvious symbol of that process. Developing that haka and having deep understanding of what it meant – it gave us a massive sense of what this All Black group is all about. We wanted to respect history but we wanted our time to be remembered.'

No doubt this re-evaluation would have made a few old-school All Blacks a little uncomfortable. It was all very new age – the players were encouraged to role-play and there were confessional seminars. But the old dogs needed to take caution before they scoffed at these efforts to learn new tricks. Even though Benjamin Disraeli was absolutely correct when he surmised there were lies, damned lies and statistics, the All Black results of recent years painted a clear picture that couldn't be disputed.

In 2000 they lost two games: one in South Africa and one in France. In 2001 they lost once in New Zealand and once in Australia and were a whisker away from losing in Argentina. In 2002 they lost in Australia and England and drew in France. In 2003 they lost once in New Zealand and once in Australia, and in 2004 they lost once in South Africa and once in Australia. Of the eight games they had lost since 2000, six had been away from home. Nobody wanted to be critical of the previous regimes, but at the same time it had become apparent that certain standards had been allowed to slip when the team travelled. Playing away from home came with inherent difficulties. Players are creatures of habit and like to be familiar with their surroundings. Familiarity does not breed contempt when it comes to test match preparation. Test football is a stressful business and much of that can be reduced if the players feel comfortable in their surroundings. It's easier to minimise the stress when playing at home.

Once the team gets on the road though, that's when the trouble can start. That's when the culture of the team gets tested. That's when it becomes apparent whether they are unified or divided. They have to spend all their time in each other's pockets and if there are rifts, they get inflamed. That's why a strong culture was imperative. The team needed a guiding set of principles that would act as glue when they travelled. Henry told the *New Zealand Herald* in January 2005 about what he and his coaches had concluded the previous year: 'I don't think we're strong on our nationalism. We're not nearly as strong as many of the countries overseas, like Australia, who are very open about wanting to be the best sporting nation in the world. We're inclined to be a bit shy on those things. We learned that we had to develop leadership. We learned that we didn't have the composure and togetherness on the field when it really mattered, under real pressure against good rugby sides. And the Australians and the South Africans were good rugby sides. And we learned that we needed to take the pressure off the players physically. We needed to make sure that we didn't over-train.' If there was any truth in the saying that leaders are born not made, by August 2004 Henry was on a mission to disprove it.

Before England went to the 2003 World Cup, Sir Clive Woodward took his team to train with the army. He wasn't particularly interested in exposing his players to the legendary physical regime of the land-based armed force. What he wanted his players to learn was how army personnel made instantaneous decisions under the most ferocious pressure. Senior officers in the army are trained to be meticulous in all aspects of their planning. When it comes to organising manoeuvres in combat situations, absolutely every detail is discussed and understood. Every officer and soldier knows what he is to do and when he is to do it. And then the instant the regiment steps into the combat zone, almost without fail they will encounter a situation that is radically different from the one they expected.

Combat is fluid. Enemy troops make surprise decisions, people get killed or injured. Plans have to be changed, except the decision-makers can't run back to the safety of headquarters to review their next move. Decisions have to be made on the spot. They have to be made while the enemy is firing live ammunition. And that is what Woodward wanted his team to learn – he wanted them to understand that rugby is not dissimilar to war. He wanted his players to learn they could spend six days planning for a test but once the game kicked-off, things might unravel in a manner they hadn't thought of. To be able to cope with that fluidity, they had to be confident they could make decisions on the field. They had to be able to think clearly under pressure and understand the game well enough to make spontaneous calls. It was probably England's greatest strength. In Martin Johnson they had one of the best leaders of men the rugby world had ever seen. He was ably supported by Jason Leonard, Lawrence Dallaglio, Neil Back, Richard Hill, Matt Dawson and Jonny Wilkinson. England had leaders across the park – men who could react in time to adapt the game-plan and affect the outcome. That was exactly what Henry wanted.

He had tried to instil leadership through the selection of players such as Xavier Rush, Keith Robinson and Jono Gibbes. But Robinson was on the long-term injury list and Rush had pretty much proven he was not quite test quality. Gibbes was just about there but the game-plan was not suited to his skill-set and he was always going to be on the periphery of selection. So there was no choice really but to try and improve the leadership of the players who the coaching panel believed had long-term All Black futures.

The plan was to select a core group and then empower them with the responsibility to govern various facets of the team culture. It was logical to believe that if individuals were encouraged to make decisions off the field they would feel more confident about doing it on the field. Leadership is as much about confidence as anything else, and Henry wanted players to feel comfortable about controlling, owning and directing facets of team policy. There were some obvious candidates to take up posts within the leadership group. Aaron Mauger had been an age-group captain and was one of those rare individuals who appeared entirely comfortable with the burden of responsibility. Richie McCaw was destined to captain the All Blacks, such was his natural charisma and ability to inspire with words as well as action.

But the essence of the leadership group was more about encouraging those who had not quite found their voice. The modern rugby side can't rely on the skipper alone to make decisions. And history had shown that the All Blacks, at times, couldn't even rely on their skipper. There needed to be leaders across the park. Greg Somerville and Keven Mealamu had played some big tests but were from the front-row school that said they should rarely be seen on the field and barely heard off it. Chris Jack was naturally shy but full of smart ideas. Byron Kelleher had been in the side for five years and in that time had matured and upskilled but was still living in the shadow of Justin Marshall who, the selectors knew, was heading to Leeds in June 2005. Mils Muliaina, in just two years, had established himself as one of the best fullbacks in world rugby but still felt at just 24 that it was not his place to be imposing himself. In total, 11 players were appointed to the leadership group.

'Between the Tri Nations and the end of season tour we established a leadership group,' said Darren Shand. 'We had seen through other sports similar types of things. We took pieces from other sports we knew about and put something together. The focus was on picking the best performers, the best players; that was one of the really early criteria – you needed to be a player who was going to be on the paddock most weeks and, through the development of your leadership skill, you would provide us with the outcomes we were seeking. In any campaign there is always a link between the management and the players and where that line in the sand is changes. What we decided was we really needed a player-centred model where we gave them real responsibility and accountability.

'A lot of the campaigns that we had all been involved in did that to a lesser extent. They were more about committees and built around fun and entertainment. There was no real accountability about delivering something that the team needed to get the win each week. Taking it to the next level was a big part of it. We gave these guys a whole load of resources and stripped leadership back to the most basic form. What does it mean to be a role model? How are you going to behave for others to perceive you as a role model? What are the different leadership styles? We had to agree on what was going to be our style and how we would go forward with that, and that is when we decided that we would work as a management group with the senior players contributing side by side.

'What we decided was that to lead you have got to understand self. Our players are exposed to a massive number of external factors that we can't influence but impact on them and create expectations. We said we have to park that and what we have to do is come back to the core and say, "What is it about me that makes me a great player and what are the strengths that I bring to the group? And how can I improve on those strengths?" In creating a leadership model we wanted leadership excellence in time. But we had to start with the individual being self-aware, understanding himself – knowing what his peers thought of him, what his strengths were, what his weaknesses were and it was only in the individual knowing that would he be able to lead others. There are some key portfolios where we need feedback in terms of what we are doing as a management group. So around training, around the medical side of things, our activity with sponsors, activity with media – that has been good because we are getting the players' side constantly fed into the management group, so we are getting an understanding of what they are feeling about those sorts of issues. They are helping manage those portfolios and briefing the players about the level of commitment.'

In addition to the key portfolios, some in the group were appointed responsibility for setting team protocol in such matters as alcohol intake, while others would canvass views about bigger-picture themes such as what it meant to be an All Black. That last point developed into a more significant project as there was a feeling within the wider squad that the haka was being performed purely because it was traditional. The players wanted to connect with it, to understand the Maori heritage and history. Everyone, even the coaches, were encouraged to learn more, and once the players had grasped the meaning, everyone agreed they would like to develop an alternative haka to the traditional 'Ka mate'. They wanted a haka that reflected the ethnic mix within the team. They wanted something that was definitively theirs and had significant meaning for them. The new haka, 'Kapa o Pango', didn't get its first public outing until August 2005, but the process of formulating it proved a powerful bonding-tool.

The grand plan was for the leadership group to be the catalyst to create a self-governed entity. Peer pressure is arguably the most powerful tool at a coach's disposal. If a player breaks a team edict on alcohol intake he could probably just about handle being ragged out by the coach behind closed doors. It's a far harder, more emotional exercise if he has to front up to his peers and explain why he broke the code. But the objective wasn't about replacing one dictatorial approach with another. That was exactly what the coaches were trying to move away from. They were reasonably confident that most of the world's leading rugby sides in the last few years had adopted management models that would not sustain results in the long run. Most sides relied on heavily structured and sequenced game-plans that saw players follow a prescribed order of events. It could be effective, but only up to a point. If the opposition countered some of the set-plays, many teams reliant on this model lacked the ability to adapt. They weren't equipped with the skills to make spontaneous decisions based on what they saw happening in front of them. The All Blacks were certainly not guilty of playing robotic rugby, but they were prone to climbing into their shells at crucial times. Henry and his team felt that was because the management team were still the dominant decision-makers.

The players had become used to being told what to do and when to do it, both on and off the field. There was an appreciation after August 2004 that not only would the players have to be encouraged to step forward, but the coaching team would have to step back. No one had a problem with that. Henry, Smith and Hansen all agreed that their egos could cope with player empowerment. The line in the sand was going to be moved, and to fully understand where it now was, individuals were not only going to have to become better players, they were also going to have to become better people.

The Brits could never get their heads around the fact that former All Black captain Sean Fitzpatrick could play like a thug and then speak with the eloquence of a lord. The Poms had plenty of players during the amateur era who had the plummy voice, but very few who could combine it with a bit of old-fashioned mongrel out on the paddock. That was possibly New Zealand's greatest advantage – they produced individuals who were not only rugby savvy, but were bright, enterprising and articulate too. Maybe it was down to the egalitarian way of life in New Zealand. Maybe it was down to the natural enterprising spirit that had been forged during the pioneering days. Whatever, the pre-professional era saw the All Blacks produce an inordinate number of good players who also enjoyed hugely successful careers away from the sport. David Kirk, Wilson Whineray and Jock Hobbs are just three examples of men who captained the All Blacks and succeeded in the corporate world. Was there a connection? Was it natural to assume that if an individual was capable of making high-quality decisions under pressure in the workplace, he was also likely to be a natural and gifted leader on the field?

Certainly Henry thought so. In his days coaching Auckland he had been fortunate to have in his side both Fitzpatrick and Zinzan Brooke – two great players, two great leaders and two men who had done pretty well for themselves off the field. By 2004 the demands of the sport had made it almost impossible for players to pursue a meaningful career outside rugby. Everyone accepted that. But what Henry didn't accept was that players should waste what free time they did have. He was concerned on two fronts.

First, while the coaches had quickly latched on to the increased physical demands of the sport, they had maybe been a bit slower to realise the mental toll. So much time was being spent in the rugby environment that it was easy to become stale, to feel overloaded with the demands being imposed and to switch off mentally. When the team had been playing at home there were more distractions for the players to keep themselves amused. But when they were away from home, it was much harder to find things to do to afford an escape from the constant diet of rugby. Too many players were not taking the opportunity to switch off and broaden their horizons. It could be a long week if players didn't allow themselves some form of emotional release outside the confines of the team hotel.

The newly imposed leadership group would be charged with making sure there were plenty of distractions for the players when they were playing both at home and away. Individuals needed to be encouraged to switch off mentally at various points of the test week and to actively enjoy the experience. To do the hard yards at training, but then to get out and about. It was a brutally long season, way too long for individuals to focus on rugby alone. The players were encouraged that time off from rugby should be exactly that. These were micro-management solutions to the problem of mental burn-out.

The second concern, though, was that the issue of mental burn-out needed to be managed on a macro level. The majority of professional players were coming into the sport having known no other life. They had left school already belonging to an Academy programme where they spent most of their existence in a team environment. By the time they signed professional contracts some players had never cooked a meal or done their own washing. It wasn't a realistic way to live. The likes of Fitzpatrick and Brooke were armed with a range of life-skills that could see them adapt and thrive in any situation, while many of the current All Blacks couldn't boil an egg. The players needed to become self-reliant and adept at solving problems for themselves. 'When I was coaching Auckland back in the amateur era, the guys worked nine-to-five before coming to training and I think that helped them develop skills and experiences that were useful in rugby,' Henry explained in October, 2004. 'I'm sure there is a huge link between developing these skills off the field and being able to apply them on the field.'

The pampered world of professional rugby was not going to teach the players to be self-reliant, not when they had so much done for them. If rugby couldn't foster those skills, Henry felt that community work, part-time jobs or academic study could.

Each Super 12 franchise already had a professional development manager who was there to provide, among other things, advice and guidance to players on how they could prepare themselves for retirement. But there was a sense that some players needed to be pushed more aggressively into the arms of the professional development manager.

Many of the players in the England side that won the World Cup had straddled the amateur and professional eras and, therefore, had enjoyed meaningful careers outside rugby. Johnson had worked in a bank, Josh Lewsey was an army officer and Will Greenwood had been a trader in the City. These were men who could think deeply about the game and also about matters far more important than rugby. They were self-reliant problem-solvers who always took the initiative. The likes of Johnson, Lewsey and Greenwood weren't just good players, they were good people. Of the players that Henry had used in 2004, very few could say hand on heart they were pursuing interests outside rugby. McCaw was trying to gain his pilot's licence. Nick Evans was a fully qualified physiotherapist and Kees Meeuws had a deep love of fine art. Carlos Spencer opened a coffee franchise in Auckland and Xavier Rush, an apprentice builder before winning a full-time rugby contract, had some property projects on the go. There were other devoted family men and some players involved in part-time study. But the coaching panel wanted to see the life-skills enhanced across the group. They wanted more emphasis placed on players bettering

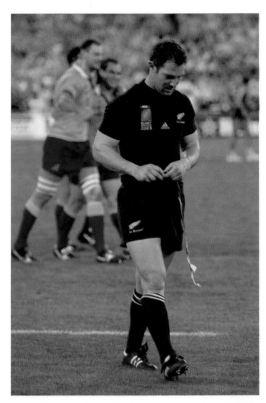

Leon MacDonald trudges off the field at Sydney on 15 November 2003 after the All Blacks' World Cup semi-final loss. He was picked out of position – something Graham Henry said could never happen again.
(New Zealand Herald)

Daniel Carter became the world's best first five-eighths under Graham Henry. Here he cuts inside Jonny Wilkinson, the man who had previously been considered the best in the position. *(New Zealand Herald)*

English lock Simon Shaw was sent off seconds after placing his knee into All Black Keith Robinson. The All Blacks went on to win the test 36-12 and the series in June 2004 – the first under Henry's command. *(Suburban Newspapers)*

Forwards coach Steve Hansen has a word with Ali Williams in August 2004 after the big lock was recalled to the squad. *(New Zealand Herald)*

Tana Umaga, in his second game as captain, beats England's Josh Lewsey to the high ball. *(Suburban Newspapers)*

Kicking coach Mick Byrne takes his first session after joining the management team in June 2005. *(New Zealand Herald)*

Byron Kelleher (No 9) makes way for his long-term halfback rival Justin Marshall to play his last test in New Zealand. *(Suburban Newspapers)*

Graham Henry, flanked by Steve Hansen and Wayne Smith, explains why he made changes to the side that played the third test against the Lions. *(New Zealand Herald)*

Conrad Smith – one of the finds of Henry's reign – was called up to play in the third test against the Lions due to the major injury toll, scoring a stunning solo try. *(Suburban Newspapers)*

A pensive Graham Henry watches his side warm up before they play a crucial test against the British Lions in 2005. *(Suburban Newspapers)*

The giant frames of Chris Jack and Ali Williams wrap up Sitiveni Sivivatu after the winger scored against the Lions in the final test. *(Suburban Newspapers)*

Graham Henry's initial choice of captain, Tana Umaga, applauds the crowd at Eden Park after defeating the Wallabies to win the Bledisloe Cup. *(Suburban Newspapers)*

Graham Henry surprised everyone when he selected 19-year-old Isaia Toeava for the Grand Slam tour. Here the coach has a word with his star pupil at training. *(Suburban Newspapers)*

Graham Henry prowls the All Black training base at Waitakere Trusts Stadium in West Auckland as his side prepares for their first test of 2006. *(Suburban Newspapers)*

Graham Henry and his skipper, Richie McCaw, assess the troops on the training paddock before the first test of 2006 against Ireland. *(Suburban Newspapers)*

Troy Flavell trains with the All Blacks in June 2006 – six years after making his last of 15 appearances. *(Suburban Newspapers)*

The All Blacks spent time reconnecting with the haka so they could perform it from the heart, as they clearly did before playing Ireland in June 2006. *(Suburban Newspapers)*

Graham Henry embraces his captain, Richie McCaw, after the All Blacks secured the Bledisloe Cup in 2006. *(Suburban Newspapers)*

Richie McCaw holds aloft the Tri Nations Cup (left) and the Bledisloe Cup (right) at Eden Park in 2006. *(Suburban Newspapers)*

Scrum guru Mike Cron lends a helping hand at Wanganui training. Under Henry, all specialists were posted around the country to help wherever it was needed. *(Wanganui Chronicle)*

The emotion on the players' faces shows how much it meant to perform Kapa o Pango – the haka they devised to reflect the changing ethnic mix and new values of the team. *(Suburban Newspapers)*

Graham Henry, Wayne Smith and Steve Hansen watch the 22 chosen All Blacks go through fitness testing before flying to Europe in October 2006. *(New Zealand Herald)*

themselves off the field. And in respect of becoming better people, there was one more major change the squad had to make.

Alcohol has been part of rugby culture for as long as the game has been played. Booze has been the lubricant to oil the wheels of the sport. In a perverse way, rugby players have always prided themselves on smashing the living daylights out of each other on the field then becoming best pals over a few beers afterwards. The sport has always been about so much more than what happens on the field. The social aspect has been critical. Lasting friendships have been forged in clubrooms around the world – friendships between players from different teams and friendships within teams. Former players who toured overseas for months at a time don't seem to have such a great memory about specific events on the field. They all, however, have legendary tales to tell when it comes to the booze-fuelled antics of their team-mates. Those big nights out were deemed hugely important for teams like the British Lions. A big session on the sauce was a way to get to know your team-mates. It was a way to break down inhibitions and gain a quick insight into the personality of the guy who might in a few weeks be playing alongside you in a test. It was a way to bond – to share songs, stories and adventures. Booze was very much part of rugby and it was very much part of the All Blacks.

Before professionalism, the All Blacks were no different from any other rugby team. Of course they were probably the most consistent side in the world and probably the best known, but they had signed up to rugby's code of ethics the same as everyone else. They were a side full of young men just like every other. And so booze was part of the bonding process. The players, drawn from across the country, needed to get to know each other. The culture had to be strong – everyone had to belong and, as a consequence, certain rituals became ingrained and therefore dutifully honoured throughout the ages.

The All Black court sessions were a focal point of any get-together. The formula was pretty simple. Players would gather in one room and be called to stand trial with an appointed player serving as judge. Individuals were accused of acts that were usually exaggerated, sometimes fictitious but always humorous. The penal sentences were drinking forfeits, and the end result was that, to a man, the team were well oiled and in good spirits. Management had pretty much accepted this ritual and some had even encouraged it. Most court sessions were usually held after a test and they almost served as a reward for all the effort that had gone in. These sessions had survived into the professional age and were alive and well when Henry took over. He wasn't a fan. He was uncomfortable with the attitude to alcohol consumption in general.

Individuals had to be treated like adults and be free to make responsible decisions. Yet the interpretation of what was reasonable could differ hugely from player to player. If the reins were not held tight, it was easy for heavy booze consumption to become endemic within the team. Young players coming into the side could see a culture where it was deemed appropriate to drink heavily and feel that was the message they must grasp and then pass to the next generation.

There were some players involved in previous professional regimes who felt the reins might not have been held tightly enough. Anton Oliver was a big critic, claiming in his autobiography that excessive drinking was rampant. He said he got hideously drunk after his All Black debut and several times after that. He felt that when Wayne Smith and Tony Gilbert took charge in 2000 they made efforts to reform attitudes and encouraged the players to aim for higher standards. But Oliver claimed there was a regression under John Mitchell.

He recalled the team assembling at Edinburgh Airport on the Sunday after they played Scotland in November 2001. The Saturday night had been major, starting with the infamous court session where team manager Andrew Martin was forced to consume unhealthy amounts of beer. Oliver felt disgusted at the airport when he clocked team-mate Ben Blair's shoes – they were sticky with stale beer and flecks of sick. The amount of drinking was also a concern for Martin, who spoke out about the culture of excess shortly after his employment was terminated.

Oliver, who was unceremoniously dropped by Mitchell in 2003, and Martin, who was forced out of his post, had axes to grind. Their respective testimonies about attitudes to alcohol under Mitchell have to be considered with those grievances in mind. Mitchell had an 83 percent win ratio with which to defend himself. There were no major incidents reported of his players behaving in a drunken and disorderly manner in the public domain and there was no obvious sign that individual levels of fitness were deteriorating as a consequence of too much juice in the system. But Mitchell did introduce breath-testing at the World Cup – where players were tested at the training ground and had to record an acceptable blood-alcohol level before they could play. Mitchell always denied the testing was introduced amid fears some players were living it up too much. But whatever the truth about what had gone on before, whatever standards had been set, Henry was going to set new ones and create a new culture towards booze.

Senior All Blacks within the leadership group were tasked with driving through a cultural shift to end binge drinking. Henry felt the message had to get across that, just as the public awareness adverts claimed, it wasn't necessarily the drinking that was the problem, it was the way the All Blacks were drinking. He wanted to get away from the booze-as-reward culture and therefore couldn't encourage or condone the institutionalised court sessions. That particular ritual gave the message to the players that it was acceptable to abstain during the week and then get hammered. That was where the cultural shift needed to take place. Most NPC and Super 12 teams had a binge culture where the players stayed off the sauce until game night. Once they had played, the beer would flow. The social problems associated with binge drinking can be viewed on any Saturday night in every town and city across New Zealand.

Binge drinking also damages health and is the enemy of athletic performance. Any player pouring a couple of gallons down his neck once every few weeks was not going to be able to say he was preparing adequately for the demands of test football. Research has shown that the 24 hours after a test are crucial in terms of recovery. That recovery can be totally derailed by a heavy night on the turps and athletic performance can deteriorate significantly. Shand explains the attitude towards booze.

'We wanted to create a culture where saving up all week to binge drink on the Saturday night was not going to be tolerated or accepted by the team,' he said. 'We work at the extremes – we either binge or we don't drink – whereas in Europe they seem to have found that middle ground. That is what we want. We still want people to enjoy themselves and feel like they deserve a drink. But the players need to manage that. Things like court sessions, that was something we decided we were not going to tolerate in our environment any more. We wanted guys to feel comfortable when we went out socially during the week. We wanted to make that middle ground the norm, rather than have it how it has been in the past.

'In professional rugby, the first 24 hours are the most critical in terms of getting your body in a state to train again and go through the whole process of a training week. We have got data that shows us how moderate to significant amounts of consumption impact on your recovery. We are looking at that more closely and have been able to chart that and say to players, this is how you did last week when you didn't drink and this is how you did when you had a few drinks. Pretty quickly, people realise how important it is to take care of yourself. We have got a player responsible who is the role model for the group. He talks post-game about what is coming up, how we need to behave tonight, what he thinks would be acceptable for the evening. It's an internal mechanism driven by the players, putting pressure on themselves about how they have to perform.'

By October 2004, Henry had made an indelible mark on the All Blacks. His critics would accuse him of having no respect for tradition. He would argue he had made every cultural shift exactly because he was so respectful of tradition and the great history of the team he coached. To win in the professional era the All Blacks had to observe the highest standards of preparation. They had to know in their own minds what the jersey meant to them, what they stood for, how they were supposed to behave and what values and codes they wanted to honour and uphold. They had to become more rounded, more balanced people – aware that in 'normal' life there was a bit more fending for yourself. They needed to develop wider interests so they had an escape from rugby in the short term, and something more solid to take over from rugby long-term. And they needed to accept that while the rest of the nation's young people were gripped by a binge-drinking epidemic, they would have to apply greater fortitude on the social front.

All this had to happen to preserve and enhance the All Black legacy. Without a cultural shift the brand would be tarnished. The All Blacks had the raw talent. Henry hoped he had given them the environment to use all that raw talent. He hoped he had empowered his players to lead on every front. He hoped they would now stand up and take the initiative, whether it be at the breakdown or at the bar. With a tour to Italy, Wales and France coming up in November, he didn't have to wait long to find out.

8   C'est magnifique!

WHEN THE All Blacks set off for Rome on 6 November 2004, it was a massive relief for the 32-man tour party finally to be able to play rugby. There had been a lot of talking in the past couple of months. There had been meetings here, there and everywhere. Souls had been laid bare, promises made and new ideas to get heads around. But by the time they took off, every man was ready to do his bit in shifting the culture of the team to a player-controlled environment. The coaches, though, had not made themselves redundant. They still had to come up with the strategic direction and game-plan and they still had to select the squad. And the selections for this trip were going to be crucial as the All Blacks were not just in need of a cultural makeover, they also needed new heroes.

There were five major vacancies that needed to be filled. The most obvious was at first five-eighths. Carlos Spencer had struggled with the whole flat backline experiment and his confidence had been drained. He'd played in the NPC for Auckland after returning from South Africa but he had done so through the pain barrier. He had a degenerative knee injury that needed rest and recuperation. Henry and Spencer agreed in September that it would be best if New Zealand's most instinctive player stayed at home during the summer to build his knee and his confidence.

Andrew Mehrtens, a legend in his own lifetime, had replaced Spencer in the final Tri Nations game. Mehrtens had a range of skills, but at 31 he was hardly one for the future and there was also the very real problem that his defensive frailty would become more ruthlessly exposed as the years went by. Mehrtens was slight, almost to the point where Charles Dickens, had he been alive, would have called him a waif. Even five years ago, an international first-five had no reason to worry that being a bit shy in the tackle would stop him winning test caps. The game had moved dramatically in the last few years though, and the volumes of traffic heading down the first-five's channel were heavy. Think Auckland rush-hour heavy and a guy like Mehrtens would become a liability. The new deal was that whoever wore No 10 had to be able to tackle, and well enough that opposition teams weren't encouraged to target him. So Mehrtens was not going to be the man to lead the backline in Europe.

Nick Evans had earned four caps earlier in the year at fullback. The North Harbour and Highlanders player saw himself as a first-five, however. The selectors saw him in that role long-term too, but weren't bowled over by his work in the NPC. It wasn't so much that Evans had been scratchy when he had returned to Harbour colours after the Tri Nations. There was greater concern that he had occupied a head-space that wasn't conducive to producing his best form. The selectors felt he needed the proverbial boot to the derrière and his name was not read out on 24 October. After those three, options were a little thin on the ground. Very thin, in fact, so they took what they saw as a gamble, and named Daniel Carter as a first-five.

Carter had dropped jaws in 2003 when he waltzed into the Crusaders Super 12 team at just 21 and looked as if he had played there all his life. He barely looked old enough to drive and there he was wearing Mehrtens' No 10 shirt and playing as if he was never going to give it back. The only reason he did give it back was so he could wear the No 12 jersey. He marched into the All Black squad on the back of that splendid campaign and again looked as if he was born to be there. He made his debut in Hamilton against Wales playing at second-five. He was so relaxed that when he came to take his first kick at goal, the referee had to tell him to hurry up. John Mitchell and Robbie Deans believed Spencer at first-five and Aaron Mauger at second-five was their premier inside pairing, but when the latter was injured for the early pool games at the World Cup, Carter stepped in and probably would have stayed there had he not picked up a knee strain.

By 2004 Carter had leap-frogged Mauger and was the preferred starter at second-five. His distribution, vision, acceleration and defence were a compelling package, topped with world-class goal-kicking. Carter was blessed with all the skills to play at No 10 and had featured there at Colts, NPC and Super 12. While Henry and his coaching panel acknowledged that, they felt when they came back from South Africa that Carter's next move would be out rather than in.

Assistant coach Wayne Smith could see Carter becoming a world class centre. At 31, Tana Umaga was only ever one injury away from retiring. Even if he was able to recover, who would replace him in the short term? Carter could have been the answer had it not been for the late run made by Wellington's Conrad Smith. A total unknown plucked from club rugby in 2003, Smith had been a revelation in Wellington's midfield alongside Umaga. The capital side had been in poor form but Smith provided a shining ray of light. His distribution was clever, his angles of attack varied and his defence solid. He and Umaga, who had shifted to second-five, developed a telepathic understanding and the All Black selectors could see those two pairing up in Rome. Smith also came with the added bonus of being exactly the sort of person they were looking for in the new culture. He had completed a law degree, was smart, urbane and self-reliant.

The arrival of Smith as a test candidate prompted a rethink about Carter. Everything screamed 'move him in' but there was one worry – the coaching panel wasn't sure Carter had the force of personality to take control. He was one of those enviable laconic types whose droopy eyes made the girls swoon and led rugby coaches to wonder if he would stay awake for the full 80 minutes. The backline general had to impose himself and call the shots. The selectors had their doubts whether Carter was naturally inclined to take control but they reckoned there was only way to find out. The 22-year-old would travel to Europe as a first-five and would be given every opportunity to prove that leadership was one of the skills in his bulging armoury.

As Simon Maling had departed overseas and Keith Robinson was still injured, lock was another concern. Ali Williams had been the first-choice partner for Chris Jack in 2003 but had gone missing for most of 2004. Educated at the prestigious King's College in Auckland, Williams had the ability to be engaging and insightful. He also had the ability and desire to play the clown, and for much of 2004 he seemed to be focusing too hard on the latter. Unsure whether Williams had put his court jester phase behind him, the selectors called in the ever-reliable Norm Maxwell. The 28-year-old Maxwell had hamstrings tighter than piano strings and so much random scar tissue he looked as if he had been scribbled on by an enthusiastic toddler. Still, big Norm reckoned he had a bit left in the tank and if he was carefully managed it wasn't inconceivable he could push on for a few more seasons. Maybe he could, maybe he couldn't, but the coaches didn't have any alternative and Maxwell was going to be, at the very least, a short-term solution to the locking problem.

The departure of Kees Meeuws to Castres had left the All Blacks looking for an explosive, versatile prop who could handle both sides of the scrum and also carry the ball. Greg Somerville had been on the scene for a few years and had specialised on the tighthead. The selectors were trying to convert him into a dual option which was always going to make him an ideal man for the bench. With Somerville effectively replacing Meeuws as the versatile option, there was an opportunity for a specialist loosehead to nail down the No 1 jersey. North Harbour and Blues prop Tony Woodcock had been capped as a 21-year-old in 2002 and then disappeared as quickly as a Scotsman when the bill arrives. He'd been pushed into test football before he was quite ready. By 2004, however, he underwent a renaissance and had done enough to be given the chance to prove he was now ready. He'd be battling with Saimone Taumoepeau, the man who only a few months earlier had been working full-time in an Auckland freezing works. Taumoepeau, at just 105 kg, had been a scrummaging sensation for Auckland after he broke into the team. Lacking in bulk, he was reliant on explosive technique which was exactly what forwards coach Steve Hansen was looking for.

Xavier Rush had fallen out of favour, having started seven of the eight tests in 2004 at No 8. He had leadership qualities and was a cheeky sort of bloke, having been educated at the University of Life. But with the greatest will in the world he just wasn't test class. He'd been a decent stopgap in the absence of any other candidates, but the net had to be thrown wider to find a long-term option in this crucial berth. Waikato's Steven Bates was called up after tireless campaigns with both the Chiefs and Waikato. He was in a similar mould to Rush, just that bit bigger and that bit more capable of making a higher impact. Mose Tuiali'i, having scored a debut try earlier in the year, was the player in whom most hope had been invested. His relative inexperience was offset by his blistering acceleration – he had reputedly been timed as one of the quickest men in New Zealand rugby over 10 metres. At 110 kg, he could cause a whole heap of damage blasting off from the base of the scrum.

Wellington's Rodney So'oialo earned a recall after leading the capital side to the NPC final. Capable of playing in all three loose-forward positions, So'oialo earned his first cap in 2002 and was a regular squad member in 2003. Mitchell had been attracted to So'oialo's athleticism and ability to cover the ground. Those talents were undisputed. However, when he was tossed around like a rag doll by England's Lawrence Dallaglio a few months before the World Cup, there were big question marks over his ability to duke it out. Henry certainly didn't think it was there when he first came on board and So'oialo was given clear instructions to go back to Wellington and prove he could graft and scrap. Impressed by the way he so obviously took that message on board, Henry duly called him into the party.

The final vacancy was at halfback – except it wasn't really a vacancy. Justin Marshall was the incumbent, in great form for Canterbury and available for selection. He wasn't going to be travelling though. Marshall had told the coaches he would be leaving for Leeds after the Lions series in June 2005. Assurances were given to Marshall that his decision to quit would not be held against him – Henry would pick the best players to play the Lions and as long as Marshall maintained his current form, he was likely to be in the side. But the coaches had to have one eye focusing beyond June 2005. If they were going to be losing the man who had dominated the No 9 jersey since his debut in 1995, they needed to be thinking about a long-term replacement. And the forthcoming tour would be an ideal opportunity to give that replacement some extended game-time. The identity of the replacement was already known.

Byron Kelleher had been Marshall's long-time understudy. The 27-year-old had occasionally bumped Marshall from the starting line-up, but it was only occasionally as Kelleher could never quite produce the consistency required to keep a man as good as Marshall at bay. It seemed as if operating in the shadow of Marshall sometimes overwhelmed Kelleher. So Henry saw his chance to leave Marshall at home and allow Kelleher, a signed-up member of the leadership group, an opportunity to clamber out of his shell and be the main man for a few weeks.

It wasn't just an opportunity for Kelleher. Henry explained to the *New Zealand Herald* why Marshall and to a lesser extent Mehrtens had been left at home. 'We were in a situation where we had two 30-year-olds who had played for the last decade for the All Blacks, and we needed to move on. We needed to find others who could play in their positions. In Marshall's case, he is such a dominating personality – and I mean that in a positive way – that other guys look to him to lead and don't take the initiative themselves. So without Marshall it gives us some space to develop other people.'

Omitting Marshall and Mehrtens was not universally applauded. Colin Meads wrote in his column for the *Herald on Sunday* that he was uneasy about so much experience being left on the beach when it should have been helping the team hold things together in the intimidating cauldrons of the Millennium Stadium and Stade Français. Henry and his management team were looking at the big picture. The problem when you are the All Black coach though, is that everyone else is stuck in the present, focusing on a much smaller picture: the results. If this brave new world of player empowerment was going to survive, there needed to be immediate proof the All Blacks had absorbed the lessons of the Tri Nations.

Anyone standing outside the away changing room at the Stade Français close to midnight on 27 November 2004 would have felt the hairs on the back of their neck tingle. All Black captain Tana Umaga had opened the door to make sure everyone, and in particular the chaps in the home dressing room, could hear. He then ordered his team to perform a haka and not to hold back. The noise was deafening. The passion obvious – it was a haka that said All Black rugby was back on top of the world. It was a haka that signalled the new unity within the All Black squad. And it was a haka to celebrate the fact that France, one of the best teams in the world, had just been hammered 45-6 on their home patch. The French, brooding in their own dark place not so far away, must have felt the pain of every word emanating from their opponents. The French are notoriously erratic, capable of self-combusting in a manner befitting their Latin temperament. The score suggested the self-destruct button must have been pushed at some stage in Paris. But they didn't even get the chance to think about it as the All Blacks had them rattled even before the game kicked off.

During the modern era, the honour of leading the All Black haka has always been awarded to one of the Maori players in the team. In Paris, though, there were no Maoris in the match 22. The leadership group gave it some thought and decided they would like Umaga to lead the haka. The skipper, in his typically humble manner, was unsure about accepting the honour. He agreed though, and then delivered one of the most enduring performances of the professional era. For too long there had been uneasiness that the haka had been held to ransom by corporate agendas. It was such a convenient marketing tool for companies that had bought a slice of the All Blacks, and even the players had begun to wonder whether they were doing it because it made sponsors feel good about backing the brand.

The team had spent the last few months reconnecting with the haka and acquainting themselves with the history. They had to let the words infuse their soul so they could be performed from the heart. Umaga left no one in any doubt the emotion was pouring from his core. The intensity of the haka left the French playing emotional catch-up as the All Blacks were fizzing when the game started. And it was an advantage the visitors never once looked like relinquishing.

The score-line was obviously something special, but it was the performance more than the outcome that warmed the cockles of the coaches' hearts. Woodcock had fronted with an enormous performance in both the scrum and the loose. It had been a close selection between Woodcock, Somerville and Taumoepeau. The latter had scored a debut try against Italy, while Somerville was an experienced campaigner who had shown himself capable time and time again. Scrum coach Mike Cron, however, had pushed for Woodcock's inclusion after the Harbour player had been effective the week before against Wales. Woodcock got the nod and, alongside Anton Oliver and Carl Hayman, destroyed what was rated a fearsome French front row. The fact Oliver was there at all was a classic fairy tale.

The 28-year-old former All Black captain had been dropped by Mitchell in 2003 and then told by Henry in June 2004 that he was probably only fourth choice and should take up an invitation to play for the Barbarians rather than hang around for the All Black trial. By mid-way through the NPC, Oliver decided he'd had enough of rugby and would try and win a place at either Cambridge or Oxford University, probably to study some form of Art History. As Otago's forgettable season ground to a close, Oliver conducted the obligatory farewell media interviews. It turned out to be a bit like Mark Twain's oft-quoted remark about reports of his demise being greatly exaggerated.

Oliver might have been disillusioned and might have checked out emotionally, but the All Black coaches saw a totally different future. They had been impressed with his work-rate and effectiveness and were planning a dramatic recall. Oliver, as a former All Black captain and a holder of a law and economics degree, could bring bucketloads of leadership as well as life skills. He could also bring some ballast and grunt to the scrum – something that would be crucial against France, who fancied themselves in that department.

Oliver had been preferred to Keven Mealamu in Paris precisely because of his greater scrummaging presence and it was an inspired selection. Early in the second half, the game was reduced to Golden Oldies rules where neither side was allowed to push. The French had run out of front-row cover, after both Sylvain Marconnet and Pieter de Villiers picked up injuries. The injury to de Villiers appeared a little suspicious at the time, and Oliver's look of incredulity as the Frenchman departed said it all. It showed his suspicion that the French had faked injury to bottle out of competitive scrums. It showed he was angry that the chance to wreak further chaos had been removed. And it showed he knew that for the first time in a very long time, the All Black forwards were a crew to be taken seriously. It wasn't just because of their scrummaging either.

For weeks the All Blacks had been training to develop a more fluid style. They wanted to confront and also use the innate skills of their forwards. That meant players looking to off-load in contact to allow momentum to be built up. Those weeks of hard slog came to fruition in Paris. There was not only a physical edge to the All Black work, there was also a creative slant that saw the ball transferred expertly from one steamed-up runner to the next. It was the sort of rugby France used to play, but now they were being beaten at their own game. 'It was like a tidal wave,' French captain Fabien Pelous said after the game. 'There was just nothing we could do to stop them.' While the brilliant French flanker Olivier Magne said: 'You felt it right from the start, even during the haka. You felt this was no longer just a bit of New Zealand folklore. You felt you were really getting ready for a battle. It was *Once Were Warriors.*'

It was certainly a style that suited Rodney So'oialo, who chipped in with a seriously good game from No 8 to provide the selectors with yet another dividend from what many saw as a high-risk investment. So'oialo had won the jersey after impressing at blindside the week before in Cardiff. Tuiali'i had started that same game at No 8 and didn't quite nail his performance. The Wellington skipper was elevated to his preferred berth and played like a man who was acutely aware he might not get another chance. His combination with Kelleher was tidy, largely because the halfback also decided to put a stake in the ground. Kelleher had spent the last few months working on his passing. He knew that Marshall copped heaps for the perceived sluggishness of his delivery, so he knew he could win some favourable press if he flung out some accurate bullets. What Kelleher also did was run with the venom of old. Stocky, with a low centre of gravity, he has a powerful torso that allows him to send people flying when he fends them off. The French found that out all night, and it was apparent that Kelleher's elevation to the leadership group and the prolonged absence of Marshall had given him the space to grow emotionally. 'I knew it was an opportunity. I had some time to train quite hard for that trip and I knew I wanted to grab that opportunity,' said Kelleher of that tour.

The same was true of Carter, who played so brilliantly against Italy and Wales that it seemed laughable the coaches had ever been worried. He'd prospered by the decision to dispense with the flat backline as the default alignment. There were still occasions when the backs stacked close to the traffic and pushed the ball in front of the opposition, but the policy was now the exception rather than the norm. Carter had been allowed to play with a little more depth to help him generate width and bring the deadly talents of Joe Rokocoko into the game. The change of thinking was an admission of sorts that either the strategy was flawed or that the players didn't have the ability to execute it successfully.

No one really cared, because the All Blacks had finally found their cutting-edge and were at last posing a threat in midfield and further out. Carter's performance in Paris was even better as he nudged the ball down the touchlines and ran the show as if he had been doing nothing else for the last decade. A couple of years later, Crusaders coach Robbie Deans revealed that he was surprised anyone could have doubted Carter's strength of personality and ability to lead. 'I don't think those concerns were legitimate. Dan may not be vocal but even when he first came into the Crusaders and All Black teams he was a problem-solver. He was an innovator and he took ownership of trying to find solutions. He's got incredible composure and confidence and uses his initiative. I think it was inevitable really that he was going to end up at first-five. I always saw him playing there, and his time at second-five gave him that experience to learn while having a bit more time and a bit of the decision-making pressure having been taken off.'

Those pre-tour vacancies now had strong candidates. Woodcock had come of age, So'oialo had impressed at No 8, Kelleher took his chance at halfback and Carter was supreme at first-five. Lock was still a concern, as Maxwell was being held together by bits of sticky-tape and Ali Williams, although improving, was still some way off being the force he was in 2003. As a bonus, Conrad Smith had emerged as a long-term successor to Umaga. He scored with his first touch of the ball in Rome and was defensively assured in Paris. No wonder Umaga had spontaneously ordered the post-match haka. There was a lot of satisfaction and pride within the camp. The results were testimony to the fact the entire squad had bought into the new culture. And that was handy, because for their next assignment they were going to be thrown to the Lions.

9   The great buy-in

IT WAS partly a quirk of fate and partly deliberate that 2005, the 100th anniversary of the first All Black tour to the UK, threw up a momentous fixture list. The British Lions had long been scheduled to tour New Zealand for the first time in 12 years, and the IRB had New Zealand down to play Ireland, England and Scotland at the end of the year. There was a pre-Lions warm-up test against Fiji and the usual Tri Nations to be accommodated in the southern hemisphere winter. Those 11 tests would provide the All Blacks with significant challenges with which to celebrate their centenary. When the New Zealand Rugby Union persuaded Wales to host a game in Cardiff on 5 November, it was the icing on the centenary cake.

Playing the Lions is a big deal, so big that a number of senior All Blacks had their contracts drawn up so they could hang around to play the Lions and then invoke escape clauses to leave immediately after. Once Wales had been added to the fixture list to create the possibility of a Grand Slam tour, 2005 was going to be huge – one of those years that would leave the players and rugby-watching public with indelible memories.

But it was also going to be long. Those All Blacks who had toured Italy, Wales and France in November 2004 were expected back at Super 12 training by late January before the competition kicked off on 25 February 2005. The first All Black test would be played on 10 June and the season would climax in Edinburgh on 26 November. The players were going to take a physical pounding and be pushed to their emotional and psychological limits by a season that would require them to play in three separate All Black campaigns, the Super 12 and a bit-part in the NPC. Mentally, the players were going to have to manage their emotional energy carefully so they could peak at the right times.

The new culture within the team would help to some extent. The players were confident they were going to be unified when the pressure came on, as it inevitably would with so many big games. Off the field they were confident they had the right environment. Players were encouraged to speak their minds and reveal worries or concerns they had about any issue. They had set their own standards in terms of preparation and conduct. The European venture at the end of 2004 had seen the team make significant progress in leadership, direction and focus. But there were concerns about how that progress was going to be sustained. There were six months and a full Super 12 campaign to get through before the players would be back in a team environment that they owned.

Henry, Hansen and Smith had all been involved with Super 12 teams. They knew there was no consistency in the system. The players would operate in one manner with the All Blacks and then live under different regimes with their Super 12 franchises. Ideally there would be a consistency of cultures. Ideally, the Super 12 franchises would adopt a lot of the thinking coming out of the All Black camp. If there was commonality in terms of strength and conditioning methods, scrummaging techniques and individual skill development, then it would be to the benefit of all parties. Henry and his team had seen how Sir Clive Woodward had never settled for anything less than the ideal. They were going to take the same approach. The management team believed the All Black squad had to be surrounded by expert coaches in specialist fields. They agreed the support networks needed to be world class. But where their thinking advanced from what had gone before was in their desire to give the specialist coaches roles not just with the All Blacks but with the five franchises.

If the players were going to improve they couldn't rely on just the 15 or 16 weeks a year they spent assembled with the All Blacks. Nor was it good practice to confine all that coaching knowledge and expertise to the select few who made the All Blacks. There were 140 contracted Super 12 players. As injuries, retirements, loss of form and overseas departures were all inevitable, in time many of the 140 not currently in the All Black squad would be promoted. It made sense to expose all the elite players to the best practices and the best people all year round, which is why on 21 December 2004 the

NZRU announced they would be pumping $8 million into a three-year high performance plan.

It was easy to guffaw when England announced in 2003 they had hired a peripheral vision coach. There was the obvious question of what on earth a peripheral vision coach actually did. It also had to be asked whether rugby had gone bonkers. Having kept sports science at arm's length for the duration of the 172-year amateur period, the professional game couldn't get enough of niche experts. By 2000 every self-respecting international team had a specialist defence coach – usually someone hired from rugby league. There were also plenty of specialist scrum coaches, lineout coaches and kicking coaches making a decent living, while sports psychologists, nutritionists, physiotherapists and doctors with experience in the sports field would never be out of work for long.

The traditional model used by most countries, including New Zealand, was for the expert coach to be contracted to the international team either on a full-time or retainer basis. That usually meant the specialist coach would be heavily involved whenever the international side was assembled, but left with little to do between test campaigns. It also meant the players would be exposed to one specialist coach with the international side and then might have to work with another specialist in the same field when they returned to Super 12 or NPC. It was a fickle business and precarious for the specialists.

The All Black clear-out after the 2003 World Cup was a classic example of how the domino effect could topple an entire staff. John Mitchell and Robbie Deans were shown the door, and that spelt the end for specialist lineout coach Ross Nesdale. When Henry took over, he wanted Hansen to be the man in charge of lineouts. Specialist scrum coach Richard Loe was also handed his jotters, as was kicking coach Daryl Halligan. Team doctor John Mayhew was ready for something new and moved on, as did strength and conditioning coach Mike Anthony. It was just the way it was. When someone is appointed head coach they want to work with people they know and trust.

However, the danger with a clear-out is that it is ultimately the players who suffer the most. They not only have to get used to a new head coach, but they also have to get used to a whole crew of specialists. It takes time for new relationships to be made, for the players to get on the same wavelength. Sometimes the new man in office disagrees with some of the thinking of his predecessor and tries to undo some of the technical work that has been put in place. The turnover of All Black coaches had been so high since 1999 – four coaches in four years – that the players were frustrated at the lack of continuity. The intention of the high-performance plan was to try and provide a more stable framework for expertise to flourish.

The specialist coaches would be contracted to the NZRU and required to work with Super 12 franchises, provincial teams, age-grade teams and pretty much anywhere the union said. Mike Chu, the NZRU's high-performance manager and architect of the plan, had seen that despite the arrival of ridiculed positions such as peripheral vision coaches, there was still a role to be played by specialists. But they had to be employed under the right terms and the whole programme centrally managed. If the NZRU was going to spend $8 million, it had to be for the greater good of the whole elite game, not just the All Blacks.

The first major initiative under the new plan was the full-time appointment of specialist scrummaging coach Mike Cron. His contract would see him work with the All Blacks whenever they were assembled and if Henry thought a test prospect was in need of tuition during the Super 12 or NPC, Cron would be sent to carry out an emergency clinic.

After Cron, the next big move in personnel came on 3 May 2005 when former Wallabies, Springboks and Scotland kicking coach Mike Byrne was appointed. Byrne, an Australian by birth who had played Australian Rules professionally for 15 years, was rated one of the best in the business. His role with the All Blacks would be to work with the kickers and to improve catching skills. By the time Byrne joined, nutritionist Glenn Kearney, psychologist Gilbert Enoka and bio-mechanist Mark Sayers had also been signed.

A secondary component of the plan was to re-introduce regular fixtures for New Zealand A, but under the Junior All Black banner as this had more appeal for the marketing men. For some years the Six Nations had run a successful A competition that had shadowed the real deal. It was an ideal tool for blooding players who were ready to play at a level above club football but unable to be accommodated in the test set-up. That was the appeal for the All Black management. There was a big gap in quality between the Super 12 and All Blacks, so anything that could bridge it would be beneficial.

With the Super 12 play-offs taking place in the penultimate and final weekends of May, those professional players not involved with the All Blacks would have to wait until mid August and the start of the NPC until they were involved in meaningful action again. Many would turn out for their clubs and probably have a couple of NPC warm-up games, but June and July were soft months for those outside the national frame. June and July, however, were anything but soft months for the All Blacks. In 2005, those two months would feature a Lions series as well as a trip to South Africa. If one of the squad should break a leg and a reserve have to be called up, it was going to be hard to find one who was match-fit. That was the other beauty of the Junior All Black programme – two games against Australia A and one against Queensland would keep 26 high-quality players match-fit and better prepared to advance their individual cause and the All Black collective cause should they be called up.

There was no question the high-performance plan was going to win the minds of elite coaches around the country. It would give every Super 12 and provincial coach access to a well-resourced group of specialists, and the continued exposure to the same expertise throughout the year would benefit the long-term development of the players. But sometimes logic could get lost in the system, and the real battle was going to be winning hearts.

Since the inception of Super 12, there had been a frisson of tension running between the franchise coaches and the national coaches. The franchise coaches had not always bought into the big picture. They were employed to build and prepare squads that could win the competition. That meant making decisions consistent with that aim. Sometimes though, those decisions might not be aligned with what the national coach was trying to achieve. Selection was always one of those flash points. Each Super 12 franchise is only allowed initially to select 24 of its 28 players. Once each coach has decided upon his 'protected' 24, the list is submitted to the other teams. Each franchise is then able to select another four players in the draft. It's a system fraught with frustration – not just for the franchise coaches.

There have been several instances where the All Black coach has disagreed with the 24 players a franchise has selected. In 2004, Henry was not keen to see Andrew Mehrtens, Daniel Carter and Aaron Mauger all retained at the Crusaders. With all three there, at least one was going to spend most of the season on the bench and all three had played for the All Blacks in 2004. Henry tried to persuade either Carter or Mehrtens to draft to the Hurricanes, where they were more likely to get on the paddock. Neither budged, and Henry accepted that if a player didn't want to do something there was no point in forcing him. The folly of that approach had been seen in 1998 when John Hart insisted Leon MacDonald leave the Crusaders to play for the Chiefs so he could get game-time at first-five. MacDonald didn't settle and his form slumped so badly he was ironically cheered by his own supporters when he was subbed off in one game.

It was a fine line for the All Black coach. On the one hand, he wanted to see the best players in action as much as possible. Henry might have seen a certain player as a potential All Black, while the franchise coach rated him no better than a good squad man. Without game time in the Super 12 it was going to be hard for anyone to press their test claim, but Henry had no direct powers to elevate players into Super 12 starting fifteens. Franchise coaches couldn't be told by the All Black coach who they could and couldn't select. The franchise coaches had their performance reviewed at the end of every campaign, and life would have been far too complicated if mitigating factors such as interference from the national coach had to be factored in.

The All Black coaches also held firm views about the best ways to manage the workload of certain individuals. Again, though, while the All Black coaches might have preferred to have seen various individuals rested more during a campaign, they had no jurisdiction telling the franchise coach he had to leave test stars out of action just so they could be fresher for All Black duty.

Henry, Smith and Hansen knew the frustrations – they knew how difficult it was to align the vision of the franchises with that of the national team. The dictatorial approach was not going to work. The high-performance plan was a signal of intent that the All Black panel was ready to leave the past behind and create a structure that had mutual and aligned benefits. But if the franchise coaches were going to buy in, all the new initiatives had to be supported with open and regular communication. And that is where Henry and his team succeeded where others had failed.

Henry, Smith and Hansen, as well as Cron and Byrne, were regular visitors to the various franchises. They hosted coaching seminars and were happy to hang around to chew the fat and share a few cold ones. The theme had been switched from exclusive to inclusive, so much so that club coaches across Wellington were invited to watch the All Blacks train before the second Lions test. At the end of the session Henry then addressed the assembled coaches and explained what the session had been designed to achieve and the specific drills that had been worked on. Bailie Swart, the giant former Springbok prop who had been coaching Nelson Bays, couldn't believe he was able to ring Wayne Smith direct and ask for some advice. It would never have happened in South Africa, he said.

A lot of the barriers of old had been broken. The distrust was no longer endemic and for the first time in the professional age, everyone was operating with the best interests of the players and New Zealand rugby at heart. As former Brumbies coach David Nucifora said after selecting his second Blues squad in October 2006: 'The way the system is structured here it is a lot closer to the national body, whereas in Australia the provinces have an association but it is probably not as direct and as strongly linked. It does work. You have only got to look at the number of times New Zealand teams have won the competition and the strength of All Black rugby and New Zealand rugby in general. There is good communication between the national coaches and the franchise coaches and that is a positive. They have been very inclusive and let us know what their plans are. We work with them. We all need to work together, from provincial coaches to franchise coaches to national coaches, to make sure that our players continue to improve 12 months of the year, because it is about the players and if we are not together then it is the players who suffer, and that is being done very well.'

The Lions, bless their hapless souls, were hit square between the eyes by the increasing collective power of the All Blacks. The series proved to be so much more than just a 3-0 drubbing. It was a series that showed how the balance of power had shifted in the world game. It showed how one nation had identified its inherent weaknesses and finally put in place some strategies to eradicate them. And it showed that one nation was pushing its players through a coherent and co-ordinated development programme that enabled individuals to arrive on the test scene equipped with a range of skills that were applied as if they were innate.

The hype leading into the series had been phenomenal. Somehow the Lions had convinced everyone they were going to be special. Even the TAB thought it would go down to the wire with a third-test decider in Auckland. In the event, it didn't ever come remotely close to being competitive, and that was because the Lions simply couldn't cope with the intensity, skill levels and speed of the All Blacks.

Perhaps slightly more surprising was that the Lions couldn't cope with the power and efficiency of both the All Black lineout and scrum. Particularly the scrum, and that had to be a ringing endorsement of the decision to appoint Cron. A prop of reasonable ability, Cron coached club sides in Canterbury in the early 1980s and served what he calls a 25-year unpaid apprenticeship that took him to the All Blacks under Wayne Smith and Tony Gilbert, then to Wales with Steve Hansen and back to New Zealand. He's an unlikely-looking guru, roaming the training paddock in his trademark beanie, but there was no one in the All Black camp who would argue about the value he was adding. When the All Blacks went to the 2003 World Cup they were shifting 1200 kg on the scrum machine. Before they played the Lions they were shunting 2000 kg. The Lions, who had come out roaring about their fearsome scrummaging power, barely held a single scrum steady. Even when Carl Hayman was forced out of the second and third tests with a leg infection, the All Black scrum stayed at full power. That was the added value of having Cron available to the franchises. During the Super 12 he had worked with both Greg Somerville, who started in place of Hayman, and Campbell Johnstone, who was promoted to the bench. As a consequence of those sessions, both Somerville and Johnstone were able to take up their places seamlessly in the front row without the Lions being able to gain any respite from the change of personnel.

Cron, speaking before the second Lions test in Wellington, put the All Blacks ascendancy down to several factors. 'We scrummage differently to the northern hemisphere,' he said. 'You have to be balanced and still before you engage whereas, if you look at rugby overseas, their movement before they engage is quite fluid and mobile. We're more static. We want to use our legs and they want to use their upper body. We have gone away from hitting scrum-machines, and I do a lot of work one-on-one with body awareness drills. We did live scrummaging in training last week and didn't have one collapsed scrum. That's how technically proficient our guys are. Several years ago the emphasis in New Zealand got lost a wee bit. We focused more on skills and developing athletes. We did that very well, but sometimes to the detriment of our set phase. When Graham Henry came in he was very clear that set phase was a key area. For us to play well we needed to be fit and wonderful athletes but also do our set phase work.

'I was allocated a lot of time before we went to Europe last year. From that, the boys are really getting their heads around it. About 62 percent of the power comes from the back five, yet we all think it is the front row. But we must have them all correctly aligning their spines to transfer the power through.'

With the scrum and lineout providing such a stable platform, the All Blacks were able to demonstrate how far ahead they were in other basic skills. Most of the Lions' backs looked like the only pass they had ever made was on some unsuspecting maiden. They struggled to run into space and to time the release of the pass. That was in stark contrast to the All Blacks, who executed the basics without ever giving the whole business much thought. Every back could time the pass, every back could find some space and every back could operate as an auxiliary forward when required.

Welsh flanker Martyn Williams, who struggled for form on the Lions tour, said to *The Independent* a year later: 'I think every one of us on that trip would accept we were taught a lesson particularly in the tackle area, where the modern game is won and lost. For a player in my position, it was obviously going to be a demanding tour. Everywhere you go in New Zealand, the open-side flanker is king; the fourth- or fifth-choice No 7 over there would walk into most sides here. But the thing that made them different to us, better than us, was that they all contested the breakdown, from one to 15. What was more, they were all brilliant at it. Some were more brilliant than others, but that wasn't much consolation. The intensity was phenomenal, and it took us a long time to get to grips with the fact that while we were picking and choosing when to make nuisances of ourselves, they were doing it all the time.'

The All Blacks could do the basics because the New Zealand system made sure that simple skills were drummed into the players from an early age. The Lions, on the other hand, looked as if they had spent too long trying to learn complex game-plans without ever really mastering the core skills that would be the foundation. It was the Lions who had been in camp since the end of May, but it was the All Blacks, on far less preparation time, who played as a unified force.

The feel-good factor swept the nation. The series was a showcase for all that was good about New Zealand rugby. The dark events of the 2003 World Cup were but a distant memory during that series, particularly on 2 July when the All Blacks put a big stake in the ground. They went 7-0 down after two minutes when Lions captain Gareth Thomas found a hole the *Titanic* could have squeezed through and scored under the sticks. The Cake Tin was swarming with Lions fans, and the unusual feeling of a visitors' try being met with a wall of noise could have unsettled the All Blacks. Maybe the All Blacks of 2003 would have let the emotion of the occasion get to them after a difficult start. This was a new team, though, a team equipped with leadership skills. It was a team that knew how to handle pressure and a team that believed in its own ability. It was also a team that was very much united – as evidenced by the way it handled two major off-field incidents before that second test in Wellington.

Justin Marshall sauntered out of the home changing room at Jade Stadium and gave no indication of the storm that was brewing deep inside him. He'd just played a blinder for the Crusaders in the semi-final of the Super 12. He'd been the focal point of almost every deadly attack. The iron in a huge defensive effort. The Crusaders had blown the Hurricanes away 47-7 and would be coming back to their home ground eight days later to play the final. A few weeks after that, the All Blacks would run out to play the opening test against the Lions. What Marshall wasn't sure about was whether he would be there wearing black on 24 June or whether the Super 12 final would be his last game in New Zealand before he headed to Leeds in mid-July. Not sure? That was crazy – the man was in the form of his life and probably playing well enough to be considered the best halfback in the world. He was a shoo-in for the All Blacks, having mopped the floor with all of his rivals during the Super 12. The All Black coaches had said his decision to head overseas would not jeopardise his chances to play the Lions.

But Marshall was still hurting at the decision not to take him to Europe at the end of 2004. Not travelling had hurt, and in his view the wound had been doused with salt because he was never told personally by the coaches. 'I have got to weigh up whether I'm going to be selected and whether my heart is in it,' he said. 'I'm a passionate player, pretty competitive and I would not want to be involved if I have one foot on the plane. The selectors have to decide whether they want me and I have to decide whether or not I want to be involved. There will be opportunities that come up after I leave. But I am completely satisfied with what I have got. It sounds bizarre because everyone else is already talking about the Lions but I'm really focusing on the Super 12.'

Marshall had pulled the pin and lobbed the grenade. No one had seen this coming. And when he continued, with very little prompting, he ensured that if he did choose to make himself available for the All Blacks, he would be met with a few cold shoulders. 'It did hurt missing out on the end-of-season tour and I made no secret of that. Subsequently some of the things I brought forward have come to fruition now. A lot of those players they took away on that tour who are now test All Blacks – they should be putting pressure on the players likely to be selected in the squad against the Lions. And a lot of those players have not shown the form. I don't want to single players out, that is not fair, but if you sit down and look at it you will know who I am talking about. You have got to earn the right rather than be given it, and those players who got opportunities should have pushed on and I don't feel they have. To a certain extent it justifies some of the issues I had with the players they took away on that trip.

'I have played well. That certainly helps but doesn't always mean you will get selected, as has been shown in the past. I have only been in touch with them [the All Black coaches] once. It was after the Blues game. Graham contacted me because there had been no communication before that tour left. I had never heard anything from them pre-Super 12. That was another really disappointing thing. I didn't really know where I stood, so I thought: "Bugger it. I'm just going to get out and play and put the pressure on them." That worked to a certain extent because they ended up having to give me a call and say, we know you are playing well and when we select the team for the Lions we will be selecting the best.'

Henry phoned Marshall the following day to touch base and let the player know he had been impressed with the way he had been playing. It was essentially a call to reassure Marshall he was in their plans. But Marshall launched a similar tirade to the one he had delivered on the Friday night after the semi-final, leaving Henry dumbstruck. Worse still for Henry was that later that day he became aware that Marshall's tirade on the Friday had been made to the *Herald on Sunday*. When Henry was contacted by the newspaper a few hours after he had spoken with Marshall, the All Black coach was tetchy. He was still reeling and understandably he didn't want the situation with Marshall to be played out in public. 'Some of his games this year have been pretty special,' he said of Marshall. 'I just assume that he wants to be part of it. I don't think those are the issues you discuss through the media, quite frankly. The selectors have got a high opinion of Justin Marshall as a person and as a player and we'll leave it at that. Justin's made a decision to play overseas and we totally support that. Before he goes there is a Lions series that he might be involved in. There will be 26 players involved and without going any further, I think it's pretty obvious isn't it?'

The nation's media lapped it all up and didn't focus on much else all week. In the end Marshall committed to the Lions series, his decision made after a major clear-the-air meeting with the selectors. The whole business was a distraction and potentially disruptive. But if there was any animosity towards Marshall from his peer group, it remained hidden. There was no rift, no simmering resentment and Marshall started the first test in Christchurch and played significant roles off the bench in the other two. The tools were in place for the squad to deal with the drama and not dwell on it.

And nor was the team broken by the media circus that enveloped captain Tana Umaga after the first test. In the first minute of that game Umaga and Keven Mealamu were involved in an ugly incident that saw Lions captain Brian O'Driscoll upended in a tackle that ended his tour by dislocating his shoulder. It didn't look good for either Umaga or Mealamu but for some reason neither player was cited. The Lions were outraged that two All Black players had got away with no penal sentence. Coach Clive Woodward held a midnight conference after the test to rage on about the injustice. He was back on his soapbox again the next night at the team's new base at the James Cook Hotel in Wellington. The British media lapped up his every word and let the injustice course through their veins and out into their keyboards.

Umaga had become public enemy number one. The Brits were disgusted he had neither checked on the Lions skipper as he was being put on the stretcher nor had made contact afterwards to apologise. Nothing had been heard from Umaga during the whole furore. The judicial process meant he had to stay quiet after the game in case he was cited. By Wednesday though, the pressure had reached levels where radio silence had to be broken.

There was a planned media session where all the players in the All Black starting fifteen would be available for interview at the NZRU's headquarters in Hinemoa Street. Normally the players just wandered in, sat down and let the journalists flock round. But on this particular occasion, Umaga chose to set up a top table where he could be grilled by the assembled masses. As he took his seat to excited whispers, the rest of the All Black squad trooped in and stood, arms folded, behind their skipper offering staunch support. It was an impressive show of unity. It said they didn't care about the rights or wrongs of what happened, but that they were standing by their man. It was a message to the British hacks that they could chip away, but they would not find any faultlines to get leverage or exploit further.

The final score in Wellington was 48-18, which said it all really. The pantomime that had overshadowed the rugby in the build-up had only brought the All Blacks closer together. The All Black players decided the best response would be made on the field and they duly delivered, particularly Daniel Carter, who collected 33 of the All Blacks' points in a performance so sublime that the *Herald on Sunday's* irascible columnist James McOnie famously rated the first-five 11 out of 10. Richie McCaw was not far behind and the total annihilation of the Lions had the nation smiling. The series showed much had been achieved by Henry and his coaching team in a short time. It showed that the high performance plan had enormous merit and was fast-tracking the development of the players. It showed that the leadership and ability to cope with life on and off the field was greatly improved and that the All Blacks were climbing towards global supremacy.

But the series also showed that no matter how well coached and prepared the players were, performance was going to suffer if individuals were asked to front for three consecutive tests. The Lions offered a physical challenge and the series knocked lumps out of the players. In the end, only eight All Blacks – Tana Umaga, Sitiveni Sivivatu, Rodney So'oialo, Jerry Collins, Chris Jack, Ali Williams, Keven Mealamu and Tony Woodcock – started all three tests. By the third test in Auckland, Carter, McCaw, Aaron Mauger and Hayman were all injured. By the end of the series, the All Black coaches decided no one would play three tests consecutively again. The detailed statistics being fed back from the tests showed that several individual performances dipped in Auckland.

Understandably, those players who had started in Christchurch and Wellington found there wasn't much left in the tank when they got to Auckland. The cumulative bumps and bruises couldn't be so easily shaken off. Retaining peak emotional intensity over three tests was a serious challenge that not everyone was able to achieve. It wasn't going to be a problem during the Tri Nations, when the All Blacks would only ever play two tests on consecutive weekends, but it would be on the Grand Slam tour, when the four tests would be played back to back. The Super 12 coaches had been asked to buy in to the new way. The same request was about to be made of the players.

10 Hokey cokey All Blacks

OF ALL the critical dates in the history of New Zealand rugby, 6 May 2005 might just prove to be the most important of the professional era. That was the day Graham Henry, Steve Hansen and Wayne Smith each signed two-year extensions to their respective All Black contracts. All three had initially been hired on two-year deals that would expire at the end of 2005. That was the standard way for the NZRU – they offered national coaches a maximum of two years at the helm. Such an arrangement allowed both parties room to manoeuvre at the end of the term. There was logic in restricting tenures to just two years. The brand had to be protected and if the coaching team were failing to connect with the players, there was an opportunity to oust them without need for a massive pay-out. But some hefty problems were also created as a result.

Since John Hart had resigned in November 1999, the All Black coaching position had been a hot potato. Smith came in and lasted barely two years. Mitchell couldn't get an extension on his two-year stint either. The players were unsettled by the constant swinging of the axe, because more often than not it would have a massive bearing on their test selection. Take Troy Flavell, the rugged lock-cum-blindside. He won 15 All Black caps when Smith had been head coach. Flavell's athleticism and raw power were just what Smith was after. But when Smith was let go and Mitchell came in, there was no longer any place for Flavell. Mitchell was put off by Flavell's perceived lack of discipline and subsequently never picked the North Harbour forward, not even when Flavell's NPC form before the World Cup had been first-class. Realising he didn't have an All Black future, Flavell signed to play in Japan. His bags were packed when Mitchell was booted and in came Henry, a big fan of Flavell. He wanted the enfant terrible of New Zealand rugby in his side. But Flavell was committed and when the Japanese almost doubled his offer to save face, Henry lost his battle to keep Flavell in New Zealand.

There were plenty of others who had been in favour under one regime and out on their ear in the next. Reuben Thorne went from being captain under Mitchell to not wanted by Henry. Carl Hayman was capped under Smith, ignored by Mitchell and re-introduced by Henry, while Ron Cribb was a major presence under Smith and a non-presence under Mitchell. The confusing part for the players was that many of them felt they had been playing better football under the regime that was not picking them. For many it felt like an arbitrary decision – that their face didn't fit or that the coach had a soft spot for another bloke and was going to pick him regardless.

In the aftermath of the World Cup in 2003, a few players came out in support of retaining Mitchell. They did so partly because they believed he had done a good job and also because they were fearful of what would happen if there was more disruption. Another change of coach could be a factor in some players deciding to head overseas. Selection was seemingly being turned into a lottery, and then of course there was the issue of having to learn the nuances of the new man and the people and systems he would inevitably bring in.

But there was a bigger picture at play too. Awarding coaches only short-term contracts put the emphasis almost exclusively on results. For an All Black coach, that is not necessarily a bad thing. Results will always be critical in New Zealand. There is no acceptance of brave defeats. The rugby public would take the view that a good loser was in fact just a loser. The aura of the All Blacks had been built on the scoreboard. In 102 years of All Black history there had only been two utterly dark years: 1949 and 1998. Those two years were like a drunken uncle at a family gathering – everyone denied ownership as they burned a sense of shame into the national psyche.

Henry and his team accepted there was no getting away from the burden of the All Black heritage. Winning tests would always be paramount. But they felt that both the present and the future had to be catered for. During their first year in charge and then again during the Lions series, they had seen how the massively increased physical and mental demands of test rugby had changed the landscape. The equation didn't stack up. If the best 22 players were used in every test then many of them were simply going to burn out. The consequence of focusing exclusively on results was going to see a number of world-class players end up on the scrapheap before their time. No one, not even the super-human Richie McCaw, could be expected to get through every Super 12 game, every test and play a part in the NPC. Or rather, they could, but there would be certain games where their performance would dip and inevitably, in time, serious injury would incur.

Maybe McCaw would get through 2005 being so heavily involved. Maybe he could also manage 2006. But what if by 2007 he was so bruised and battered that the edge came off his form in the same way the legendary Josh Kronfeld had slowly declined though overuse in the mid to late 1990s? Or worse still, what if he ended up seriously injured as a consequence of his major joints being overused and weakened by all the physical contact? That was the real concern for Henry – that if he kept picking the same players there was no way all of them would make it through to the World Cup. And if he kept picking the same 22 all the time, there would be little strength in depth to provide replacements for those players who did succumb to their workload.

Henry's argument was that New Zealand had never been down any other road. Since 1903 the All Blacks had picked the best side for every test. There was no criticism of that philosophy, as that is the very essence of test football. But there was a reality to be acknowledged too. The game had taken a paradigm shift in physicality. The athletes of 2005 bore no resemblance to those men who had worn the silver fern 100 years earlier. The game had gone off the scale in terms of impact and the number of collisions.

It also had to be acknowledged that the model of only worrying about the present had not served the All Blacks when it really mattered. The World Cup had been won in 1987 and never seen again. The experience of 2003, in particular, couldn't be forgotten. One injury to Tana Umaga and the All Blacks were stuffed. They ended up having to select a guy at centre who had barely played there in his life. Henry was adamant that could never be allowed to happen again.

Rugby had long ceased to be a 15-man game. It was now a 22-man game, and at the World Cup it would be a 30-man game. To win the World Cup in 2007, the All Blacks would have to play four pool games in 21 days and then win three knock-out matches on consecutive weekends. Having seen the injury toll incurred during the Lions series and the way those who did make it through all three tests suffered a drop in effectiveness, there was no way Henry could select the same 22 for all seven World Cup games. That would be a recipe for disaster, and disaster had been on the All Black World Cup menu once too often. Henry was not going to fall into the same trap as Mitchell – his vision was to have strength throughout his 30-man squad to ensure that one single injury could not derail the entire campaign.

To build that strength in depth, though, he needed to have the backing of the NZRU. He needed to be contracted through until 2007 so he could undergo some cohesive planning. Until his contract was extended, there could be no shifting of focus – the emphasis would remain on results, and selection decisions would be made on that basis alone. If the All Blacks were ever going to get their hands on the William Webb Ellis trophy they needed to be brave enough to start bringing fringe players through early. They needed to be prepared to make the odd selection gamble and trust every man in the wider squad. And that process began on 6 May 2005 when NZRU chairman Jock Hobbs said in a statement that the board had extended the coaching panel's contracts to allow them to start building towards the World Cup. The board also wanted to provide certainty to New Zealand's elite players about coaching and selection. It's hard to believe the board would have granted Mitchell the same leniency – the relationship, trust and communication were not strong enough to support the pressure of the risk.

But there was massive respect for the way Henry had handled his post and he was duly granted a licence to follow a different road from the one all his predecessors had followed. And there was a kind of irony about that. The coaches' contracts had been extended to give players certainty about selection. Yet, under the new master plan, no one, not even the skipper, was going to be certain of selection any more.

As the coaches sat down in May 2005 to plan their journey through to the World Cup they had two objectives in mind: the first was to ensure they were protecting the players from excessive workloads, and the second was to ensure they had two genuine test-class players in every position. The two objectives were neatly aligned.

The All Blacks were going to play 12 tests in 2005, probably 13 in 2006 and then a further 14 if they were going to win the World Cup in 2007. Moreover, the Super 12 would be expanded in 2006 so every team would play at least 13 games. It wasn't going to be possible to control the amount each individual played during the Super 12. Relations between the panel and the franchise coaches were at an all-time high, but the goodwill could only buy so much. The only component of the season Henry could control was the test campaigns. And the way the coaching panel saw it in May 2005, they were going to have to prioritise the various campaigns.

The Lions series was not going to be the time to experiment. There was just too much at stake. The hype building into the series had been huge. The economic benefit to the NZRU was estimated at about $20 million, while the New Zealand economy was expecting to be better off by $250 million thanks to the likely 25,000 Brits who would travel. Then there was the fact that so many experienced players had remained in New Zealand purely in the hope they would feature in the series. And there was another factor not to be underestimated – the last man to coach the Lions had been Graham Henry, and the tour to Australia in 2001 had been one of the low points in his career.

The Grand Slam tour at the end of the year was a chance to make history. Only Graham Mourie's All Blacks of 1978 had ever successfully defeated all four home nations in one trip. How satisfying it would be if the All Blacks of 2005 could emulate that feat. So that left the Tri Nations as the only possible opportunity to play around with the make-up of the team. 'With the greatest respect to the Tri Nations, it probably ranks as the third campaign this year,' said assistant coach Steve Hansen on 29 May. 'That doesn't mean to say we don't want to go out and win it. It's an opportunity to try some new players and rest some of the other guys who need a break. The Lions series is going to take a lot out of us. We have got to look at it on an individual basis. Some guys might take two games off. Some might take the whole campaign off, and others will play the whole campaign. It depends how they come through the Lions series.

'People who don't understand or agree with it are pretty upset. But we have to do what is right for New Zealand rugby. The All Blacks are expected to win and we want to win. We have to trust some of the talent in this country to do that. Rather than just 22 guys, I am happy to trust 30. History tells us we only win 72 percent of our tests. We want to get that figure higher, and expanding our squad size will help.'

The coaches had a pretty good idea of the individuals who were likely to be offered an extended rest period. Chris Jack and Carl Hayman had played big roles for their respective Super 12 franchises and never lacked commitment in physical berths. They were also world class in positions where there was not a lot of back-up. They were possible candidates to play less prominent roles in the Tri Nations. There were other senior players who would probably fall into the same category, but much would depend on the shape they were in after the Lions series.

Probably the only player the coaches knew for sure they wanted to take out for some, if not all of the Tri Nations, was Tana Umaga. The skipper had signed a three-year extension on his contract in 2004 shortly after being unveiled as captain. The 2003 World Cup had been such an unhappy experience for him that he wanted to see if he could make it through to 2007. He would be 34 by then and his World Cup knee injury aside, he had been blessed with a charmed life in terms of injury. But there was no getting away from the fact that while he was the model professional in his preparation, he was dangerously close to the top of the hill.

The reality for 30-somethings in professional rugby is that no matter how much they look after themselves, the bumps and bruises take longer to recover from. Maintaining explosive pace is a constant battle, as is keeping mentally fresh. The coaching panel knew how important Umaga was to the All Blacks both in his role as captain and as player. They wanted him to be in France. They felt he could still be a world-class midfielder in two years time, and there was no question he would be an even better leader by then.

But they felt that for Umaga to get through to 2007, he would have to be protected. 'We want Tana to last as long as he can, so we have to look after him,' said Hansen. 'I know there were a lot of people who got upset when we didn't pick the captain in Wales. But we have to grow the leadership. It's good for Richie [vice-captain McCaw] and it's good for Tana, and if this means we have Tana for longer, then it's good for New Zealand rugby.'

The problem for Hansen and the rest of the coaching team was that Umaga didn't agree. Hansen had revealed the plans for Umaga before the Lions series. Maybe in May the skipper would have been more comfortable with the idea of being carefully managed. But by July, there was more chance of turkeys voting to keep Christmas. Umaga had been in supreme form against the Lions. He had been the best back on display and his captaincy had been forceful and decisive. Off the field though, he had been emotionally drained by the fall-out following the Brian O'Driscoll incident. Umaga had been hounded by the British press in the week leading up to the second test. Even when he fronted on the Wednesday, Fleet Street was still baying for blood. The questions kept coming and it became apparent that Umaga was only going to earn a reprieve if he fell at O'Driscoll's feet and begged forgiveness, then flayed himself with birch twigs to show how truly repentant he was.

The British had lost perspective. There was no denying the incident deserved further inquiry by the citing commissioner. The fact it didn't receive it was not Umaga's fault. Nor were the British being realistic in demanding that Umaga deliver a personal apology to O'Driscoll. Danny Grewcock, the Lions lock, had been cited for biting in the first test and was duly suspended by the judiciary. The Brits were strangely reluctant to suggest Grewcock offer Keven Mealamu an apology. The whole business was unsavoury and it drained Umaga emotionally.

It was probably no surprise, then, that by the end of the Lions tour, Umaga began to evaluate his rugby future. 2007 started to seem an awfully long way off. When he'd agreed to be captain in 2004 he told Henry he would give it two years and then re-evaluate. He'd been brilliant against the Lions and the series had been won 3-0 – maybe it was the right time to call it quits. That would give his likely replacement as captain, McCaw, two years to grow into the job and the selectors two years to find a replacement for him in the midfield. It would also allow him to get out with his reputation intact and, more importantly, on his own terms. Retirement was a very real option at that stage.

The coaching panel thought it was too soon though, that there was still plenty of good rugby left in him. They felt he could make it through to the World Cup and they outlined their plans to rest him for the away leg of the Tri Nations. Maybe he could skip some of next season's Super 14 too. Umaga heard the plans to offer him special treatment and he went away to mull things over. When the leadership group were told about the plans to rest Umaga and other senior players, they too talked things through. The skipper didn't like the sound of not playing and the leadership group were not necessarily very keen either. In the end it didn't matter, as the injury toll during the Lions series and the first Tri Nations games scuppered the rotation plans.

For the first two away tests of the campaign, the selections were largely consistent, with the big names all featuring. Hansen said on 21 August before the All Blacks' home games, that Hayman probably would have been granted some time off if an infected leg hadn't kept him out of the last two Lions tests. Greg Somerville too might have had a rest, but as the only prop capable of covering both sides of the scrum, that luxury could not be extended his way. 'You have all the intentions with your planning,' said Hansen, 'but the system has to be flexible enough to cope with change. New Zealanders, players and coaches included, want to win every test. So looking at the games ahead, we have to respect those games for what they are and take the opportunities to build the squad. It is not always about game-time. James Ryan is getting a little bit of field-time and will probably get some more. It is about building momentum and making sure we win games. For someone like John Afoa to have the opportunity to walk out in his kit in front of 80,000 people, you can't buy that experience. He's had a few weeks with scrum coach Mike Cron and, again, that is hugely important. If these guys can get comfortable with all the things we do off the field, then I believe it will make the actual playing side that bit easier.'

As for Umaga, Hansen said: 'I think he is playing as good as he has ever played in his life. He doesn't know how much longer he is going to play for, so play him. While he is in the form he is in, he wants to play and lead the side and we have to respect that.' The thing was, though, Umaga had a pretty strong inkling he knew exactly how long he was going to play for. More and more he was thinking the Grand Slam would be his last hurrah. The travel, the training, the time away from the family and the demands of being captain were making him uncertain he would push past 2005. As a player he was going to be hard to replace. Conrad Smith had been impressive in his limited outings at centre, but he was not a line-busting, big-hitting presence. Ma'a Nonu had the raw power but was riddled with foibles, while Casey Laulala hadn't progressed as far as anyone would have liked since earning a place on the end-of-season tour in 2004.

There were other positions where cover was light. There was no outstanding candidate to replace Daniel Carter at first-five. Richie McCaw was without peer at openside, as the selectors had cooled on the ball-snaffling Marty Holah. Afoa had been in the squad but had not actually played, so it was still unclear whether he was really capable of holding a test scrum steady from the tighthead, and while James Ryan had emerged strongly at lock in his cameo appearances, there was still a desire to discover a fourth lock of real quality.

The coaching panel knew they had to put the emphasis back on development if they were to fulfil their objective of building depth across the squad. They had been forced partly by injuries and partly by the leadership group to be consistent in their selections throughout the Tri Nations.

They also knew from the Lions tour that UK rugby was in a dark place. England were going through an interminable rebuilding phase. Wales were struggling with injuries after winning the Grand Slam, Ireland without the injured Brian O'Driscoll and Paul O'Connell were not going to be much to worry about, and Scotland could have fielded 20 players and still no one would have ever thought they were going to win.

In the initial planning process, the end-of-season trip had been seen as a landmark tour where the emphasis would be on results. By September 2005, with the Tri Nations in the bag after just one defeat in Cape Town, the selectors saw they had a golden opportunity to use the end-of-season tour to cast their selection net far and wide.

If the theme really was going to be development, the All Black coaching panel felt they would need 35 players in the UK to test their depth. They argued that with no mid-week games to assess those on the fringes, they had no choice but to use test matches as a vehicle to evaluate some players who they couldn't guarantee were of the appropriate calibre. The traditionalists hated it – the All Blacks were not a finishing school. The jersey was reserved for those who had earned it, not those who might possibly be good enough.

The coaching panel knew accusations about cheapening the jersey would be thrown at them. But they stayed firm and on 23 October named a squad that contained two players that even those with an anorak devotion to the game had not really heard of. Jason Eaton was named as a lock and Isaia Toeava as a utility back. Eaton was a big, mobile unit who had enjoyed a prominent campaign with Taranaki, but the 23-year-old had no Super 12 experience and the year before had been playing for the lowly Manawatu in the second division. Toeava was only 19, with just one NPC start for Auckland under his belt. He'd excelled at age-grade level in the midfield, and the selectors saw a supremely talented young man with all the skills to be a global superstar – by 2011. They wanted to take a punt though, and see if they could fast-track his development and turn him into a household name by 2007.

Eaton and Toeava were brave calls as was the decision to pre-select one team to play the opening game against Wales and then an entirely different starting fifteen to play Ireland the following week. The British media were flabbergasted that any international coach had the gall to try something so audacious. No other team in the world could possibly have pulled it off, but

Henry and his team didn't see it as showing a lack of respect to the opposition. They weren't experimenting – doing the hokey cokey by putting one team in, one team out and shaking it all about – for the sake of it. They were tying to achieve clearly stated objectives.

Before the tour party departed, assistant coach Wayne Smith took the opportunity to put the rotation plan into perspective. While everyone had an opinion on the merits of making wholesale changes, it was the coaches who had the in-depth knowledge of the players. It was the coaches who had the detailed statistics on each player that painted a clear picture of what contribution each individual was making. And perhaps most importantly, each of the individual coaches had been working with elite players for more than 10 years, with Henry having almost 20 years experience. In all that time, they had presumably acquired the ability to read and understand the players – to get a feel for who was fresh, who was in need of rest and who was in need of more game-time.

It was with all those factors in mind that Smith said: 'You have got to take into account the intensity of the game. We get a feel after the game, the physical toll it has taken on the players. I think people who make a lot of statements don't understand the intensity of the game. Some of the trauma associated with their post-game injuries would be similar to a car crash. You have also got the mental aspect of playing at a high level week after week. It is a totally different environment that we are talking about. I think player welfare is critical for long-term success. It's easy to look at the now and say we will get the most out of these guys and win this test and that test, but you must look further ahead. I've felt for a while that a case-by-case scenario was the way to go rather than a blanket policy, and if anyone in the world could manage it, we could because of central contracts.'

The Lions series had shown there were problems when players were asked to front on three consecutive weekends. The Grand Slam tour was going to require four consecutive performances. Getting through two consecutive tests was not so hard, but three, that was a problem. Some players could manage it better than others. Outside backs were exposed to less intense contact and could keep fresh for longer. In the high-impact positions of the front and back rows, however, there were few players who could still give of their best by the third week. Even allowing for a tapered and sympathetic training build-up, it was a big ask for a jumbo, hard-hitting prop like Hayman to play three games on the hoof and still be snorting fire. Even McCaw, with his enormous aerobic capacity, was going to be feeling the effects by the third week. The panel were in no doubt that come the World Cup, some players such as McCaw and Hayman would probably be asked to play three weeks in a row, but two years out from the competition, there was little need to be flogging them that hard. Henry was clear before the party left that no one would start in all four tests and it was likely that most players would only start in two.

Heading into that opening game in Cardiff, there was further concern among New Zealand's rugby fraternity that not only was Henry messing with tradition, but that too many individuals were short of match fitness. After the Tri Nations had ended in early September, the 26-man squad had been granted a couple of weeks off. Some players such as Mils Muliaina and Mealamu barely featured for Waikato and Auckland respectively during the NPC. Others managed a few NPC games, where they appeared to be blowing a bit hard. There were fears that the majority of the side were going to Cardiff with not enough football under their belts.

They were fears that were eradicated about half an hour after kick-off. That's how long it took for the All Blacks to pop the Welsh in their pockets. Rico Gear, with just a couple of outings for second division Nelson Bays in the last seven weeks, gave a master class in finishing. Elsewhere, Neemia Tialata put in a huge scrummaging shift on debut, Ryan was aerially strong and mobile and Carter was, as usual, in a different class. Wales were blown away – hammered 41-3 on their home patch, and the side that had swept away all of Europe earlier in the year never once looked like scoring a try. Surely such a definitive performance would force the coaching panel into a rethink for the Irish game? No chance. The panel had committed to their selections before they left New Zealand and the result in Cardiff was going to have no bearing on the team they named to start in Dublin. And sure enough, out went hat-trick hero Gear, Ryan made way for new boy Eaton, Carter had to stand down for Nick Evans, and even the skipper had to take his turn in the stands to allow McCaw to build his leadership portfolio. Henry named the team at the Castlenock Hotel on the Tuesday before the test, and when he was badgered about making fifteen changes, even suggested that results were not all that important on the trip. He might have been serious, but he made the point with every confidence the All Blacks were going to win.

It took all of 30 seconds for the All Blacks to prove in Dublin that the old saying about never changing a winning side is not always true. With his first touch of the ball inside his own 22, first-five Evans, who was a late tour party call-up for Luke McAlister, saw the Irish were not getting off the defensive line and pushed a long pass to Ma'a Nonu. His opposite that day, the far more experienced Ronan O'Gara, received his first touch, never once looked outside him and hammered the ball into touch. The difference in approach epitomised the gulf between the two teams. The All Blacks were full of instinctive footballers who had been encouraged to assess what was on before making a decision. The Irish, on the other hand, played by numbers. O'Gara was in his own 22 so he booted it – that was the way he was programmed. The All Blacks went on to win as comfortably as they had in Cardiff, 45-7, and there was barely a peep heard about the folly of rotating players so heavily.

England were always going to present the sternest challenge of the four opponents and Henry duly selected what would be considered the All Blacks' strongest side. It was an epic battle at Twickenham, with England scoring early from one of their famous rolling mauls and the All Blacks picking up three yellow cards. The numerical disadvantage forced the All Blacks to dig seriously deep and they did well to cling on for a 23-19 win. It was another triumph for the leadership group – the side was under huge pressure, not helped by the late withdrawal of McCaw, and they didn't fold the way they might have in the past. The All Blacks were also aided, quite considerably, by the English backs being almost totally devoid of any creativity.

A very experimental side secured an error-strewn, relatively easy win in Edinburgh a week later to clinch the Grand Slam. It was a huge achievement, something of which the players could be enormously proud. But even with their place in history secure, the coaching panel insisted the mission had always been about player development. And there was plenty of progress on that front to keep the coaches satisfied. Props Afoa and Tialata had come through strongly. Ryan and Eaton had been big successes and would be putting pressure on the established pairing of Jack and Ali Williams. Chris Masoe, a surprise choice, made an impression as an all-action openside. Elsewhere, Evans was assured at first-five and competition for wing berths became red-hot with Doug Howlett, Joe Rokocoko, Sivivatu and Gear all displaying classic try-scoring instincts.

But perhaps the most important breakthrough on the tour was getting the penny to drop in a few minds that were stubbornly refusing to see the big picture. The staunchest critics realised there was method in all this selection madness and it was possible to work the dream ticket of catering for the present while developing for the future. Results had been achieved by using the full strength of the tour party. Everyone had been trusted to play a part and everyone had repaid the faith. There was no one who could say that wholesale rotation was cheapening the jersey when Wales, Ireland, England and Scotland were all toasted in consecutive weeks. And it wasn't just an external realisation either. If there had been some trepidation within the leadership group about the rotation policy during the Tri Nations, those doubts evaporated in the UK. Everyone was now towing the party line. The coaches presented a compelling case that the policy was in every player's long-term interests. Some players might have been frustrated. Some might not have wholeheartedly agreed with the idea of giving their jersey up to have a rest. But that was the way things were going to be and the players began to speak publicly about the situation, with everyone careful to voice their support, understanding and commitment to the concept.

There was maybe only one real downer from the trip – and that came when Umaga did indeed decide to call it quits after winning his 74th cap against Scotland. The skipper was going to be a huge loss, and not just because he was a world-class player and leader. Umaga's retirement came in the same year that Justin Marshall, Andrew Mehrtens, Carlos Spencer and Xavier Rush also decided to head off to pastures new. There was a huge amount being done to develop strength in depth throughout New Zealand rugby, but no country could afford to haemorrhage that amount of talent and experience. In an ideal world, Henry would love to have seen Spencer and Mehrtens stay in New Zealand to battle Carter for the No 10 jersey. They were the kind of players who could guide emerging talent through NPC and Super Rugby campaigns, and who could be called on at any time to slot into the test team. What if Carter broke his leg a month before the World Cup and then Evans popped a shoulder a week later? Given the increasing physicality of rugby, such a scenario was not unimaginable.

Plenty was being done to build the emerging talent pool, but more needed to be done to retain those older players approaching the twilight of their careers. They still had plenty to give New Zealand but too many were being lured overseas. That was about to change though, because just as the All

Blacks were romping through the UK, discussions were being held that would make New Zealand a more attractive place for senior professionals to end their careers.

11 One for all and all for one

EVERY AMBITIOUS corporation in New Zealand knows how hard it is to retain the best talent. The so-called brain drain is arguably the greatest impediment to New Zealand's productivity. And since the inception of professionalism in 1995, player retention has arguably been the greatest impediment to New Zealand rugby fulfilling its potential.

The NZRU board that created the Henry clause were right in their belief that New Zealand would continue to come under threat from foreign predators. The exodus of talent has been constant. Every All Black coach since 1996 has had to operate in the shadow of lurking suitors. John Hart had some of his best men picked off by overseas bounty hunters. So too did Wayne Smith and John Mitchell, and if anything, the threat to New Zealand's players was even greater by the time Graham Henry took over.

In Henry's first year, Otago lock Simon Maling and Auckland prop Kees Meeuws both departed. Maling had been a key man in the Tri Nations, and Meeuws played all eight tests before the end-of-season tour. Maling was 29, Meeuws 30, and both had plenty of good years left. Meeuws in particular was only just coming into his prime.

Those two were joined in the Koru lounge by 22 others who had played Super 12 rugby that year. With 140 players contracted to play Super Rugby in any one year, that figure of 22 represents a turnover of 15 percent. Losing Maling and Meeuws meant the All Blacks were denied their services on the end-of-season trip to Italy, Wales and France. They had to dig deep into the talent pool to find replacements.

The queue of locks waiting to step into Maling's place was not terribly

146

long. In fact, there wasn't a queue at all. There were plenty of young hopefuls, but no one was ready for a black jersey. In the end, Henry had to persuade Norm Maxwell that his body could just about make it through one last hurrah. Maxwell was 28 and being held together with sticky tape. His body had been pounded to the point where he didn't really train at all, he just played – and usually only for 50 minutes at that. It was a productive 50 minutes, but he hardly represented the future, and while he toured in November 2004, by April the next year he had signed to play in Japan.

Meeuws was slightly easier to replace, although the coaches would still have preferred that he come to Europe with them rather than take up his contract with Castres. Tony Woodcock was an emerging talent behind Meeuws. *Emerging* wasn't quite what the selectors were after though. They wanted *emerged* so there could be a seamless transition. Again, as with Maling, they were forced to look hard for alternatives, and they opted to take the totally unknown Saimone Taumoepeau as well as Woodcock. Loosehead prop and lock were crucial positions and the selectors had to trawl the net along the ocean floor to find the right candidates. The conveyer belt was working; it was just that when New Zealand had to supply its own teams and half of the European market as well, it wasn't working fast enough. That was life for All Black coaches – every player on their watch could be snatched from under their noses.

Some Super 12 teams were losing as many as 10 players a season and seeing almost a complete turnover in the space of three years. Constantly losing players puts pressure on franchises to maintain standards. As a consequence, in some years the quality of particular teams has been noticeably lowered, or, as the franchise coaches prefer to couch it, has resulted in a rebuilding phase. The constant drain of talent in the professional age hits New Zealand rugby with a double whammy – the overall quality of the competition is lessened and the number of players ready to step up to the next level is reduced.

The starkest example of the All Blacks being punished by the global market was probably 1998. In the early days of Super 12, about 70 percent of players only managed three seasons in New Zealand. In marriage the itch comes after seven years, but in Super 12 it was coming after three. That statistic bit the All Blacks hard in 1998, a year that remains an ugly blot on an otherwise impressive landscape. The All Blacks had remained largely unchanged between 1995 and 1997. But in 1998 New Zealand lost Sean Fitzpatrick, the hugely talented Zinzan Brooke and the abrasive Frank Bunce. They offered a combined total of more than 200 test caps and each would have been recognised as about the best in his respective position. Hart had a difficult job finding replacements. The market had failed him. The defection rate was so high it denied him and his fellow Super 12 coaches the opportunity to groom successors. No one was hanging around for long enough and Bunce in particular was proving irreplaceable. It was the mother of all rebuilding years.

By 2005, off-shore migration remained high. After Maling and Meeuws in 2004, there was a rush for the door in 2005, and another 22 of the 140 contracted Super 12 players left. Justin Marshall and Carlos Spencer both headed to the UK after the Lions tour in July. They had been Henry's first-choice inside pairing until the end of the 2004 Tri Nations, when Spencer fell out of favour. Marshall, though, after a stunning Super 12 in 2005, remained first-choice halfback and arguably the best in the world. Andrew Mehrtens, an All Black legend and the man to whom Henry threw the No 10 shirt when he lost patience with Spencer, joined his old pal Marshall in the UK. Xavier Rush, Henry's initial pick at No 8, went to Cardiff. Maxwell went to Japan, and of other recent All Blacks, Dave Hewett went to Edinburgh, Sam Broomhall to France, Carl Hoeft joined his old pal Meeuws in Castres and Paul Miller went to Japan. The list was completed by Sam and Tom Harding, Keith Lowen, Adrian Cashmore, Taufa'ao Filise, Michael Collins, Grant McQuoid, Wayne Ormond, Grant Webb, Riki Flutey, Joe Ward, Isaac Boss and Sailosi Tagicakibau.

By 2005 the European and Japanese appetite for New Zealand players had shown no signs of abating. If anything, it had become stronger, partly because there is a belief in global markets that if you are buying Kiwi, you are buying quality. This assertion hasn't always been true, but the perception has been hard to shake. And that appetite has remained insatiable partly because it has been relatively easy for European and Japanese clubs to flash their chequebooks and acquire their All Black of choice. The size of the chequebooks has of course been a factor. The Japanese clubs are bankrolled by some of the world's biggest and best-known corporate giants. The added attraction of Japan is that their club championship is virtually over before it starts. An All Black warhorse like Maxwell can head to the land of the rising sun, drag his weary bones through a 12-match campaign that is less physically intense than either the Super 14 or NPC, and be paid generously for the pleasure.

The European clubs, particularly the French, have a fair bit of the folding stuff too. It helps that in the UK components of a player's salary can be deemed image rights and paid into offshore tax havens. If the exchange rate is favourable, a whole heap of money ends up in Mr Former All Black's account back in New Zealand.

It's not just about the money though. Professional players are denied the opportunity to fulfil what is a rite of passage for most Kiwis and embark on their OE. While their mates are heading off to London and Paris to pull pints and drink gallons, New Zealand's premier rugby players are being bashed to bits on rugby fields. Anyone who is serious about making it to the top in New Zealand can't reach their early 20s and disappear overseas in an attempt to find themselves. So when a European club comes knocking further down the line and offers the chance to experience a foreign culture while being paid handsomely, there are plenty of New Zealand players who don't need to think about it. The pull factors, then, are considerable. But until the end of 2005, so too were the push factors.

The birth of professional rugby had been both premature and traumatic. By the World Cup in 1995, it had become apparent rugby was going to have to stop pretending to be amateur. The International Rugby Board couldn't seriously expect the players to give up seven weeks of work every four years to take part in a competition that generated millions of dollars with not one cent flowing into the pockets of those who were making it all happen. Professionalism was coming – everyone agreed on that point. It was just a case of when. As it happened, the timescale was never a matter for debate, as before the end of the World Cup, Australian media mogul Kerry Packer sent his stooge, Ross Turnbull, to sign up the world's best players to his organisation, World Rugby Corporation. Turnbull pitched the idea to the All Blacks and they were sold on it. Those who signed with WRC would have to kiss goodbye to their All Black careers. Or they would have done so if the NZRU hadn't quickly realised the threat was real and sent in former All Black captain Jock Hobbs to lure the players back. And the only way to do that was to revoke amateurism and put hard cash on the table. The situation was saved, but it meant rugby had been rushed into professionalism without having thought through all the consequences. The sport's administrators would have to learn on the hoof, and that is the main reason why New Zealand's players were offered what was essentially a raw deal in those early days.

Rob Nichol, the head of New Zealand's Rugby Players Association

(NZRPA), probably knows better than anyone how the employment market has evolved for New Zealand's elite players. 'Rugby went professional in 1995, and what emerged out of that was that some players benefited because of who they were and because they sought good advice,' says Nichol. 'But for the majority it was a case of "here you go boys, sign it if you want to play for us." When you look at the contract, it was heavily in favour of the employer at the time. It still rewarded the players but it also had the players bearing a lot of the risk. After a while the players naturally had a few questions, particularly around player payments and welfare.

'All things considered, they held it together on the field well. The game received great public support, there was a massive drive for knowledge, for coaching, extra resources and expertise. But outside the training and playing environment, professional rugby presented some real challenges for the players. Some players handled it well but a lot of players struggled to achieve a balance and feeling of control off the field. When you have a high-performance athlete trying to work for the team, if his environment and state of mind away from the team are not good, it is going to undermine his ability to perform. Success can happen in short bursts but it is not going to happen long-term. You can throw all the money you want, all the resources you want, but unless the athlete feels organised, capable and in control, he is going to struggle to perform to his potential. It is not much different to any other profession in that respect – and that is what rugby had become, the players' profession.

'In the early days I would suggest a number of good players experienced difficulties and frustrations off the field and at times that may have contributed to them looking elsewhere and heading overseas. Concerns around loss of income due to injury, illness or non-selection, post-rugby career prospects, their families' future, public expectations and perceptions and of course what they are being paid are all important factors a player thinks about when deciding where to play. Creating the best possible employment environment became something New Zealand rugby as a professional sport needed to work on.'

It's hard to build an All Black legacy when star players keep disappearing overseas. The NZRU was adamant that it wouldn't go the same way as other countries and allow overseas-based players to be eligible for the All Blacks. The Europeans could make it work. In what was effectively a borderless market, all the major rugby countries were in the same time zone and their club competitions aligned, so availability was not going to be a problem. Such a scenario would have been disastrous for New Zealand though. Any All Black playing for an English club would not be released for the Tri Nations because the southern hemisphere's premier competition overlaps with the Guinness Premiership in the UK, the Celtic League and French Championship. It wasn't just the logistics, though, that were driving the NZRU's policy.

They felt they needed to make the All Black jersey sacred in the battle to retain players. If the players could line their pockets with foreign currency and still have the honour of playing for New Zealand, it would have killed the domestic structure. It would have been a world where the players could have had their cake and eaten it. So a policy was put in place to instigate choice. Players could have the foreign lifestyle and the big bucks, but that would mean giving up the All Black jersey. It was one or the other, and whether inadvertently or deliberately, it gave the NZRU an easy stick with which to hit the players during contract negotiations. Invariably those players who opted to head overseas were portrayed through the media as mercenaries, Judas types who had turned their back on their country. They had put money before the All Black jersey – the greatest honour in the game.

This emotive portrayal of those who departed was hugely disingenuous as it failed to take account of the bigger picture. It simplified the choice to an unrealistic extent. Rugby players weren't just balancing money on one side against test caps on the other and trying to work out which one they valued more. Rugby was their career, and New Zealand's top players needed help adjusting to life as professional athletes. They needed support structures, direction on how to manage their finances, how to rest and prepare properly. What about life after rugby? There were concerns that not enough players were readying themselves for the day when they could no longer earn a living running around a muddy field. Being a professional didn't just mean you were paid for doing what you had always done as an amateur. It came with a whole new set of demands, responsibilities and pressures, and the professional players needed an organisation to represent their interests and their interests alone.

'In 1999 the players became aware of the concept of player associations,' says Nichol. 'In conjunction with the NZRU, they said maybe it's time we thought about getting the players organised. Everyone else was organised – the administration, the training and playing environment, but the athletes, the crucial component, were not. The Australians had established a player association in 1996 and in that period Australian rugby performed well. That's how it came to be started in New Zealand.

'In the late 1990s, if the players got an injury, there was a lot of uncertainty around if they would get paid or not. If a player missed selection to Super 12 his payments stopped. As a result of playing rugby, though, he had forgone other career options because rugby was all-consuming. While it was a great opportunity to play professional rugby, it was highly competitive, very public, required dedication and hard work to succeed and was not going to last forever. It carried significant risks and uncertainty. So realisation amongst the players set in that they needed a voice, and the only thing they knew for sure was that the game depended on them. In the meantime, commercially, professional rugby was doing very well and so were those involved in the commercialisation of it. It probably doesn't take a lot of science to conclude that unless they got organised and started to represent themselves around the new commercial table, the players were at risk – if they were not already – of being undervalued.'

From 1999 it became Nichol's job to work for the newly formed NZRPA – to put support structures in place for the players; to protect the players from misfortune and look out for their welfare; to help them develop alternative career ideas and networks; and maybe most importantly, to make sure they were not being undervalued.

In those early professional days, it was virtually every man for himself. Most of the top players earned roughly the same. The NZRU made them an offer, they haggled a bit and then signed. The really big stars, though, such as Jonah Lomu, did command more money. While the majority of the top players would be taking home between $200,000 and $300,000, Lomu supposedly was earning in excess of $900,000. That was understandable – the giant wing was rugby's only global superstar. There were offers from various sports from a range of different countries permanently on the table. The NZRU needed to be competitive or they would lose their prize asset.

But when Nichol assumed his role, there was going to be a more egalitarian approach. If everyone went it alone, the NZRPA would be rendered toothless. That wasn't what the players wanted. Rugby has always fostered a team ethos. It has never been a sport tolerant of individuals who operate on their own terms. It's probably because it is one of the few sports where teams can't survive on the work of a few individual superstars. The fat prop needs to do his bit in the scrum so the glory-boy first-five can wiggle his hips to allow the hair-gelled winger to cross for the try. Different characters, different attitudes, but 15 men all chasing one goal. That was how it was on the field and that is how the players wanted it off the field. Negotiations were going to be conducted on a collective basis.

'The collective approach is an acknowledgement that to align your interests and act collectively you get a much more responsible outcome. It is one that, if done correctly, everyone will feel they have some input into, and it is one that over time and in particular in sport, has resulted in things being achieved far more quickly than if players went it alone. If you look at some sports, their player associations will never function properly because they have left their run too late. The elite players are actually too elite, and for them to say they are going to sacrifice themselves, to come back and help the masses in the knowledge that it is going to be better for the game and the athletes in the future, that is going to be very hard.

'The senior payers here have all been prepared to say that they can see the bigger picture. They know that they could go off and do an individual deal and possibly do better but ultimately, long-term, that undermines the other players and the game in New Zealand and the players have understood that.'

It was going to be a long process redefining the environment for New Zealand's professional rugby players. There was still a lingering hangover from the amateur days in some of the administrative thinking. In the pre-professional days, the players had obviously been massively undervalued – they generated millions of dollars for the sport and were paid nothing. That attitude of doing it for the love of the game prevailed even in the early professional years. Persuading everyone that rugby was now a career, similar to going into legal practice or dentistry, was a hard battle. Too many observers believed the players were just playing a game and those who represented the All Blacks didn't know how lucky they were. Nichol was not going to accept that argument. Not for one second.

'The business of sport generates significant funds, and organisations within New Zealand and internationally were doing very well out of professional rugby and its players. It is unreasonable to expect the players to sit back and allow that to go on without asking the question of whether they were fairly valued. We had young talented New Zealanders leaving our shores and we wanted the opportunity to retain them and reward them fairly for being part of an industry that generates significant revenue.

'By acting collectively, the professional players were saying the dynamics have changed and that they needed to stake their claim in the partnership and make sure it was a fair claim. And the only way you know whether it is fair is by going through a robust negotiation process, where all the information and ideas are put on the table. We are a small country in a big world, and if we start encouraging a culture where we don't stand up and take responsibility for ourselves, then we are doing ourselves a disservice.'

Since 1999, Nichol and his team have asked questions and stood up to the NZRU. The voice of the professional players is being heard and enormous progress has been made on all fronts. Professional development managers have been attached to every franchise to help and advise players on alternative careers or study routes and any other form of personal assistance, support and guidance a professional rugby player may require. There is a benevolent fund, a pension scheme and vastly improved injury cover. But while the employment conditions had substantially improved for New Zealand's professional players, the market, even by 2005, was still clearly not quite right.

The ability to retain players was always going to be the litmus test of whether the environment was all it should have been. Or, more accurately, the ability to retain players that the NZRU wanted to retain was always going to be the litmus test. Marshall, even at 31, was still a player any coach in the world would have wanted. Spencer, at 29, was allowed to leave with far too much good rugby still in his system. In previous years the scenario had been the same. Christian Cullen went to Munster in 2003 when most of New Zealand thought he should have been going to the World Cup. Todd Blackadder joined Edinburgh in 2001 with enough gas in his tank to turn the club around, while Craig Dowd went to London Wasps in 2000 and matured into one of the best and most destructive props in the world. There was a common thread linking all these players – they had all gone overseas when they perceived their All Black careers were over. Also on that list was former All Black captain Taine Randell. He led the All Blacks on their end-of-season tour in 2002, realised in 2003 he was never going to find his way back in and signed for Saracens. Josh Kronfeld was another to see the writing on the wall and head north, as did Ron Cribb, Troy Flavell, Pita Alatini and Mark Robinson. The list goes on.

There was a pretty simple reason why this pattern evolved. For all the improvements made since the inception of the NZRPA in 1999 in employment terms and conditions, the value of every contract was entirely dependent on being selected.

It didn't matter who you were, the deal was that every player sat down with the NZRU and worked out what they were worth. Both parties agreed, but the money would only be paid if the player was selected in a Super 12 franchise. Since 2002 the NZRPA had negotiated a minimum payment of $65,000 for anyone picked to play Super 12. Obviously the more experience and ability a player had, the more he would be paid. The scale went up to around $120,000 for someone with 3-5 years Super 12 experience, to around $200,000 for the best players. That was pretty reasonable money, certainly enough to live comfortably and put a bit in the bank.

The process was the same for the All Blacks. A value would be determined at the signing of a contract and it would kick in when the player was selected. The values were roughly similar to those at Super 12. A rookie All Black would be offered an agreed minimum of $85,000, ranging up to about $200,000 for the senior professionals. There was definitely money to be had. A senior All Black could possibly command more than $200,000 for playing in the Super 12, another $200,000 for making the test squad, and anything from $40,000 to $100,000 on top of that from a separate contract with his provincial union. The total package could be as high as $500,000 – a salary that would be in line with what was on offer overseas.

Meeuws is understood to have joined Castres on a deal that was worth about 300,000 Euros ($560,000) a year. Marshall negotiated an extraordinarily good package at Leeds, possibly £160,000 ($480,000) a year. Mehrtens went to Harlequins on a deal reputed to be worth £140,000 ($420,000) a season, while Spencer, on account of his undisputed ability to entertain, is thought to be earning about £190,000 ($570,000) at Northampton. When those packages are converted into New Zealand dollars, they come out roughly on a par with what the respective players were earning in New Zealand. Except there was a massive caveat attached – to earn the equivalent figures in New Zealand they had to be selected in the All Blacks, and even then it wasn't that simple.

What if a player was selected for the end-of-season tour but not the Tri Nations or the in-bound internationals? Or what if he played the in-bound tests and the Tri Nations, but not the end-of-season tour? There was a formula in place that calculated how many days of the year the All Blacks were assembled and paid players pro rata depending on how many days' service they gave.

The bigger problem with that set-up was exposed in 2001 when Cullen was left out of the tour party to Ireland, Scotland and Argentina. Cullen said he was unavailable due to injury. New coach John Mitchell said Cullen had been available and had therefore been dropped. It wasn't just a matter of pride. If Cullen had been dropped, he would not have been entitled to any payment. If he was unavailable due to injury, he would be paid. Under the collective, a player who made the All Black squad for one campaign would be entitled to receive full pay for 12 months if he was not re-selected due to injury. If he was simply dropped due to a loss of form, that was it, he would be paid only for those days he had been assembled with the team. The system was ultimately flawed in that coaches were making selection decisions that also carried huge financial and lifestyle ramifications.

The NZRU reckoned it had no choice though. It didn't have bottomless pockets and there had to be a big incentive to play for the All Blacks. The package had to say to players that if they made it all the way to the top, they could earn massive financial rewards. It was a big carrot to dangle and the incentives to win test selection were strong. But once a player had bitten the carrot and become used to its taste, there were massive problems when that carrot was withdrawn.

In 2004 Spencer was selected for the first two All Black campaigns of the year and then declared unavailable for the end-of-season tour due to injury, which secured him full payment. Given his experience, talent and value to New Zealand, his payment for 2004 from his provincial, Super 12 and All Black contracts would have been somewhere between $480,000 and $500,000. The following year, when it was apparent he was not going to make Henry's All Black squad, his income would have been cut by about half. Not knowing what he was going to earn made planning hard. The uncertainty was stressful, so when Northampton came knocking with a package that was not necessarily that much more, but guaranteed for three years regardless of his performance, he signed. The same was true of Meeuws. He has made it clear that if there had been a higher guaranteed component in his contract, he would have been happy to stay. So when Nichol sat down with the NZRU to hammer out a new collective deal in 2005, there were some obvious issues that had to be addressed.

By the end of the financial year in 2005, the NZRU had built up cash reserves of $80 million. The union was flush and the players had done their bit in shovelling cash into the coffers. The relationship between the NZRU and the players needed to change from being parasitic to symbiotic. Nichol wanted a partnership, a structure that more closely aligned the interests of the players with the interests of the NZRU. The All Black jersey had to be lowered as a negotiating mast. If New Zealand was serious about retaining talent, players had to be able to earn a reasonable income without playing for their country.

Under the existing collective deal, there was virtually no incentive for a discarded All Black to stay in New Zealand. The guaranteed money on offer elsewhere made leaving an easy choice for a player in his late 20s or early 30s. Nichol wanted that choice to become more complex, so that guaranteed money was offered in New Zealand for the duration of players' contracts.

Says Nichol: 'Prior to 2006, coaches weren't just making selection decisions, they were making life decisions. We are talking serious life decisions – the ability of a player to pay the mortgage next month if the coach did not select him. There was a need to address the conditions under which payments were being made and make sure that every dollar spent was as effective at retaining and rewarding our players as possible. The second area to be addressed was the value of the players collectively, and a way to be able to value that in terms of their guaranteed retainers. The positive result has had a big impact. Players are now able to secure a guaranteed level of income for a period of two or three years or more.

'It is not such a financial issue if they get injured or ill or suspended; there is a level they can be guaranteed. They can work out how much money they can save over the period to put aside. They budget for a mortgage and their future with a better degree of certainty. When you combine that with the other improvements, such as the coverage if you lose your career, the welfare fund, other insurances we are putting in place, the professional development programme assisting players on career development, personal planning and asset protection and all the other good work being done by everyone involved, then we now have an environment that is pretty compelling. The decision to go or not to go has become a bit harder for our players, more complex, and that is what we want. Having said that, the market is very dynamic, the threat is always there and we need to keep working hard to make sure we are as competitive as possible.

'In the past, the All Black jersey has been the carrot that has been held out there. The last negotiation took the focus away a bit from the black jersey. In a way it was about trying to quarantine the All Black jersey from the money discussions. We have a few more players now who are seeing out their careers in New Zealand, and it isn't about whether they were going to be picked for the All Blacks. Being in the All Blacks for a number of players now is not a prerequisite to stay, but is still a goal that drives them.'

The new collective became effective on 1 January 2006, and from then players would be guaranteed a level of income for the duration of their contract. The formula put in place saw the guaranteed retainer for players earning less than $100,000 a year from their potential All Black fees set at the level they were earning for playing Super Rugby. That meant a player under the old system who earned $120,000 if he made Super 12 and $85,000 if he made the All Blacks would now be guaranteed to earn $120,000 a year, regardless of whether he was selected for Super 14 or not. If a player was earning more than $100,000 from his All Black fees under the old collective, his retainer would be his Super 12 fee, plus his All Black fee, minus $100,000. That meant a player earning $150,000 from Super 12 and potentially $150,000 from the All Blacks would now be guaranteed to earn $200,000 a year. A player's provincial union payment was on top of this, and there were plenty of senior players who had been consistently playing Super 12 without much hope of making the All Blacks who enjoyed a $30,000-plus pay rise overnight. Just as important was the fact that the money would be paid if they failed to make Super 14 or were invalided out of the game.

Proof that guaranteed retainers were doing their job came at the end of 2006, when only 11 contracted Super 14 players signed for overseas clubs. Ben Blair, Neil Brew, David Hill, Aleki Lutui, Sean Hohneck, Seilala Mapusua, Mark Ranby, Joe McDonnell, Mike Noble, Loki Crichton and Deacon Manu were the only men to leave in a year that saw European bounty-hunters significantly up the ante. The year leading up to a World Cup is historically a turbulent one for New Zealand in terms of personnel. The major European clubs can't get their hands on the biggest names because they are all staying put until the end of the World Cup, so they come shopping for players who are not certain to make the All Black World Cup squad and offer them serious money. That usually leads to a major clear-out. But it didn't happen in 2006.

There were a number of former All Blacks who turned down big deals in favour of committing to the NZRU. Chiefs captain Jono Gibbes had a major offer from the Ospreys in Wales, but in the end opted to re-sign with the NZRU on a three-year deal. Highlanders captain Craig Newby was another who felt he could remain in New Zealand with uncertain All Black prospects. Anthony Tuitavake also said 'no' to some big European clubs but 'yes' to North Harbour, Rua Tipoki turned down Munster for Canterbury, and at the end of 2005, Auckland and Blues stalwart Gus Collins signed to see out his playing days in New Zealand.

Guaranteed retainers were only one part of the jigsaw. To change the dynamic of the relationship between the NZRU and the players, there needed to be a greater sense that they were working for each other. As Nichol saw it, the best way to do that was to strike a deal that would see the players own a direct share of the NZRU's revenue. It was a simple enough concept. The players could argue they were directly responsible for generating a proportion of the union's income and that money should be given to them. The NZRU was not averse to the idea. The issue, however, was not about the concept, it was about the detail. Exactly how much were the players going to want for the payment pool?

The other significant change was the simplification of All Black payments. The existing system had too many contentious areas. With individuals likely to be rested or rotated, not only for individual tests but for whole campaigns in 2006, the likelihood of confusion and conflict was only going to get greater. Match fees were not going to work, as a player who was rotated after doing nothing wrong would miss out on payment. In the end, the NZRU and NZRPA agreed on a standard fee of $7500 for every week an individual was assembled with the All Blacks. If he was rotated at the behest of the All Black coaches, he would still be entitled to the payment.

Nichol explains: 'We didn't want a situation where a selection decision is also a financial one. Culturally we felt that match fees were not for us, and that there needed to be recognition that the players who don't make the 22 are still contributing and a part of the team.

'We had all been thinking about revenue-sharing for a while. We knew that one day we would go down this path. We knew this collective would be the one where we said we wanted to be in a partnership. The NZRU also did extensive studies on revenue-sharing. They went around the world and checked every other model. We came to the table and said we are probably going to have revenue-sharing but everyone said it was all about detail – how do you split it up, what's affordable? The hardest part was developing a model we felt would take care of all areas of the game and be sustainable, rather than whether we should have it at all. What is unique about our revenue-sharing model, as opposed to those in the States, is that we cater for the funding of the development levels of the game, the administration and running of the game as well as the amount set aside for professional players.'

In the end, the players struck a deal where the total payment pool will be equal to 32.4 percent of the NZRU's total revenue. Not bad when you consider the NZRU turned over $145m in 2005. It was a deal that signalled that the chaotic early days of professionalism were a distant memory. The players were no longer commodities; they were valued employees in a mutually beneficial partnership. The set-up was still not perfect but it was vastly improved and the numbers choosing to stay in New Zealand were testament to that. The fact that players like Gibbes and Newby had chosen to stay was critical, especially Gibbes. He was the sort of player who would always be close to All Black selection. To have him available was a massive reassurance to the coaches. If injuries struck down Jerry Collins or Reuben Thorne, Gibbes was the kind of guy you could bring into the squad on a Friday night and know he would give you everything. Having options was exactly what Henry wanted, and the fact that players were choosing to stay in New Zealand when there were big offers to go, helped foster the belief that his was a special team that people wanted to play for.

The camaraderie between the players blossomed as a consequence of seeing senior pros commit to New Zealand and also as a consequence of the improved work environment. The new deal was fair and capable of adapting to the new thinking of Henry and his coaching panel. And that was a job well done, because such thinking was going to leap even further out of the box.

12 Player welfare

IT WAS apparent Chris Moller was not best pleased when he walked into the lobby of Auckland's Heritage Hotel on 31 March 2006. If the phrase 'face like thunder' hadn't already been coined, it would have been conceived there and then. The chief executive of the New Zealand Rugby Union was fuming as a result of not being able to agree on a date with the Australian Rugby Union for the third Bledisloe Cup test that season.

The game, potentially a series decider, had a definite venue: Auckland's Eden Park. It had a choice of dates, though, either 18 August or 19 August, and that was highly irregular. Since the inception of the competition in 1996, every Tri Nations test had been played on a Saturday. In the early years there had been some variation in the timings, with a mix of afternoon and evening kick-offs. But for the last few years the formula had been fixed: New Zealand played home games at 7.35 p.m. local time on Saturday nights, Australia played home games at 8 p.m. local time on Saturday nights and South Africa played home games at 3 p.m. local time on Saturday afternoons. The NZRU's proposal to play on a Friday night was radical.

Moller had proposed playing the game on 18 August after consultation with the All Black coaching panel. If 2005 had been an epic season, 2006 was going to trump it in volume, if not prestige. The All Blacks would open their season on 10 June with a two-test series against Ireland before flying to Buenos Aires to play Argentina on 24 June. The extended Tri Nations would begin in Christchurch against the Wallabies on 8 July, with South Africa in Wellington on 22 July, Australia in Brisbane on 29 July, Australia again on either 18 or 19 August and then consecutive tests in the Republic on 26 August and 2

September. There would definitely be a two-test series in France, with the first game on 11 November in Lyon and the second a week later in Paris with Wales in Cardiff on 25 November finishing the season. There was also a good chance that an additional test against England in London would be arranged on 5 November to land the All Blacks with a record 13 tests in six months.

When the coaches sat down to plan the season, they gulped. There was also an extended Super 14 to factor in, and they saw a fixture list that looked as if it was designed to kill the players. There was no way, in their view, that any player was going to be able to get through every game and still be standing at the end of it. It would be madness even to try.

There were specific parts of the season that concerned them. Given the form of both the Hurricanes and Crusaders, there was a good chance both sides could make the Super 14 final on 27 May. That would give the test stars in those two teams only one week off before having to prepare to face a very good Irish side. If it had been the Highlanders and Chiefs pushing for glory it wouldn't have been such an issue, but the Hurricanes had Neemia Tialata, Andrew Hore, Jason Eaton, Jerry Collins, Chris Masoe, Rodney So'oialo, Piri Weepu, Ma'a Nonu and Isaia Toeava who were all likely to be in the squad, and the Crusaders had Greg Somerville, Chris Jack, Richie McCaw, Mose Tuiali'i, Dan Carter, Aaron Mauger, Rico Gear and Leon MacDonald. Between the two teams there were 17 players who had been on the Grand Slam tour. Making things even trickier was the fact that the test against Argentina would be in Buenos Aires, a notoriously brutal place to play and a stinker of a flight with major time differences to be negotiated. With the All Blacks playing Ireland at 7.35 p.m. at Eden Park on Saturday 17 June, the squad wouldn't be able to leave for Argentina until mid-day Sunday 18 June and the preparation time for a seriously tricky test on 24 June would be reduced to five days.

The other danger period was the run of three consecutive Tri Nations games that would start with the Bledisloe decider in Auckland. The All Black coaches had made their views known to Moller about the impact on performance when individuals had to front on three consecutive weekends. And the problem during the Tri Nations was going to be more acute. If the All Blacks had to play Australia at the usual time of 7.35 p.m. on Saturday 19 August, the players would not get to bed much before 1 a.m. after the test. They would then have to get up at 4.30 a.m. to fly to South Africa and be ready to play two tests in a country where they had not won under Henry.

The traditionalists could accuse the modern lot of being soft but the reality had to be acknowledged. The first 24 hours after a test were crucial in terms of recovery. That's when players needed to be rehydrating, stretching, having massages, eating well and sleeping well. As Wayne Smith had said before the team travelled to the UK in 2005, some of the injuries the players picked up in tests were similar to those incurred by the victims of minor car-crashes. Asking the players to put their bodies on the line against the old foe, have a couple of hours' sleep and then endure a 13-hour flight to South Africa would delay recovery times and seriously hinder the chances of the team giving their best. So Henry pushed the case for Moller to shift the game in Auckland forward 24 hours.

Moller was supportive. He wanted to see the All Blacks win, and to win they needed the best possible preparation. He was also aware of the wider theme of player welfare. When Henry said it was a serious issue, Moller took that on board. He also took on board that the NZRU had to be proactive and put in place effective policies to protect the players. Hence the frustration that after months of negotiation, the Australians were still refusing to budge.

The way Moller saw it, the ARU needed to do some bridge-building. Relations between the two Sanzar allies had turned decidedly frosty when the ARU revealed it had not voted for New Zealand's bid to host the 2011 World Cup. New Zealand had won the vote on 17 November 2005, but Moller was still steamed up that New Zealand's closest ally had voted for Japan. With that lingering bitterness, and frustrated at the stalemate over the Bledisloe test, he sat forward in his chair at the Heritage and said with no little exasperation: 'Australian executives have listened, but we have seen no tangible evidence to bridge the gap. The relationship has been dulled. Our view is that player welfare is vitally important. But either it is not important to them, or they have a different view on player welfare, or there is another issue that affects the decision for them. There is a belief that what Australia wants, Australia gets.'

When Moller's opposite number at the ARU, Gary Flowers, heard Moller's accusations he took it all in his stride. He felt the NZRU were using an emotive argument to force an outcome that was never going to be possible. He felt the NZRU were using 'player welfare' as a smokescreen, when really the issue was preparation for two tests. As Flowers made clear, the situation was not ideal but the players would not actually be in any long-term danger if they had to play on the Saturday night. No one would want to see such a short, sharp turnaround become commonplace, but on a one-off basis it would have to be tolerated. He felt that Henry was simply looking to pick up an extra day of preparation before having to face South Africa. He also revealed that alternative measures to help with the tight turnaround had been explored, such as allowing New Zealand to travel with four extra players.

The deal-breaker for the ARU, though, was the contract they had with their domestic broadcast partner, Fox Sports. Fox had put their cash on the table to buy the Tri Nations rights and had a clear preference for 7.35 p.m. kick-offs in New Zealand. With the time difference that would be a 5.35 p.m. kick-off on the east coast of Australia. Shifting to a Friday night with a 5.35 p.m. Australian time kick-off would have been a disaster. The vast majority of the rugby-viewing public would be at work or on their way home from work. There was no way Fox would tolerate that and the ARU had to respect the deal they had signed. 'We take player welfare very seriously,' said Flowers, 'but we have to balance that against the contractual obligations we have with our broadcast partners. It has to be remembered that a Friday night game has never been played in the history of the Tri Nations. It's a really big call.'

The Australians had the support of South Africa, who were vehemently opposed to a Friday night game as it would kick off during business hours their time on the Friday morning. The ARU had actually proposed kicking off at 3 p.m. New Zealand time on the Saturday, but the NZRU rejected that as it would see them fall foul of their domestic broadcaster, Sky TV.

With at least one party destined to be disappointed, the whole future of the Sanzar alliance was under a cloud. But Flowers, perhaps because he was confident the ARU would not emerge as the disappointed party, played down any fears of a bust-up. 'We are fundamentally committed to the Sanzar concept,' he said. 'I think it has been good for all three parties. We are clearly having operational issues but we still value the concept. I think, though, it is important we don't keep having every problem come back to the 2011 World Cup.'

In the end a compromise deal was struck and the game would be played on Saturday 19 August with a 5.30 p.m. local kick-off time. It was a tiny victory for the NZRU, and the battle over the scheduling of the Eden Park test hardened the desire to thrust the issue of player welfare further into the public domain.

It was one of those occasions that required a double-take. On 16 April the All Black coach revealed he was going to select two separate sides to play Ireland

and Argentina. He didn't mean he was going to select a squad of 30 players and mix and match his options as he had done on the Grand Slam tour. He meant he was going to select a total of 39 players and actually handle the three tests with two separate teams.

A total of 24 players would be available for the two-test series against Ireland, and preferably none of them would have featured in the Super 14 play-offs. An entirely separate starting 15 to play Argentina would be named on the same day as the Irish squad was announced, and 11 players from the 24 named to play Ireland would travel to Buenos Aires. The 15 named to play the Pumas would actually fly to Argentina on the Friday before the second test against Ireland at Eden Park. 'We are trying to look after the players and are also working hard to get depth across the board,' Henry said as he announced the plans. 'We are trying to get the balance right.'

There were plenty who didn't feel he was getting the balance right. If there had been uneasiness about the level of rotation on the Grand Slam tour, it went off the scale with a plan that really would see the All Blacks used as a finishing school. This was test football – and the jerseys got handed to the best 22 players in the country. Henry was taking a huge gamble in handing them all the way down to the 39th best player. Even allowing for the increased physicality of the game, there was an overwhelming sense that Henry was not respecting the ethos of test football. Nor was he respecting Ireland, who were a dangerous side, especially with Brian O'Driscoll and Paul O'Connell restored to full health. Argentina in Buenos Aires were an entirely different proposition from Argentina in Hamilton. In 2004 the All Blacks had cruised to a comfortable 41-7 victory at Waikato Stadium. In 2001 they had needed a very late Scott Robertson try to win the game.

But against all this, Henry kept coming back to the point he had made again and again – if the same players featured test after test, the casualty toll would be disastrous and the All Blacks needed depth in every position. It was the first point that was driving the thinking in regard to the two-team policy. Player welfare was the key objective rather than player development.

The selectors were in their third year and had had a long, hard look at all the talent. They had taken a punt on both Jason Eaton and Isaia Toeava on the Grand Slam tour, but they were considered special projects and there wasn't an appetite to take on more work of that nature. Included in the 39 would be some reliable performers whom the selectors trusted to step up, do the job and not have their confidence crushed when they were inevitably discarded for the Tri Nations.

Henry obviously felt he needed to keep the emphasis on player welfare, as it was apparent he was not best pleased at the way some of his key players had been handled during the Super 14. While in Edinburgh six months earlier, he had spoken of his desire to see the franchise coaches follow his lead and rotate their resources more than they had in the past. The expansion of the competition was going to place a greater physical burden on the players, and he wanted to see some of the top All Blacks granted a couple of weeks off during the competition. He couldn't order specific rest periods or enforce maximum quotas of games any individual could play. He was powerless to do anything other than hope he struck a chord with the franchise coaches.

But by mid April, despite improved relationships, Henry's words had fallen on deaf ears. Or maybe it would be fairer to say the franchise coaches were listening but couldn't oblige given the nature of their own goals. The Blues struggled upfront all season, and as a consequence Keven Mealamu and John Afoa started every game, as did Joe Rokocoko. Fellow Grand Slam tourist Sitiveni Sivivatu started all 13 round-robin games for the Chiefs. At the Hurricanes, Nonu, Weepu, Masoe, Tialata and Hore started every game, with Toeava, Eaton, So'oialo and Collins starting 12. MacDonald, Gear, Carter, Tuiali'i and Somerville started all 13 for the Crusaders and Carl Hayman and Anton Oliver were in the No 2 and No 3 jerseys respectively for 12 of the Highlanders' matches.

Of the 35 players who had toured the UK at the end of 2005, 20 of them had featured in all or all bar one of their side's Super 14 games. It was more than Henry wanted them to play. He told the *New Zealand Herald*: 'I think we have learned from the Super 14 that it is a very long continuous competition and there is a real need for player rotation. Otherwise players are just going to fall over, and I think there have been some signs of that lately.'

One of the signs to which he was referring was that a number of senior All Blacks were showing obvious fatigue by the latter stages of the competition. But the biggest sign of all that there needed to be some active management of player workloads had come earlier in the season when four 2005 All Black tourists incurred serious injury.

In mid February Conrad Smith broke his leg playing for the Hurricanes against the Western Force. It was a bad break and he would be out for a minimum of 12 weeks. A few weeks later, and Nick Evans was hit hard by a big South African and heard the awful crunch of his collar-bone breaking. Next it was Angus MacDonald, who had the misfortune not to see team-mate Troy Flavell as he flew into a ruck, and the ensuing collision snapped knee ligaments and ended his season. When James Ryan's shoulder disintegrated in March, it gave enormous credence to Henry's insistence that catastrophe loomed for those ostrich coaches who tried to bury their heads in the sand when it came to player welfare.

Henry was not going to bury his head. He was going to find innovative solutions to cope with a calendar that was doing its level best to quite literally grab a pound of flesh. With innovation came risk, and there was a danger he was being too ambitious in trying to win tests against decent sides with what were clearly going to be under-strength All Black teams.

By 16 April it was a safe bet that the Hurricanes and Crusaders were going to make the play-offs. If Henry stayed true to his word that those players involved in the finals would not play against the Irish, then he would be without 17 high-quality test footballers. That was a huge number of quality players to turn his back on.

But Henry was sure the long-term interests of those players would be better served by not being available for the Irish tests. His preferred option was for those players involved in the play-offs to come into camp and get through two weeks of basic conditioning work and run through the game-plan for the Pumas test. That was the ideal. In the end, though, it was deemed too big a risk to tackle the Irish without any Hurricanes or Crusaders. A balance had to be struck.

The All Blacks had strung seven consecutive victories together since losing in Cape Town in July 2005. The week after they had lost in South Africa, they played in Sydney and found themselves 13-0 down after 15 minutes. They were playing their bogey team on their bogey ground, but they managed to settle after a rocky start and went on to win 30-13. The composure, so obviously lacking in previous visits, was now in place and the All Blacks even managed to weather the loss of Carter who broke his leg shortly after half-time.

A classic game in Dunedin against the Boks a couple of weeks later provided the highlight of the competition, with both sides playing thrilling rugby in a contest that ended with a 31-27 New Zealand victory. A week later, and the Wallabies were put away 34-24 at Eden Park. As Hansen said during the 2005

Tri Nations: 'The difference between the team now and last year is immense. We saw that in France and we saw it in the Lions series. It's ongoing, though. As soon as you get comfortable, you find someone comes along and hits you on the head with a big hammer. But that is the job of me, Graham and Wayne to make sure things keep going and the leadership keeps growing with it.'

The All Blacks were building momentum and confidence, and while it was deemed vital to give key players some breathing space in an incredibly long season, that momentum had to be maintained. The Irish series still had to be won and Argentina put away, so the squad of 24 to face Ireland included new skipper McCaw, Mauger, So'oialo, Nonu and, after an injury to Ali Williams, Jack was called up. The inclusion of these players added a touch of class to a squad that had the feel of an A team. Included in the 24 was David Hill, who had earned his place on the back of solid rather than spectacular performances. Craig Newby, Jerome Kaino, Clark Dermody and Casey Laulala were in there too, and while they were all committed professionals, they were not going to be required for the Tri Nations. Even with McCaw and the other Grand Slam tourists, it was a brave ploy to take on the Irish with so much ability and experience sitting on a plane bound for Buenos Aires.

With 20 minutes remaining at Waikato Stadium, the two-team ploy looked more stupid than brave. The Irish had rattled the All Blacks from the kick-off and had a famous victory within their grasp. When it really mattered though, they lost belief in themselves, and a lucky try to the recalled Troy Flavell after 70 minutes allowed the All Blacks to get out of jail and seal the win 34-27.

The Irish had previous when it came to making a fist of the first test and then lying down to die in the second. The expectation was strong heading into the Eden Park test that history would be repeated – that the Irish had emptied their tank in Hamilton and had played above themselves. The All Blacks would surely raise their game and ease to a comfortable victory. It didn't happen. The Irish had some juice left and had grown in belief that they could grab the scalp that had evaded them for 101 years. Again, though, despite having the All Blacks at sixes and sevens for much of the game, the Irish couldn't locate the jugular. The All Blacks pulled off another late escape, this time 27-17.

A week later the other All Black team delivered an equally unconvincing performance to stagger home in Buenos Aires 25-19. In three tests the All Blacks had played some ordinary rugby. Neither side had convinced, with the lineout work shoddy, tackling suspect, the handling inaccurate and the overall direction and authority that had been in evidence in 2005 sadly missing.

The overall objective of running two sides had been achieved: key players had been rested and the tests had been won. The coaching panel were far from happy, however. They felt it was necessary to remind the squad of 30 that was chosen for the forthcoming Tri Nations of the standards they had set themselves. As far as the coaches were concerned, the eye had come off the ball. The lack of quality produced on the field was perhaps symptomatic of preparation not being all it should have been.

After the Super 14 final between the Hurricanes and Crusaders, many of the Wellington players went out to drown their sorrows and to celebrate the 33rd birthday of Tana Umaga. In the very, very late hours Umaga considered it necessary to bash team-mate Masoe over the head with a handbag to bring the flanker into line. Umaga had seen Masoe get into an unnecessary altercation and had reached for a patron's handbag to administer a peculiar form of deterrent. A mobile phone in the handbag was broken by the impact and Masoe reduced to tears. The story ended up on newswires around the world and, while it had a humorous side, it really didn't look good that so many senior All Blacks were out drinking well past 8 a.m. the following morning.

Wind of other alcohol-related incidents reached the ears of the coaching panel, and Henry reckoned the proverbial kick up the derrière was required before the squad headed into the Tri Nations. That blast, and the fact the All Blacks would revert to the more traditional format of running just one team, grew the public's confidence that the missing spark would be restored.

Their faith appeared well placed when the All Blacks opened their campaign with an aggressive win against Australia in Christchurch. The forwards found their cohesion and tidied the set-piece. They were rampant in the loose and Australia couldn't compete. The final score of 32-12 might have flattered the All Blacks, but there was no denying that the determination, intensity and accuracy had come up several notches from where it had been against Ireland and Argentina.

On 15 July the Wallabies hammered the Springboks 49-0 in Brisbane, which set Henry thinking. It had always been the plan to make some changes for the fixture with the Boks on 22 July, but no one really thought that would involve replacing 10 of the fifteen who started in Christchurch. Development and welfare were not fads – Henry and his team were committed to their goal of building 30 test players and preserving individual careers. The new boys came in and were good enough to win 35-17.

A week later in Brisbane, the selection blade was wielded again. What looked suspiciously like a top team, if there was such a thing, was pushed all the way by a committed Wallaby outfit. Again, though, there was ample evidence that the leadership across the team was growing and that the ability to make good decisions under pressure was now something that was coming naturally to most of the players. The All Blacks won 13-9 and the unbeaten run was now 13 games.

The selectors saw the final Bledisloe clash at Eden Park as the ideal opportunity to give starts to both Eaton and Toeava. It was vital to see how they handled the big occasion. Eaton relished the opportunity and played a senior role at the lineout, but Toeava wilted and was removed shortly after half-time. This was disappointing after investing so much time and effort in him, but on the plus side, the All Blacks weathered an early onslaught and never panicked. Mauger had been a late withdrawal and Luke McAlister slotted in as if he had always been destined to start.

The 34-27 win at Eden Park pretty much secured the Tri Nations with two games to spare, and Henry had every reason to be grinning. The dual objectives were being achieved. The injury toll during the first four games had been remarkably low. There were bumps and niggles but nothing major. The squad of 30 was fresh and everyone itching to play, and if the panel had ever been pushed into publicly declaring what they believed was their top fifteen, they would have had to make some really tough calls. McAlister was emerging as a useful inside back, Eaton was starting to look comfortable at test level and Tialata was a beast at prop. There were four victories in the bag too, and apart from the lineout, which continued to be a source of concern, there had been some good football played.

There was plenty of ammunition for Henry to fire back at those critics who harped on about the rotation policy. And Henry needed evidence that his strategy was working, because the morning after the Wallabies were beaten at Eden Park he was back at the same ground revealing plans to take player welfare to yet another level.

It turned out that swapping the entire starting fifteen on the Grand Slam tour, the debate over the kick-off time for the third Bledisloe test, operating two teams in June 2006 and the heavy rotation used during the Tri Nations were all just scratching the surface. The definitive statement on how seriously the panel were taking player welfare came on Sunday 20 August when Henry revealed that a maximum of 22 All Blacks would not be available for the 2007 Super 14 until early April.

After consultation with strength and fitness coach Graham Lowe, Henry believed that what his leading players would need most at the start of 2007 was a prolonged period away from the game. They would need some rest and then an extended period to lay down a conditioning base that would allow them to address their various niggles and also become bigger, faster and stronger.

Back in the amateur days – even the early professional days – when the season didn't start until March, the players had an extended off-season where they could put in the hard training yards. That period was vital for the athletic development of the players. With an uninterrupted pre-season, players could get through enough work in the gym to become stronger and more explosive. They could improve their aerobic capacity and also become faster and able to maintain their speed over longer periods and distances.

The problem in the current environment was that the extended pre-season window had been lost. The end-of-season tours generally finished in the last weekend of November, sometimes the first week of December, and then the All Black tourists had a month off before beginning conditioning work in early January. That window was only ever about three or four weeks though, as they were expected back with their franchises by late January. And once they reported back, most teams were working extensively on their collective skill-sets, set-pieces and basic game-plans, as the training regimes were tapered so as that the bulk of the conditioning work was completed in December.

In 2006, because of the introduction of two new teams, the competition was pulled forward to start on 10 February and in 2007, because of the September start at the World Cup, the first game was scheduled for 2 February.

In Henry's view that was a suicide mission and a deal he just couldn't accept. If his best players started playing Super 14 on 2 February and then tried to get through seven tests before the World Cup on just a few weeks conditioning, too many wouldn't make it to France. Lowe explained the thinking of taking the extended break. 'This year [2006], the guys who went on the end-of-season tour had two or three weeks of true conditioning. I don't think we can say there's a correlation between a reduced conditioning window and the increased injuries.

But there is evidence that you increase the chance of getting injured if you carry an injury from one season into the next. Because the number of games is increasing and therefore the amount of training is increasing, there is going to be an increase in injuries. That will grind the players down mentally and it is obvious the players are getting younger. With players also getting bigger, faster and stronger, I think that will reduce the chances of players having extended careers at the top level. Even carefully managing these guys, I still think the length of time players remain at the top will be shorter.'

The short off-season was not the only problem. Once the players got into the game cycle it became almost impossible for them to advance athletically. They would, hopefully, become better rugby players as a consequence of regular game-time, but they were barely holding on to their conditioning base during the season. The actual workloads during the season were all sympathetic and didn't make excessive aerobic or strength demands of the players. There were ample rest periods and the whole week was geared towards keeping players fresh for the next game. Following that formula over the course of the season saw most players flatline in terms of their strength and fitness. At best the forwards could fit in two but more usually just one weights session during a test week. And as Lowe said: 'The guts of it is that it is a lot easier to lose strength, speed and power than it is to gain them.'

Having planned so meticulously to get 30 genuine test players to the World Cup, there was no way Henry was going to come unstuck in the final year. Excuses just wouldn't wash with the New Zealand public if the All Blacks failed to perform in France. There would be no one listening if Henry blamed another World Cup failure on his players being tired and mentally drained. There would be no point crashing out and then saying it was down to inadequate preparation. It was Henry's job to get the preparation right and because he was acutely aware of his responsibility, he knew he had to push for a scenario where he had total control.

Earlier in 2006 he heard all the franchise coaches talk about being supportive of the All Black cause, and then play key test players in 13 games consecutively. Having been a Super 12 coach himself, he knew how it worked – you made all the right noises and then did what was right for your team. Henry knew he couldn't set a protocol where test players were to be rested for a specific number of Super 14 games. Once the season was up and running, coaches would make compelling cases each week why they had to break the protocol. It was, in the brutal world of professional sport, always better to ask for forgiveness than permission.

So Henry laid out his vision to Moller. It was radical and it came with problems, but Moller had backed his man so far and had been delighted with the outcomes. The All Blacks had gone undefeated for 14 games, were developing talent across the board and looking after their prime assets. What Henry wanted, as far as Moller was concerned, Henry could have.

The plan was to rest a nominated 22 players from the first seven rounds of the Super 14. Henry had initially wanted to keep them out for longer, but compromised with a three-month window. The 'protected' players would be announced shortly to give the franchise coaches plenty of warning as to who would be off limits.

Moller confirmed the agreement was made after extensive negotiation with the individual franchises, sponsors and broadcasters. Everyone had agreed to the plan as they all wanted to see the All Blacks win their first World Cup in 20 years. With the announcement made, Henry and his team jumped on a plane to South Africa. A few days later and a chipper Moller jetted off to join them in Pretoria. But by the time he landed in the Republic his mood had darkened. Not every member of New Zealand's extended rugby family had been sold on the idea.

13 End of the love affair

IT WAS hard to know whether it was an oversight or a deliberate snub. An oversight reeked of incompetence, while a snub would have been arrogance beyond belief. Whatever the reason, there was widespread astonishment when it was revealed, five days after the Eden Park announcement, that the NZRU had failed to consult News Limited about the plans to withdraw test stars from the Super 14.

Moller had been at pains to stress how the NZRU had been through a detailed consultation process with all the relevant parties. New Zealand's key Super 14 sponsors Rebel Sport and Ford had been sounded out and kept in the loop almost from the instant Henry first raised the idea. They were supportive on the basis the withdrawal was a one-off. An All Black victory at the World Cup could only be good for the profile of the game, and the Australians had found that there were huge commercial spin-offs after the Wallabies won the tournament in 1999.

The five franchise executives and their respective coaches had to be consulted as they were going to be directly and significantly affected. There would be obvious selection issues to be negotiated. The coaches would have to know who was going to be in the 'protected 22' and they would have to be allowed to pick extra players to plug the holes. There would also have to be an agreement to change the key performance indicators in their contracts and a guarantee of sympathetic reviews. The Hurricanes and Crusaders were likely to be the hardest hit and would have fairly compelling reasons to justify any underperformance. The protected 22 was almost certainly going to include Chris Jack, Richie McCaw, Daniel Carter, Aaron Mauger and Leon MacDonald from the Crusaders. Denied the services of so much quality for seven rounds, life was going to be tough for coach Robbie Deans.

It was also going to be tough for Crusaders chief executive Hamish Riach. The people of Christchurch might be reluctant to turn up at Jade Stadium if there was no Carter and McCaw. If the Crusaders were struggling to win – and it had been a long time since that was the case – the normally well-visited Jade could become a ghost stadium. And local sponsors might reckon they needed to renegotiate their commitment, given the Crusaders brand was clearly going to be less attractive without the big stars turning out.

These were issues the NZRU took seriously and spent months negotiating. Coaches were offered the guarantees they were after, and if they lost seven players they would be allowed to select an extra seven players. Financial compensation was offered to the franchises to make sure the move did not leave them out of pocket.

The New Zealand Rugby Players Association also had to be involved as someone needed to pay for the 22 extra contracted Super 14 players in 2007. The All Blacks who were required for conditioning work would still be paid as per the terms of their guaranteed retainers. The players drafted in to cover for them would be offered a minimum payment of $65,000 and would be retained when the All Blacks returned to action in late March. Should the extra money required to pay those new players come from the NZRU, or come out of the player payment pool (the 32.4 percent of NZRU revenue set aside for the players)? It was an NZRU-driven initiative, so surely they should stump up? A compromise was reached, again after lengthy discussion.

Moller and Henry had been at Sky TV's Mount Wellington headquarters to brief chief executive John Fellet on the plans. Sky TV had paid good money for the broadcast rights and were now being told the NZRU wanted to take out the best players. There was an obvious risk that viewership figures would drop. Sky TV, however, were not convinced the risk was so great. They had seen how viewing figures had held up when All Blacks were removed from the NPC. In 2003, when the All Blacks were absent for the whole competition because of the World Cup, viewing figures were even slightly up. The loss of the big names allowed the Bay of Plenty, Southland and Taranaki to mount exciting challenges. There was less certainty that the same scenario would pan out in a cross-border competition, but nonetheless Fellet was willing to go with it. Just like all the other stakeholders, Sky TV could see the long-term value in having the world champions in the Tri Nations.

Given the lengths to which the NZRU had gone to get the process right, it was utterly unfathomable as to why News Limited, the company that owned the Sanzar broadcast rights, had not been directly consulted. It was News Limited that made quarterly payments to the NZRU as part of the broadcast contract – money that was absolutely vital to the financial well-being of the game in New Zealand. Keeping News Limited in the dark while negotiating with all the other stakeholders was a bit like making all the wedding arrangements before popping the question to the bride-to-be.

News Limited had known about the NZRU's plans, as two executives from News, Peter Macourt and Michael Miller, were on Sky TV's board. But that, in a sense, only made their outrage greater. They had known what the NZRU was planning and sat in silence waiting for contact to be made. That contact never came, as instead, the NZRU sought legal advice to determine whether their plans could be considered a breach of contract. The NZRU's legal advisers were sure they were on solid ground. The removal of 22 All Blacks would not constitute a breach of contract.

By the time Moller touched down in Pretoria on 25 August, the day before the All Blacks played the Springboks at Loftus Versfeld, News warned that suing for compensation was a real possibility. The media group argued the contract was clear – all three Sanzar unions were obliged to field their strongest teams in every game in both Super 14 and Tri Nations. Head of corporate affairs for News, Greg Baxter, was licensed by his executive team to make it known that the media conglomerate was far from happy about either the proposal or the snub. 'If you have a relationship with someone, wouldn't you go to that person and talk to them rather than seeking legal advice? We are now looking at the options available to us. We don't see why a contract we have in good faith should be dishonoured.'

Moller was unrepentant once the storm broke. He refused to say why News had not been consulted and insisted the NZRU was acting within its rights. Backing down was not an option. Moller had been convinced by the All Black coaching staff that if they were serious about winning a World Cup they couldn't compromise. Taking the top players out for three months was not negotiable. The players were staying out and the NZRU was not going to be intimated by News.

News, of course, had a different view. It was not going to be treated with such disdain. News didn't feel it had ever been a broadcast partner that had just signed the cheque and handed it over. There was a relationship in place, one which it thought was being tested by Moller. It was more than just that though. There were also serious concerns with what the NZRU was proposing. News had bought the rights, then on-sold the packages to the various domestic markets. In selling those rights, News had made contractual obligations that it would be providing premium content. If 22 All Blacks were missing until late March, the various domestic broadcasters would have a right to suggest News had not supplied them with the top-level content they had promised. And if the content wasn't premium, there was a fair chance viewing figures would fall. And if viewing figures fell, advertising revenue might drop with it, subscriber revenue might decline too, and the various domestic broadcasters might have a strong claim to make that they were due compensation.

Sky TV, having been kept in the loop and believing their viewing figures would just about hold up, informed News that they were relaxed with the situation. The word coming out of Australia, perhaps unsurprisingly, was not offering any endorsement of the plans. Andrew Oakes, marketing director at Fox Sports, said: 'If the 22 players are taken out, it will absolutely be a big problem. Losing that many players will have a major impact and we have paid a significant amount to buy the rights. Take golf, for example. When Tiger Woods plays, a lot more people watch than when he doesn't, and we think that will be the same in rugby. We want to see the best players fielded each week. A mate of mine has a 12-year-old son who has just switched allegiance from AFL to rugby because he loves Daniel Carter. There are a number of Australian kids growing up here who want to be All Blacks. There will be a big impact on the ratings taking those players out, and that is a concern for us.'

The NZRU was trying to lessen those fears with talk of the conditioning window providing an ideal opportunity for the next generation of superstars to emerge. The absence of McCaw would open the door for a new champion openside. Carter probably wouldn't be missed. The Crusaders had built their success on their seamless ability to wave goodbye to established legends like Andrew Mehrtens one season and hail the arrival of a genius like Carter the next. With the Crusaders and to a lesser extent New Zealand rugby, no one was ever mourned for long. That was the NZRU's argument, but as Baxter retorted: 'I don't think there is any doubt New Zealand has a stunning depth of talent, but we are talking about 22 players for seven weeks. The issue is whether there is a difference between what we've paid for and what we're being offered.'

Unfortunately for the NZRU, their argument that they had the talent to ensure the Super 14 would not be materially affected was deflated by a force more significant than Baxter. Just as they were bragging about a rugby culture that appeared to have superstars growing on trees, the All Blacks lost for the first time in 15 tests.

There was a double sadness when the All Blacks lost to South Africa on 2 September at the little-known Royal Bafokeng Stadium in Rustenburg. There was the obvious disappointment for New Zealanders that the unbeaten run of 15 games had come to an end. The All Blacks had moved in sight of a number of records as a consequence of winning every test since their defeat in Cape Town. If they had won in Rustenburg, they would have travelled to England in November with an opportunity to equal the world record of 17 consecutive test victories and might well have set a new record in Lyon the following week.

It wasn't to be. After a convincing win in Pretoria on 26 August with yet another experimental selection, the All Blacks were fancied to inflict more damage in Rustenburg.

An advance party had flown to South Africa on the Sunday morning after the final Bledisloe test. Having lost his fight to have that game shifted to the Friday, Henry had known for some time that the team he selected to play in Pretoria would be significantly different from the one that had played in Auckland the week before. That made sense. The guys who had started in Auckland would need time to recover after what was a physical test against the Wallabies. Fresh legs would be the order of the day, playing in the afternoon on the rock-hard surface at Loftus. The game in Pretoria would be the ideal opportunity for squad men like Greg Rawlinson, Luke McAlister, Anton Oliver and Reuben Thorne to get a start. Henry and his team of selectors were confident they could leave a lot of firepower in the stands – they made 11 changes in total – and still win the test. That would allow for the triple whammy of the unbeaten record being maintained, a number of fringe players travelling further along their development curve and an opportunity for some senior players to recharge their batteries ahead of the closing Tri Nations game.

In Henry's time, he was yet to win a test in the Republic. That was a monkey he was particularly keen to get off his back, and the leadership group spent some time ensuring the attitude and motivation for the final leg of the Tri Nations was every bit as focused and professional as it should be. Winning both tests in South Africa was a goal the players desperately wanted to achieve. They might have already had the Tri Nations trophy in the bag, but that did not diminish their appetite for success. Henry didn't perceive his team selection in Pretoria as the slightest bit detrimental to achieving victory. He was proved absolutely right when the All Blacks finally found their groove in the last quarter and carved the Boks at will. The final score of 45-26 flattered the hosts.

Rustenburg should have been more of the same. The Boks didn't have any magic personnel they could draft in to turn things around. They were stuck with what they had, and that didn't appear a whole lot. Coach Jake White was under pressure to quit, and as usual the wider management appeared riddled with political rifts. As for the All Blacks, they were able to recall the big-hitting Jerry Collins, the rock that is Carl Hayman, put Aaron Mauger back in the midfield, select the deadly wing combination of cousins Sitiveni Sivivatu and Joe Rokocoko and introduce the very fresh legs of Jimmy Cowan and Andrew Hore. There were 10 changes from the previous week, but with the exception of hooker, halfback and fullback (wing Doug Howlett was standing in for the injured Leon MacDonald), it was probably the All Blacks' strongest line-up.

Interestingly, Carter and McCaw had been retained, even though both would be playing their third test consecutively. The panel felt both men could handle the workload. It was perhaps also an acknowledgement that while the All Blacks had been building strength in depth, the back-up quality at openside and first-five was not quite there yet. Or maybe it would be fairer to say that Masoe was a seriously good player – but he wasn't world class – and the difference when McCaw played was significant. The same was true of Carter. McAlister could do the job but he couldn't grab the game in the same way as Carter. No question, there was an intriguing mix of fresh legs and experience to put the Boks away big-style at Rustenburg.

It didn't happen like that at all. The Boks dug deep and found some inspiration. They were brilliant at the lineout and for the first time in many games actually looked capable with ball in hand. They got off the line quickly to pressure the All Blacks, and it turned out to be one of those days when the gods smiled upon the men in green and gold. The All Blacks were clumsy and laboured, failing to convert their opportunities. Even with so much emphasis on player welfare, the side looked jaded. They appeared to be lacking sharpness, and as a consequence they lost the game 21-20 in the dying minutes when Andre Pretorius kicked a tricky enough penalty. Gone went the chance to make history with a record-breaking run of victories, and while Henry had previously hinted the players were being distracted by the possibility of establishing a new record, there was still obviously major disappointment at the loss.

But more disappointing than the result were the thousands of empty seats. Only a few days previously the NZRU had been trying to convince News Limited they had the depth of talent to take 22 of their best players out of the Super 14 and no one would really notice. It turned out that the All Blacks didn't have the strength in depth even to win a two-test series against an ordinary South African side. Not only that, the NZRU wanted to risk viewing figures at a time when it was apparent rugby was failing to engage its market.

The expansion to Super 14 and the extra Tri Nations rounds had placed a huge burden on the players. It had placed an even bigger one on the viewing public, made worse because 2006 was also the first year of the expanded provincial championship. Rugby was being crammed into every available nook and cranny. There were Friday night double-headers during Super 14 and quadruple hits of football on Saturdays. During June, July and August it felt like Groundhog Day with so many tests against the Wallabies and Boks, and then things just got out of control when the provincial championship started in mid August.

There were tests and provincial programmes to be shoehorned into the weekend. Even when the Tri Nations finished, the expansion to 14 teams in the provincial format meant there were Friday night double-headers, Saturday triple-headers, Sunday double-headers and, unbelievably, that still wasn't enough to accommodate all the games. Thursday night football came into existence, and unsurprisingly the viewing public opted to instigate a rotation policy of its own.

It wasn't so long ago that a clever wit visited New Zealand and on his departure facetiously remarked the country had been closed. It was a gentle poke at the sleepiness of New Zealand, a country dominated by sheep and mountains that only came alive when rugby was played. The travel guides loved pushing the line that rugby was a religion. The perception was given to the rest of the world that when the All Blacks played the whole country stood still. The

NZRU was happy to push that theme in its bid to win the hosting rights for the 2011 World Cup. A stadium of four million people was the line that won the vote.

By 2006, the myth of rugby as religion was being exposed. Stadiums might have replaced churches as the new place of worship, but they were struggling to hold on to their congregations. For most of the professional age it was a mission for anyone to get their hands on Bledisloe Cup tickets. In 2006 it was a mission for the NZRU to get rid of them.

The first Tri Nations test in Christchurch was not a sell-out. On the Monday before the test there were still a few thousand tickets available. By the time the game kicked off, the vacancies were down to a few hundred. This was the All Blacks playing their biggest rival, the prime fixture in Sanzar's showpiece event, and they couldn't fill what was only a modest capacity of 36,000.

The NZRU blamed the weather. New Zealand was in the middle of its coldest winter for 32 years and snow lay thick across the South Island. Faced with the prospect of sitting in uncovered seats in Antarctic conditions, the people of Canterbury opted for watching the game in front of the box.

It got a little harder for the NZRU to explain why, on the Monday before the next test against the Boks in Wellington, there were again thousands of unsold tickets. Normally Wellington tests were sold out an hour after tickets went on sale. The weather was markedly improved in the capital and the All Blacks had turned in a convincing 80 minutes in Christchurch to build a level of excitement. There was again a late surge of sales in Wellington, leaving only a couple of hundred unfilled seats on the night. Sales in Auckland for the final clash were just as sluggish, but a full house was eventually secured. The Wallabies had played the Boks in front of a half-empty stadium in Sydney, and then of course there had been the shame of Rustenburg where only 28,000 made it along on a beautiful day.

The malaise and indifference towards the bloated rugby calendar were made to seem worse in New Zealand because the early rounds of the new provincial championship were also played to a depressing backdrop. The most prominent feature in every game was the sea of empty seats. Auckland, the reigning champions, could only muster a staggeringly pathetic 12,000 to their local derby against Waikato, the same number against Otago and only 11,000 to watch the quarter-final against the Bay of Plenty. Even with most of the All Blacks in action, the potentially thrilling clash between Canterbury and

Wellington pulled only a paltry 15,000 people. Some of the games between the smaller unions were barely creeping into four figures.

Plummeting attendances were not definitive evidence that New Zealand's love affair with rugby was waning. It could have been that the overall number of people watching rugby was holding up, but that more and more people were choosing to watch on TV.

That notion was blown out of the water when viewing figures for the Tri Nations were released by the media firm AGB Neilsen. The figures showed that each All Black Tri Nations test in 2006 attracted an average of 404,000 viewers on Sky and 221,000 on Prime. That compared with 458,000 for Sky and 425,000 for TV3 in 2005. The figures were down partly because of a switch in the free-to-air rights from TV3 to Prime, which cannot be accessed in some parts of the country, but even so, no one was expecting the drop in numbers to be as significant as it was. The combined loss of 258,000 viewers per test represented a decline of 30 percent in the overall numbers of people watching the All Blacks play. The NZRU were able to extrapolate some positives from the numbers. Deputy chief executive Steve Tew said: 'We actually had an eight percent increase in viewers for the first three (Tri Nations) games. We always knew this was going to be a challenging year and we steeled ourselves for it.'

But it was a comment that brought to mind the doomed Dutch boy with his finger in the dyke. The NZRU could blame the weather, the increased price of oil, the growing desire for sedentary, couch-based pursuits and the ever-increasing choice of alternative entertainment options. The reality had to be faced, though, that the rugby public were bored by a season that had far too much rugby. They were bored by a season that featured so many unmemorable games against the same old faces. And they were bored by the incessant revolving door when it came to All Black selection. The last point was acknowledged by Moller when he was in South Africa. 'We recognise the World Cup is the jewel in the crown and as New Zealand hasn't won it for 20 years, it would be nice to win it. But there is a danger games in other competitions are becoming more like friendlies and we need to look at the domination of the World Cup. [Rotation] is definitely a balancing act. We want to build depth and experience, but that comes with a risk at the other end around the audience appeal that drives the sport.'

Rugby couldn't survive if the World Cup became the only meaningful tournament. If every test in between became solely about building for the next

World Cup, the game was doomed. There needed to be a focus on the here and now. News Limited were paying top dollar for premium content. They hadn't paid top dollar to watch test sides experiment for a competition that News didn't hold the broadcast rights for. There needed to be some bite put back into the traditional fixtures that had made the game as popular as it was long before the World Cup came into existence.

The paying fans needed to be treated with more respect. They were handing over as much as $100 to attend a game, and for that kind of money they wanted to see Daniel Carter play – not find themselves sitting in the stands next to him watching an inferior version of him playing in the All Black No 10 shirt.

But there was no point blaming Henry and his coaching team. They were not the bad guys – they were simply managing a bad situation as best they could. They hadn't been behind the expansion of Super 14 and Tri Nations and they hadn't asked to play 13 tests in 2006. They had been charged with winning games and, in 2007, going to France and coming home with the William Webb Ellis trophy. The choice, as the All Black coaches saw it, was to accept that the administrators had stuffed up and put the players through hell. Or they could work round the bad hand they had been dealt. They could take a few selection risks every week and rest the big names when they felt rest would be beneficial. They could experiment more when they assessed the opposition wasn't up to much.

By the end of the Tri Nations, Henry had amassed a win ratio that was better than all those who had gone before him. Under him, the All Blacks had won 29 of their 33 tests and were undefeated at home. There was also a previously unseen strength in depth. By September, with Conrad Smith, James Ryan, Sione Lauaki, Nick Evans and Keith Robinson all playing again after long-term injuries, it was apparent that some seriously good players were not going to make the end-of-season tour to England, France and Wales. In 2004, Henry had been scrambling to find locks; now he had six. There were four world-class wings and some mighty fine props coming through behind the world class Carl Hayman and Tony Woodcock.

And yet, despite the 29 victories, despite the obvious talent developing across the country, and despite the fact players were being afforded sensible recovery periods to get through a long season, it was obvious from the attendances and viewing figures that the rugby public were struggling to embrace the new way of doing things. It was a worry for the NZRU. They couldn't brand their paying supporters Philistines, lecture them on the fact rugby had changed beyond recognition in terms of athleticism and physicality, and then tell them they would have to like rotation or lump it. The experimentation of 2006 had to be a one-off – a season of indulgence where the means justified the end. Empty stadiums wouldn't fund the game in the long run. If News sensed the public were drifting, the big cheque would not come at the next broadcast rights renegotiation. Henry found a way to manage a bad situation. But rather than have it become the norm for the All Black coach to duck and dive, it was deemed a better ploy to improve the situation and dramatically rework the structure of the season.

By the time the All Blacks arrived back from South Africa, the stoush with News had still not been resolved. There had been discussions between Jock Hobbs and Macourt during the two weeks the All Blacks were in South Africa, but the deadlock was proving hard to break. Both sides wanted a resolution, and while there was obviously some tension and a little bad blood, both parties were committed to the relationship. There was too much at stake for the whole deal to break down over one squabble, and in the end News agreed to sanction the move on the proviso that if viewing figures slumped while the All Blacks were missing, they would bill the NZRU for compensation.

It was a compromise of sorts and it allowed both parties to move on, which was a relief for the NZRU as they needed to name the list of protected players to give the franchise coaches ample notice of where they would need to strengthen their squads. The list of protected players was eagerly awaited, as no matter how much Henry insisted Super 14 exemption was not a guarantee of selection in the World Cup squad, there was a seriously good chance everyone on it would end up in France. Woodcock, Hayman, Mealamu, Ali Williams, Chris Jack, Jerry Collins and Rodney So'oialo were recognised as the strongest pack and were duly in the 22. Byron Kelleher, Carter, Aaron Mauger, Mils Muliaina, Rokocoko, Sivivatu and MacDonald were possibly the first-choice backline and to no one's surprise were on the list. Greg Somerville, Oliver and Thorne had been around for a fair while and had not had a decent off-season for years so they were listed, and Chris Masoe, Jason Eaton, Piri Weepu and Hore took the final four places.

The announcement of the protected players didn't quite put the whole issue to bed, as the NZRU had still not given any indication why they had chosen to keep their broadcast partner in the dark. Everyone was left to work their own theory but two factors emerged as the most plausible.

The NZRU had kept News out of the loop as a means of establishing who controlled the game. News provided a critical source of income but was not there to advise or dictate to the three unions how they should go about their business. The NZRU rightly assessed that if they had asked permission to withdraw 22 All Blacks, News would have said no. And the NZRU didn't see this as something up for negotiation.

Henry was convinced an extended reconditioning window was imperative if the All Blacks were going to arrive at the World Cup in prime physical condition. Former strength and conditioning coach, Mike Anthony, says that John Mitchell had contemplated running a few conditioning camps in early 2003 to prepare his key players for the World Cup that year. In the end he didn't feel it was a move that would be fully supported by the Super 12 franchises and he didn't want to get offside with his colleagues in such a critical year. Instead, he famously opted to leave a host of senior players at home when the All Blacks toured England, France and Wales in November 2002. By doing so, he afforded those players in New Zealand an extended reconditioning window.

Henry could have done the same thing and taken a much-reduced squad to England, France and Wales at the end of 2006 to allow the likes of Carter, McCaw, Hayman, Woodcock, Mealamu, Collins and Muliaina to rebuild through November, December and January. Henry felt it made more sense, though, to have them play the tests and recondition on someone else's time.

With the decision made that a full-strength squad would tour Europe, the only option to recondition was the early months of 2007. When the lawyers said the move was kosher, Moller was not going to back down. As far as Moller knew, he and his executive team, not News, still ran the game of rugby in New Zealand.

That stance also explains why the NZRU ended up in the soup with their Sanzar partners. According to Baxter, the Sanzar unions had held a meeting earlier in 2006 where they agreed to declare their plans to manage the convoluted 2007 season. Supposedly it was agreed that all three unions would discuss possible strategies with their domestic sponsors, broadcasters and franchises and then reconvene. Once all three had declared their intention, the Sanzar board, which in 2006 was chaired by the Australians (the secretariat swapped between the three countries every two years), would sit down with News and negotiate an agreement.

Again, as New Zealand was proposing something far more radical than their partners (Australia decided that leading Wallabies would miss one Super 14 game, while South Africa opted to rest key players on their 2006 end-of-season tour) they couldn't reveal their hand in advance. Rather than report back, the NZRU chose to go public with their intention. Moller was irate that one of the Sanzar partners had clearly snitched to News. But it wasn't just that someone had talked out of school that had Moller all hot and bothered, it was the fact they had, in his opinion, peddled misleading and potentially damaging information. 'We are adamant there was no agreement to come back together [before making an announcement],' said Moller. 'We refute those claims and are not happy information has been passed to News. They have taken that information in good faith and we have concerns with that.'

The other possible reason why the NZRU kept radio silence was the need to make a major statement about player welfare ahead of a critical IRB board meeting in mid September. Moller had never made any secret of his desire to see a more structured, shorter season. Player welfare was being managed from campaign to campaign, but if all the furniture was shifted and the season made shorter, progressively structured and sympathetic towards the increased physicality, then player welfare would become less of an issue as the game would be permanently set up to look after the players. Creating a conditioning window was a powerful statement. New Zealand was sending a message to its fellow IRB board members that permanent change was required to stop countries who were serious about looking after their players from having to take such dramatic action that put them at loggerheads with other members of the extended rugby family.

'The Professional Players Association has made some powerful submissions to us on this issue and we think it is very important for players to have a break from the game,' said Moller when he was in South Africa. 'We recognise we are talking about human beings here and that it is critical we are not just preparing players to win today but are looking after them long term. I haven't had a proper look at the agenda for this month's IRB board meeting but I'm sure the issue of an integrated season will be on it.'

It was indeed on the agenda, and as Moller flew back from that IRB meeting in Dublin, he could smile the smile of the righteous. A global season was no longer a fantasy – it was a distinct possibility.

14 Global season

ANY PROBLEM burdened with the label 'global' seems destined to be discussed in serious terms with no real prospect of definitive action ever being taken. Take global warming. For the last decade scientists have insisted the phenomenon exists and is a real and present danger to life as we know it. Politicians accept the evidence is irrefutable, agree that global warming is a massive concern and then do absolutely nothing about it until their next major get-together, when they agree again it is still a major concern that needs to be addressed.

It was much the same in the rugby world when it came to the prospect of establishing a global season, or as some preferred to call it, an integrated season. By 2000, the entire rugby fraternity was agreed there needed to be a major re-organisation of the rugby calendar to protect the players and the commercial value of the sport. Administrators, coaches, medics, players, sponsors, broadcasters and fans could all see the increased physicality of the sport, and the burgeoning fixture lists were at odds with each other. The season had somehow been stretched to an 11-month slog, with players wondering when exactly it was they would find the time to fit in a summer holiday or a long weekend or even just a cheeky sick day. Without a real off-season, as Henry had made everyone aware, the players were unable to prepare adequately. And when corners were cut in conditioning, the injury toll mounted. Somehow the season had to be condensed so there was an extended break for the world's best players. There was no way that Henry or any other All Black coach could get away with pulling players out of the Super 14 a second time. It was absolutely a one-off and there needed to be a rest and reconditioning period permanently built into the calendar.

The problem was most acute in England, where the players served under dual paymasters. At least in New Zealand, the players were centrally contracted, with an agreement under the collective that everyone was entitled to one month away from rugby when their season ended. That was untouchable. But in England the situation was a mess.

The players were contracted to their clubs and, if selected for England, paid on a match-fee basis. Most players earned the bulk of their money from their club contract, which became problematic when more and more international demands were made of the players. The club season in England is so convoluted it's almost impossible to keep track of what is going on. Three separate competitions are played concurrently, so a team can play in the cross-border Heineken Cup one Saturday, the Powergen competition featuring English and Welsh teams midweek, then dog out a local derby in the Guinness Premiership the following Saturday. With so much rugby to get through, the club competition can't take a break during the Six Nations or when England host in-bound touring teams in November. It is not uncommon for an English test star to play for England in the Six Nations one week, play a crucial game for his club the next and then return to international colours. The international coaching staff hate this scenario, as they would rather retain their players in camp and allow them to rest and prepare for the next test. It doesn't happen that way, though, as the clubs want their pound of flesh and they have, after all, paid handsomely for it.

The club season doesn't end until late May, giving some players barely any break before England have to fulfil their touring obligations in June. Supposedly all players who tour are entitled to extended rest and recovery periods, but unlike the situation in New Zealand, the agreement is not untouchable. The club season kicks off again in mid August and the sugar daddies who have emptied their pockets to buy ownership of the game don't really like to see their best assets on the sidelines. All the clubs say they take player welfare seriously and care about the athletes, but have no hesitation in selecting an English tourist way before he's had sufficient recovery and reconditioning time. The upshot is the top English players are asked to front more than 40 times a season and have no one looking out for them. The demands are excessive and, while it would not be a panacea, an extended off-season where the players were untouchable by either club or country would certainly alleviate some of the burden.

By 2000, every Tier One nation – England, Scotland, Ireland, Wales, France, Italy, Australia, South Africa, Argentina and New Zealand – agreed that condensing the season was of paramount importance. The term global season was used as there needed to be a harmonisation between the hemispheres. If one season could be established globally – so that in England, France, Japan, Argentina, New Zealand or wherever, the rugby season started, say, in February and ended in October – then the demands on the players would be contained. There would also be greater opportunity to establish cross-border competitions at both provincial and international level. Agreeing to the principle of a global season was all well and good. But how exactly could this be done in practice?

It was hardly going to be an easy process rearranging the furniture when there were established competitions in both hemispheres with attached commercial arrangements. Something had to give. There needed to be compromise in both hemispheres if the objective was ever going to be achieved.

The IRB opted to move cautiously and set up a Tours and Tournaments working party. This group had a brief to examine the way the IRB scheduled tests and to determine whether there were ways in which the season could be restructured. The creation of this working group coincided with Sanzar's decision to commission consultancy firm Accenture to explore avenues of expansion for both Super Rugby and the Tri Nations. With so much resource being devoted to the issue, there was genuine hope that constructive changes were just around the corner. This was important, as by the late 1990s the bigger unions had become increasingly frustrated with the cumbersome nature of the IRB. The committee-based management group gave the organisation the speed of an oil tanker. There would be endless meetings, neverending discussions about the same topics, but very little decisive action – or policies would take so long to be formed they were rendered redundant immediately they came into force.

There was a prevailing view within the biggest unions that the only way major change would ever happen was if they revoked their IRB membership. A breakaway was seriously discussed, but in the end the big five unions – England, France, New Zealand, South Africa and Australia – agreed to stay loyal to the IRB. But all the optimism that had been generated by the decision to stay loyal and the research being conducted into a season restructure was wiped out in March 2002 on the eve of a crucial working party meeting in Treviso, Italy. The Australians and South Africans unilaterally withdrew their support for the Accenture Report, and the momentum that had been building promptly stopped in its tracks.

By September 2002 there were still no concrete proposals on the table. It had become a global-warming issue, where it seemed everyone was happy to keep acknowledging the magnitude of the problem as long as they didn't actually have to get serious about coming up with ways to fix it. It was becoming increasingly difficult, however, for the administrators to keep the problem at arm's length. In September 2002, the IRB held a two-day player welfare conference in Dublin where the issue of a global season was debated at length.

Then All Black coach John Mitchell was one of the speakers and he told the *New Zealand Herald* the gist of his speech before he left. 'These guys [the players] need three months away from the contest so they can establish a better fitness foundation, so they can be prepared and can have some of the operations many need. I will probably only need one slide to explain it and will do so to anyone who wants to listen. If the international window could be aligned between the Super 12 and NPC, then we could get a break in November, December and January.'

A powerful presentation from no less an authority than the All Black coach was clearly going to carry some weight. It was surely going to kick-start the IRB into hammering out some detail on how the northern and southern hemisphere seasons could be aligned to give all players the break they so desperately craved.

The promise of action seemed real when IRB chief executive Mike Miller said after the conference: 'The issues discussed stem from the phenomenal growth in rugby over the last seven years. Fans and sponsors all seem to want more and more rugby and that puts demands on players.' Miller then revealed that a range of proposals from the conference would be put forward to a meeting of the IRB council in November. The proposals would include setting up a four-week holiday slot for players to escape the pressures of top-flight rugby, followed by an eight to 10-week pre-season period. There was a sense that momentum was building again, that more and more resource would be devoted to the problem of working out how to achieve the objective of a shorter, less convoluted season in both hemispheres.

But the following month, Miller, who had only started his job in April, was in New Zealand to meet key executives at the NZRU. Having given the impression a couple of weeks earlier that change was on the medium-term agenda, he went on to dispel all the optimism by saying: 'What we have are two seasons and debates for the next few years about whether it is possible to have a unified season. We don't want to make the mistake of moving traditional times around and then finding they have lost their impact.' He confirmed that the IRB would press ahead with its plan to host an exhibition game at Twickenham on 30 November between a southern hemisphere select fifteen and a northern hemisphere select fifteen.

It didn't add up. Here was the IRB setting up conferences and devoting significant resources to address the issue of player burn-out and the need to protect the game's prize assets, while also arranging what was deemed a needless fixture that would put yet more of a physical burden on the best individuals.

With 2003 being a World Cup year, the issue of a global season would inevitably drift down the agenda. That would mean the square root of zip would have been achieved in the four years since the Tier One unions accepted the need for action. No wonder the major unions had given some thought to going it alone. But the IRB finally appeared to get itself into gear by the middle of 2004.

On 24 June 2004 Miller wrote to the chief executives of all the Tier One unions. He told them: 'I wanted to update you on the work that has been ongoing regarding a potential global season for rugby. You will recall that at our Heathrow governance workshop meeting last March this was one of the priority issues identified. The feeling was that a global season based around a series of clearly defined windows for the top end of professional rugby could produce a more structured flow to the rugby season, could help alleviate player availability issues and would ensure a proper close season for player recuperation.

'Since that meeting there has been consultation with the Tier One and Tier Two Unions on this issue, a tender process has been conducted amongst a number of the world's top consulting firms to carry out work on a global season, and background work has been carried out by our governance consultant in conjunction with IRB staff. This work was reviewed by both the governance working party and the executive committee last week. A global season discussion proposal was put to both the governance working party and the executive committee. Both groups felt that prior to engaging a consulting firm, another round of consultations with Tier One Unions was necessary. The hope was that this round of consultation, based around the global season discussion proposal, might show an emerging consensus among Tier One Unions.'

It was not exactly definitive but it was a step in the right direction. A consultancy firm would at least produce a document that would contain firm proposals that could be debated and voted on. Miller proposed a timetable that would see the unions get the consultant's document by 18 October and then make a decision about any course of action a month later when the full board met in Dublin on 18 November.

It was enormously disappointing, then, when the document produced by Deloitte & Touche failed to offer more than a starting-point. It reeked of being a rushed job, which it was, given that Deloitte weren't commissioned until July and delivered their findings by mid October. If this document was actually going to be strong enough to result in action, it needed to be formed after discussion with all the relevant parties. Obviously all the Tier One unions had to have their say, but so too did all the broadcasters, sponsors, associated medical staff and player union representatives. To come up with theoretical constructs that didn't take into consideration the views of all those with a stake in the game was not going to advance the debate far enough. All the IRB were going to do on 18 November was say more work needed to be done.

When Deloitte did report back they suggested four distinct scenarios. The IRB was keen to call them scenarios rather than proposals – a further indication that more research and more discussion was going to be required.

The first scenario proposed keeping the southern hemisphere season pretty much as it was, with the traditional European touring window in November pulled forward to September and maybe extended. That would allow elite players in the south to rest in November, December and January before the February start to the Super 14. In Europe the plan was to play domestic club competitions in uninterrupted blocks to avoid confusion and enhance the attraction to broadcasters. The bulk of the Heineken Cup – the equivalent of the Super 14 – would be played in December and January with the final taking place in March to close the club season and heighten interest in the Six Nations, which would be pushed back to a dedicated slot in April and May and serve as the grand finale to the season. Europe's elite players could rest in June, July and August. This scenario proposed fixing the World Cup in an October/November window and scrapping the rule that said teams couldn't play tests within five weeks of the tournament. That way the southern hemisphere nations could still tour the north in September. This was crucial, as hosting in-bound tours netted the European nations serious cash, as rugby still followed the traditional formula of the home side keeping the gate money.

The second scenario would see the Super 14 kick off in late February, with the Tri Nations coming forward to June and July. There would be just one extended international touring window of seven weeks, where teams would play in both hemispheres during August and September. The NPC would kick off in early August and end in late October to allow the southern hemisphere players to rest and prepare in November, December and January. In the north, the Six Nations would start in late February and run through to mid April, with test players missing the first two weeks of the Heineken Cup, which would be played in a straight block in April and May. June, July and early August would be rest time ahead of the touring window in August and September, with club league championships commencing in August as well. The World Cup would be played in September/October, which would force the truncation of the tour window every four years.

The third scenario was largely the same as the first proposal, and pretty much consistent with how the current season is set up, the only real difference being the existing November touring window being pulled forward to October. There would be significant tidying up of the European competitions so there would be more flow and less overlap between international and club commitments. In World Cup years, the tournament would be fixed in October/November with only one touring window in that year. That window would be in September and the direction of travel dependent on where the World Cup was being played. If it was in the northern hemisphere they would act as hosts, and vice versa when the tournament was played down under.

The fourth scenario was easily the most radical, particularly for the southern hemisphere. The idea was to start the Super 14 in mid January and run it through until late April. The players would have a three-week rest period before commencing the Tri Nations in May and June, which would be played concurrently with the Six Nations. The southern hemisphere would host tours as usual in June and then the test players would be released for the bulk of the NPC, which would start in late July. The All Blacks would, though, miss the conclusion of the provincial championship as they would tour the northern hemisphere in October. In World Cup years, however, it was suggested that the

Super 14 start in February and run, uncompleted, to the end of March. The Tri Nations would start in April and May with the World Cup played in June/July. The remainder of the Super 14 would be played out in August and September, with a touring window in October.

The critical factor was that every scenario offered a minimum off-season of eight weeks, with some proposals allowing up to 10 weeks. Some of the proposals were perhaps going to be more favourable to the southern hemisphere, while certainly the fourth was going to work out better for the north. The other important point was that each scenario cleaned up the mess in the north where disjointed, concurrent club competitions overlapped international commitments.

On the plus side, after four years there was finally a document on the table which could serve as a focus for discussion. There were, however, problems in using the document as a tool for achieving decisive action. There were four options to mull over, which meant it was going to be hard for one scenario to gain majority backing. There had also been little input from the commercial backers of the sport. So when it came to 18 November, there was once more healthy discussion and debate, but no firm agreement on how the issue could progress. For the umpteenth time the creation of a global season was put in the too-hard basket. And because the IRB only met sporadically and had plenty of other business to get through, creating a global season would slip down the agenda for some time unless the most influential unions kept driving the issue. By mid 2006, there was no shortage of administrators banging their fists on the table demanding that once and for all this business of a global season be finally settled.

Chris Moller had never given up hope that one day he would see a restructuring of the rugby season. Ever since he had come into the job at the end of 2002 it had been an issue he felt strongly about. As he watched the players grow bigger and faster every year and the sport become more brutal, he knew player welfare was not something that could go on being ignored. He knew that at some stage the game would implode if ever greater demands were placed on the players.

He'd spent time with Graham Henry and had heard the All Black coach tell it straight. He'd listened to Henry express his increasing anxiety about the state of his athletes. And a guy like Henry, who'd been around for ever and a day, could not be easily ignored. Moller had a strong working relationship with him. It was a relationship underpinned by trust and respect, and Moller wanted to do what he could to help Henry continue to deliver a winning brand. By 2006 Moller had seen and heard enough to know it was imperative to build in an off-season to protect the players.

But the desire for a global season was being driven by more than just concerns about player welfare. Moller, like every other administrator, was always worried about where the game's next pay cheque was coming from. The contract with News Limited still provided the NZRU with almost half its income. The sponsorship deal with adidas was another significant component. It was a stated aim and wise practice for the NZRU to grow other revenue streams to reduce the reliance on just two contracts.

Moller believed in using the power of the brand to grow the brand, and since 2003 had tried to arrange additional All Black tests played under commercial arrangements. That is to say, he tried to arrange overseas tests where the All Blacks received a significant portion of the gate money. The NZRU had long chased a restructuring of commercial practices to split test revenues, but it was yet another issue that could never get the traction it needed at IRB level. So rather than wait for a blanket change in the set-up, Moller looked for one-off games where terms could be struck. The All Blacks could sell out any ground in the world and the Europeans knew it. A game at Twickenham, say, between New Zealand and England would be guaranteed a full house of 82,000. That put about £4 million in the coffers of the RFU. In 2006, the NZRU approached the RFU outside the confines of the IRB and offered to play a test in the first weekend of November for a fee of about £1 million ($3 million). Although the test fell outside the IRB window which would start the following week, both sides were happy to play and the deal was done, thereby extending the All Blacks' end-of-season tour from three tests to four.

The same thing happened in 2004, when the NZRU agreed to play the Barbarians at Twickenham after the All Blacks' three-week tour of Italy, Wales and France, and again in 2005 when the Welsh agreed to play at Millennium Stadium in the first weekend of November. It was an easy way for the All Blacks to cash in on the power of their brand. But of course it increased the burden. It was adding yet more high-intensity rugby and extending the season further.

Commercially, though, there were not a lot of options for the NZRU. They had a family of sponsors and there was little room to extend that family. They had sold the TV rights to all their competitions, were selling out grounds (just) in New Zealand and merchandising opportunities were being fully exploited. Playing more tests was an option that had to be pursued, and Moller could see it was going to be made easier and more viable with the introduction of a global season. If the players had longer rest periods, a more defined and logical flow to their season where they finished Super 14 and then effectively stayed in camp with the All Blacks, then it would be possible for more tests to be arranged.

It would also be possible to leverage better commercial terms with existing broadcasting and sponsor partners, as well as potentially make the game attractive to new geographic and corporate markets. All the clutter and uncertainty in the rugby world was not a turn-on for potential investors. No money men liked the uncertainty of the season every fourth year. Unlike football, the Rugby World Cup was not fixed in a window, which made planning and financial evaluation hard. Every World Cup year there had to be considerable replanning of the season. If it was held in June/July, as it was in 1995, the southern hemisphere missed out on hosting northern hemisphere opponents. Likewise, if it was in October/November, as it was in 1999 and 2003, the northern hemisphere lost its in-bound hosting rights. The loss of those respective hosting rights was costly – gate revenue was a major part of every nation's income – and there were further complications.

What were broadcast packages worth if no one could be sure what they were actually buying every fourth year? And surely what everyone wanted was the best players turning up to play in the best possible physical and mental condition? It also couldn't be ignored that the Super 14 and Tri Nations had been a little stale in 2006. The viewing figures – while there were some big positives to be extrapolated – were not brilliant. The difficulty in selling match tickets in all three countries was troubling. Sanzar could bury its head in the sand and focus on those abstract positive figures, or they could face up to reality and accept that by 2010, when they would have to renegotiate a new broadcast deal, something exciting involving new teams from different places would have to be proposed. If the season was streamlined, more integrated with the northern hemisphere, then the possibilities would be greatly enhanced.

It wasn't as if Moller needed any convincing – he'd been sold from the off – but by mid September 2006 he had the global season bit between his teeth. Now was the time to push for change, and for the first time since 2000 when the whole issue began to be taken seriously, there was a real chance it could at last make it all the way to shore. The ill wind blowing through England was certainly going to help.

The new club season was in its infancy in England and already, after just a few weeks, there was barely a first-choice test player standing. The injuries kept coming. Each weekend would see another big star break this, break that, pull this or dislocate the other. It was carnage, and while no one could stand up and make a direct link, every sports scientist knew the crux of the problem was that the players had been forced back into action without sufficient rest and preparation time. The problem was too severe to be ignored, especially when a damning report was released which highlighted exactly how badly the players felt they were being treated.

New Zealand academic Scott Cresswell produced a detailed report after three years of research that revealed elite players' attitudes towards player burn-out and the season structure. Cresswell's research dovetailed with work commissioned by the Players Association in England, and the two projects effectively canvassed the opinion of every player in the Guinness Premiership.

The most worrying finding was that 58 percent of players said they had been pressured to play by their clubs even if they were injured. Each player spent 19 percent of the calendar year injured, and four out of five players felt injuries were becoming more severe. Ideally, players felt they needed an off-season of 11 weeks, where five would be spent away from their club. One of the concerns raised by the test players was that while they had four weeks off under the current regime, they came back to their clubs and were thrown straight into contact work. Almost 60 percent of those interviewed felt the season was too long.

The RFU were now firmly in Moller's camp. The English civil war between the clubs and the national team was killing the players and it had to stop. The best way to do that was to create a global season, or integrated season as Moller preferred to call it. Maybe he was keen to drop the global part as he was aware of the unfavourable reaction 'global' problems invoked. Whatever the reason, by September 2006 there was unanimous support among the IRB member countries to restructure the calendar. Moller came back from Dublin in late September after meetings with the so-called Group of 10 – Six Nations, Tri Nations and Argentina – as well as a full IRB board meeting, and rated them the most positive and constructive get-togethers he had enjoyed during his tenure.

The IRB was not going to lose momentum this time. The deal was going to be secured because New Zealand, England, Australia, South Africa and France were all driving it. There was also the added incentive of ridding the guilt over Argentina. The Pumas were the bastard child of world rugby, unloved and unwanted by either hemisphere. The union had no money, the players only ever managed to assemble a few days before every test, yet the Pumas hammered Wales twice in 2006, then went close to the All Blacks and would finish the year with a deserved first win at Twickenham. The IRB wanted them to be included in regular, meaningful competition but Sanzar said 'no can do'. Argentina had no professional structure and all its best players were based in Europe. They would not be released by their clubs to play in the Tri Nations and there was no way the All Blacks could be expected to take on Argentinian amateur players. The Six Nations made more sense, with Argentina arguing they could be based in Barcelona. Their players would have to be released according to IRB regulations and that would be a solution of sorts.

A better solution, though, was discussed in Dublin. There was a commercial risk in messing around with established and successful competitions such as the Six Nations and Tri Nations. They were the bedrocks of the rugby calendar. But there was an opportunity to revamp the respective June and November touring windows. Those two windows were responsible for elongating the season, and they were no longer producing classic encounters that engaged the rugby public. The modern formula of playing three separate opponents or a two-test series plus one other test in the respective three-week windows had become decidedly stale.

But what if a biennial competition was created involving the world's best nations? Rather than have endless meaningless tests every June and November, why not have a structured competition every second year, or re-introduce tours where mid-week games were played? That would at least provide the opportunity for an off-season every other year, and as IRB chairman Sid Millar told the *New Zealand Herald*: 'It would enable us to fulfil the needs of unions to produce the necessary finances. There are a lot of test matches now compared to what there used to be. But there is a requirement for income. Players have to be paid and rugby is a very expensive game to play with all the back-up staff. We have to look maybe at some other formula than just having the southern hemisphere countries coming here in the autumn and playing a few matches and the northern hemisphere sides going to the southern hemisphere in June.

It would solve many things, such as concern over player welfare and number of matches. It would create more relevant games and be a more effective way of increasing revenues.

'But people will have to compromise and change to create these things. There is no need to tweak the Six Nations or Tri Nations to any degree, but we have to look at the autumn internationals and summer tours so there are enough games that generate sufficient revenues.'

After six years of discussion, there was at last a definitive route to the promised land. It wasn't ideal. The ideal would have been a global season – a shorter, more structured season with a definite start- and end-date for all players. But an integrated season with a biennial competition involving the best teams would be a massive improvement on the status quo.

Moller returned to New Zealand enthused by a desire to make his dream come to fruition. No doubt he waxed lyrical to Henry about the plans in the pipeline and the prospect of change further down the line. But Henry, while pleased to learn that a more sensible season structure could be in the offing, had already taken matters into his own hands by awarding his top 22 the off-season they were after. His players were not going to be affected by burn-out. They would not turn up in France virtually dead on their feet with almost nothing left. The game was killing the English and taking big chunks out of everyone else. Henry was vaccinating his side against the various diseases that could be caught by playing too much rugby, and by the end of November 2006, every rugby follower on the planet could see exactly what rude health the All Blacks were in.

15　The last crusade

IF THERE was lingering discontent pervading New Zealand rugby circles during the Tri Nations, it evaporated on 11 November 2006. That was the day even the staunchest critics of Graham Henry had to concede he was on to something. In May 2005 Steve Hansen first mooted the idea of resting senior players. Neither the public nor the players thought it a great idea. When Henry persevered and continued to talk of the need for depth and player preservation on the Grand Slam tour, still the public seemed lukewarm at best. When every campaign in 2006 had development as the core theme, clearly a lot of honest rugby folk started to lose interest. The sluggish and in some instances poor ticket sales and reduced broadcast figures were evidence of the fatigue being felt by some weary souls. Henry's rotation policy was fingered as an accelerator of that fatigue. The expanded Super Rugby and Tri Nations formats were a chore to get through, and the latter was certainly not helped by the continued selection experimentation.

But on 11 November at the Stade de Gerland in Lyon, all that changed. That was where the All Blacks delivered the definitive performance not only of 2006 but of the Henry era. That's when the strategy of the last 18 months finally made sense. Against the same opponents two years previously, the All Blacks had been clinical and ruthless in hammering France 45-6 in Paris. It was hard to imagine how they could ever top that.

Since that game in 2004 the French had waited patiently for revenge. They had been psychologically damaged by the power and pace of the All Blacks, and the final score was too much to bear. Slowly they had exorcised the demons of that night and regained their poise and panache. They returned somewhere close to their best by the end of 2005, won the Six Nations in 2006 and then shortly after achieved a rare victory against South Africa in Cape Town. By November 2006, the French were the number two-ranked side in the world, and the build-up to the first test in Lyon crackled with anticipation. It was going to be tight, no-nonsense, old-fashioned test football, where a bit of claret would be spilled in the forwards and some champagne cracked open by the backs.

The pre-match forecasts were hopelessly wrong. The All Blacks produced a performance even more compelling than the one in Paris. Sitiveni Sivivatu scored down his left flank within four minutes and set the tone. It was one of those rare nights when passes stuck, kicks bounced the right way and pretty much everything went in favour of the All Blacks. The lineout, a shambles for much of the Tri Nations, was suddenly running as smoothly as a German-engineered car. The transformation was astonishing. The lineout had in fact become a national obsession for much of 2006. Everyone had a theory why the All Blacks were frequently losing their own ball and why, when they did get their hands on it, the quality was not as high as it should have been. The All Black coaching panel also got hung up about it. Before the third Bledisloe Cup test, former All Black lock Robin Brooke was called in to work with the forwards. There were moderate improvements at Eden Park after Brooke's crisis session, but they quickly disappeared in South Africa.

There were plenty of former players who used their newspaper columns or TV shows to suggest that a specialist coach was required, but Henry insisted they already had a lineout specialist – a bloke called Steve Hansen. That bloke spent most of September and October analysing videos, taking advice and working his own thoughts to establish a panacea for the lineout ills. It actually turned out that the ailment was fairly straightforward to cure.

The whole process needed to be speeded up and simplified. For some reason New Zealand rugby teams at all age-groups and levels had got into the bad habit of taking forever to get the ball from the touchline back into play. As a general rule, the pre-throw routine was too fussy and the deception overdone and elaborate. Hansen wanted his players to break the habit of a lifetime and make the call quickly, reduce the amount of deception by the jumpers and get the ball in earlier, with a flat, hard throw as the preference. A subtle readjustment of the hooker's body position also helped the jumpers to read the throw more easily.

It was that simple. That's all it took to get the lineout back on track, and with the ball secure on the touchline in Lyon the All Blacks eradicated the one hope the French had. France felt they had an opportunity to exploit the All Blacks aerially. It was, they hoped, the one weakness they could chip away at and subdue their opponent. Except it wasn't a weakness in Lyon at all, and when it was supported by a brutal scrum and a defensive effort that was one of the best ever seen, the French became obviously distressed.

The All Blacks nailed their set-piece work. They were phenomenal at the breakdown in decision-making, technique and application. Their attitude and organisation defensively was supreme and with ball in hand they were accurate and the ball-carrier brilliantly supported with runners on both sides. French captain Fabien Pelous, unbelievably, reckoned the final score of 47-3 could have been a lot worse. What an irony – a test played on Armistice Day and the French had to face Blitzkrieg rugby. It was a performance in line with the brief Henry set himself when he first came into the job. And perhaps most important, it was achieved by a side that showed eight changes from the one that had inflicted a record home defeat on England six days earlier.

Henry had moved a big step closer to the impossible dream of having an entirely interchangeable test side where it wasn't possible to discern any drop in quality. In Lyon, Ali Williams and James Ryan started at lock in place of Chris Jack and Keith Robinson, who got the nod at Twickenham. Ryan, in his first test for a year, handled his workload in the tight and roamed the paddock with an aggressive disposition befitting a man with a coppertop. Williams, so prone to moments of madness, was supreme in every department. In the midfield, Luke McAlister and Conrad Smith took over from Aaron Mauger and Ma'a Nonu. McAlister was so assured and played with so much confidence and vision that former All Black captain Sean Fitzpatrick rated him the best second-five in the world by the end of the tour. Smith, who like Ryan was playing his first test of the year, was his usual mix of intelligent offloads and sweeping defence. Anton Oliver had come in at hooker in place of Keven Mealamu, and his notoriously suspect darts flew true all night, while his presence was duly noted elsewhere in the loose.

It just didn't seem to matter who played now. At Twickenham the All Blacks had been a bit shaky on defence and had not played to their best. On occasions during the game they had raised their standards, but only ever in short bursts. But that was still enough to run England ragged and leave them gasping for breath at 42-21. The beauty of having so much depth was that the All Blacks could weather a six-day turnaround – the game against England had been on Sunday 5 November – make eight changes and still spank the French by an obscene margin.

A week later, four personnel changes and a positional change were made for the second test in Paris. Back came Nonu for McAlister, Mils Muliaina switched from fullback to centre to allow Leon MacDonald to wear No 15, Jack came in for Ryan and Mealamu replaced Oliver. The French raised their game, or at least improved their defence, and the All Black winning margin was cut to 23-11.

The final test of the year in Cardiff was for some inexplicable reason suddenly billed as the biggest challenge of the four-test tour. It was maybe because the French had failed to fire anything and had looked to be impostors in the IRB world rankings. Probably Wales's victories against the Pacific Islanders and Canada and their draw with Australia helped raise expectation too. Whatever reason they were being hyped, it began to look very flimsy even before half-time. The All Blacks barely needed 40 minutes to kill the game. Neemia Tialata made his first start on tour at loose-head, Oliver was back at hooker, Robinson and Williams locked the scrum with McAlister and Smith reunited in the midfield and Rico Gear restored to the right wing. There were six personnel changes and a positional switch from Paris, and Wales were stuffed 45-10.

In four games the All Blacks scored 157 points and conceded just 45. They were unquestionably the best side in the world by the sort of margin that had bookmakers wondering whether they should stop taking World Cup bets 10 months out from the competition. Even allowing for New Zealand's propensity to self-destruct at World Cups, by the end of November they were red-hot favourites finally to deliver for the first time in 20 years. They were red-hot favourites not just because in four consecutive weeks they had swallowed whole three of the best the northern hemisphere could muster. Watching All Black sides romp through Europe was nothing new. They had been there and done that, and proven success on these end-of-year soirées was no guarantee that possession of the William Webb Ellis trophy would follow.

But this was different. This was total rugby. There were no cracks for opponents to peer through and find a weak underbelly hidden by dazzling but ultimately flawed football. The psyche was no longer frail. There were leaders in various jerseys now who had been around for long enough to know how to handle themselves on pressure occasions. Of the 32 men who travelled to Europe in November 2006, 14 had been in Mitchell's World Cup squad. There was an experienced core that had the skills and ability to make accurate decisions under pressure in a manner few All Black teams of the professional age ever had.

There was now also an unprecedented strength in depth. In previous eras some All Black teams had an embarrassment of riches in certain positions. Never, though, had there been a 32-man squad of this calibre. There were three world-class props in Hayman, Woodcok and Tialata, with able deputies in John Afoa and Clarke Dermody. There was of course also Greg Somerville, a versatile prop with 50 caps to his name recuperating in New Zealand. Mealamu and Oliver were interchangeable at hooker depending on the opponents, and Andrew Hore was seriously unlucky not to be selected more. Lock was just stupid. In 2004 the All Blacks had to coax Norm Maxwell into one last tour of duty because they really didn't have anyone else. In 2006 they had Williams, Jack and Robinson, who had made a fairy-tale return after two years out with a serious back injury. All three would come close to making any side in the world. Ryan and Eaton were only marginally behind, with Troy Flavell and Greg Rawlinson, who both played against Ireland, standing by as highly capable replacements.

There was the usual log-jam of loose forwards. Sione Lauaki, Marty Holah, Jono Gibbes, Craig Newby and Mose Tuilai'i had all been capped in 2005 or 2006 but couldn't win a place on the tour. Byron Kelleher had Andy Ellis and Piri Weepu pushing him for the No 9 jersey, and McAlister and Mauger were class acts at second-five. Smith and Muliaina were options at centre, with Muliaina and MacDonald highly capable fullbacks, and no one would really mind who out of Sivivatu, Joe Rokocoko and Gear started on the wings.

The rest of the world was distraught. The All Black selectors could shut their eyes and stick a pin in the squad list to come up with a starting fifteen. They'd probably not want to be so blasé about openside flanker and first-five, where McCaw and Carter still reigned supreme. McCaw finished the year winning every major individual award going, and Carter was being talked about as possibly the greatest ever All Black first-five. On the few occasions McCaw had been rested or injured, Chris Masoe had made an admirable fist of replacing him. Masoe was powerful, rugged and one of those players you simply wound up and set free. Henry reckoned the Hurricanes dynamo was the most underrated player in New Zealand.

Carter, though, had been a thornier problem. McAlister had stepped in against the Irish. He went okay, but as his performances in November confirmed, he was a natural No 12. And that's why a 10-minute cameo appearance by Nick Evans in Cardiff kept rugby's aspirant nations in a fit of depression. Carter had been majestic in London. His timing and control in both Lyon and Paris were exquisite. Then for 70 minutes he boomed the ball all over Cardiff and looked as if he had an age whenever he was in possession. When he left the field, the Welsh thought they could at last get some respite and that the edge would come off the All Black offensive machine. With his first touch Evans scorched through a gap, accelerated past the cover and turned the ball inside to Sivivatu for a dramatic score. It sent the message that even if Carter broke his leg at the World Cup, the All Blacks could take it in their stride. Less than one year out from the tournament, the All Blacks were exactly where Henry wanted them to be. And that was hugely pleasing because they had not arrived there by chance. It was all down to meticulous planning.

It was November 2005 and already the All Black management team had the 2006 season mapped out. In fact, as Henry sat in the lobby of the Royal Kensington Hotel in London on 16 November 2005, he revealed he also knew how he wanted to handle the 2007 season. In the history of All Black rugby, no coach had ever been thinking that far ahead. In the modern era every coach had been working from campaign to campaign, or at best looking no further ahead than 12 months. That was how it had to be when coaches were on two-year contracts and judged almost exclusively on results.

But Henry had been granted a far longer leash, and with the board supporting his strategy he was able to plot an altogether different route from those who had gone before. The end-of-year tour in 2005 had been the birthplace of full-scale rotation and the plan was to maintain that theme right through to November 2006. Every campaign in that period would have the underlying objectives of developing two teams and maintaining the welfare of the players. Obviously, top of the agenda was winning tests within that framework. With those goals in mind, Henry wanted to work with extended squads and use the full depth of each. He took 35 players to the UK in 2005, and 39 players were selected for the tests against Ireland and Argentina in June 2006 before the squad was trimmed to 30 for the Tri Nations.

But the focus would be dramatically different for the end-of-year tour in

2006 and through to the World Cup. That's when the selection net would start to close. The trip to Europe would be treated as a pseudo-World Cup. The World Cup was going to be played in France and as fate would have it, the All Blacks were scheduled to play France twice in November 2006. They were also going to play Wales, which was a little serendipitous too, because if the All Blacks topped their pool at the World Cup, they would have to play a quarter-final in Cardiff. The itinerary was tailor-made to serve as a road test for the World Cup.

From a logistical point of view, they would have an opportunity to stay in the same hotels as they would 10 months later and to use the same training venues. Travel arrangements could be sussed out, which was a far bigger deal than may be realised. In 2005 the All Blacks stayed at the Royal Kensington Hotel for the full week in London. The journey from central London on match day took more than an hour, even with a police escort, and half the team fell asleep on the bus. It was far from ideal for elite athletes to be dozing so close to kick-off, so in 2006 the team decamped to Richmond – a suburb on Twickenham's doorstep – on the Thursday. Identifying similar potential problems in France would be crucial ahead of the World Cup. The familiarity would also help the players settle quickly when they arrived in France in 2007. From a playing point of view, there was a golden opportunity to treat the three tests as if they were the quarter-final, semi-final and final of the World Cup. That would mean wiping out the development theme and being more ruthless in selection.

With only 30 players allowed at the World Cup, that would have to be the number taken on the end-of-season tour in 2006. The objective would be to win each test with the best team. There would have to be consistency in selection. As Henry said in London in 2005: 'We sat down about six months ago and planned out the next two and a half years. We prioritised the campaigns and tours we were involved in and have set targets for each one of those. One of the targets for this trip was to develop two teams across the pitch and I think we are achieving that. As we get closer to the World Cup, we will reduce the numbers [in the squad]. We will use the end-of-season tour in 2006 as a prelude to the World Cup and try and simulate what we are going to do at World Cup. Hopefully we will stay in the same places and use the same facilities as we will for World Cup. We will continue to try and develop New Zealand rugby. But we will only take 30 next year and you'd hope that all those 30 will have a major influence on how we play and get plenty of game-time.'

The outstanding rugby witnessed on that end-of-season tour was exactly how Henry had envisaged his master plan unfolding. He'd kept the players fresh and hungry for more game-time. And just as frustration was possibly creeping into the squad about the constant selection changes, he flicked the switch and made everyone fight for their place. The genius of the plan was there was so much competition for places that everyone knew they had to nail the definitive performance when they got the chance. For the first time in 12 months the players knew that if they delivered they were likely to retain the jersey next week. Unlike the Grand Slam tour or the Tri Nations, there would not be wholesale changes regardless of performance and result. It got the best out of virtually the entire tour party, and that was exactly what the last 12 months had been about.

Henry had built his options and was now going to be selective about using them. There had to be a slight planning adjustment a few months before the tour when the game against England was confirmed. That had not been on the agenda during the initial planning, so Henry adapted by asking the NZRU to sanction an increase in the tour party from 30 to 32. He wanted another hooker and halfback to prevent players from backing up on a six-day turnaround. The extra players diluted the intensity of the trip and the idea it was a mini World Cup. But the big picture in regard to selection remained unchanged – the focus would now be on picking the best 22.

There was maybe some confusion as to what that actually meant. Many of the traditionalists interpreted the policy as meaning Henry was going to unveil what he considered his best fifteen and select it all four weeks. That clearly missed the point the All Black coaches had been making for the last two years – that the athleticism and physicality of the game was so intense that players just couldn't handle so many consecutive tests. 'I think we proved during the Lions series that guys playing three on the trot is almost impossible,' said Henry in November 2005. 'The ideal situation is not to play anybody in more than two tests in a row.'

So the concept of the best 22 had to fit around the demands of the sport. That's why Henry had wanted 30 genuine test players – so he could select not only according to who was in form, but also according to how physically and mentally fresh each individual was. If Mauger was struggling with an injury, then the No 12 jersey would go to McAlister who was just as capable. If Joe Rokocoko lost a yard of sharpness, no problem – in would come Gear and there would be no loss of momentum or firepower. There were five locks all playing out of their skin and bursting to prove their passion and aptitude. It was a scenario every international coach dreamed of. The new selection policy was more about tinkering. It was about using the depth wisely to supplement and support a core group who had established themselves as the best in their positions. There was maybe even a core within the core, as Hayman, McCaw and Carter were deemed indispensable.

Despite all Henry's concerns about asking players to front on more than two weeks consecutively, those three started all four tests. Carter was not initially selected to play England but had to when Evans pulled his hamstring, while Hayman was relieved midway through the second half at Twickenham and again didn't quite complete full shifts in either Lyon or Paris. McCaw, as captain, wanted to play – always. On the Monday before the final test in Cardiff, Henry approached all three to enquire if they were ready for a fourth start. Their emphatic yes convinced him that some individuals were capable of handling such a demanding workload.

Essentially, then, Hayman, McCaw and Carter were the rocks around which Henry juggled his team. Tony Woodcock made three starts at loosehead and the back row of Collins, McCaw and So'oialo was recognised as the best combination. Kelleher and Carter were the first-choice inside pairing. Those guys were the non-negotiables, and filling the holes came down to judgement calls dependent on form, fitness and opposition. If the All Blacks were playing a big scrummaging side, maybe Oliver would start ahead of Mealamu at hooker. Williams, Jack and Robinson were the first three locks in contention, with the final combination again dependent on variable factors. Gear, Sivivatu and Rokocoko were almost impossible to separate and Muliaina was the best fullback in the squad.

Where things were a little confused was in the midfield, as Muliaina was probably also the best centre. If he played at 13, that meant using MacDonald at 15, with Mauger, McAlister and Nonu all options at 12. Or Smith could start at 13, but there were concerns in pairing him with Mauger as that might create the impression of defensive frailty. The point was there were options galore and the selectors could mix and match to suit their thinking.

This wasn't quite the vision held by the traditionalists. They were expecting something far more prosaic – for the cap to be doffed to tradition and for a best team to be identified and stuck with. It couldn't be like that, though. That would suggest all the previous talk about the importance of player welfare had been empty. There were two tests against France and one against Canada to get through before the World Cup, as well as a reduced Tri Nations (it would, as a one-off, revert to the original home-and-away formula in 2007), with another seven tests to be won once they got there. There was no way any player could get through all those games and still be in prime shape by the final stages of the World Cup.

Henry and his coaching team had planned meticulously to get to the end of 2006 with a barrage of options at their disposal. Then they would place the emphasis on building combinations and honing the individual and collective skills. The goal was to keep improving the performances and keep delivering results between the end-of-year tour in 2006 and the World Cup. That would require a far greater degree of selection consistency than had previously been seen. The core group of Hayman, Mealamu, Oliver, Woodcock, Williams, Jack, Robinson, Collins, McCaw, So'oialo, Kelleher, Carter, Sivivatu, Rokocoko, Gear, Mauger, McAlister, Smith, Nonu, Muliaina and MacDonald were going to be heavily involved. The starting fifteen would most likely be drawn from those 21 players for most tests. Occasionally the likes of Masoe, Tialata, Hore, Weepu, Evans, Ryan and Thorne would appear in the team or on the bench. Changes from test to test were now going to be minimal rather than wholesale. And that had the rest of the world scared.

The All Blacks returned from Europe adamant they still had room to make significant improvements. Most pundits agreed. They could see the All Blacks had only just embarked on the final phase of their plan. There was still time for the All Blacks to really build their unit skills. They were already working well collectively, but how good would they be when the various combinations were granted extended periods together? The bookmakers had bought into Henry's grand plan and priced the All Blacks at $1.55 to win, which reflected their confidence that Henry's team would be so far ahead of the chasing pack that the biggest danger to their mission would be themselves. No one in New Zealand needed reminding that the All Blacks had been their own worst enemy at recent World Cups, and it was a thought Henry himself kept coming back to.

Henry had taken control of the physical workloads of his players. Physical burn-out was an unlikely enemy. The majority of those players who made the All

Black World Cup squad were going to have enjoyed an extended conditioning programme. That programme was designed to return each individual to active service infinitely more prepared to handle the season ahead than if they had been rushed back into Super 14 on the first weekend of February. The coaching panel had intervened to ensure the bulk of their key players were going to be in supreme physical condition by early September.

When the protected 22 returned to Super 14 there would still be a minimum of six rounds left. There would be one weekend free after the final, then five consecutive tests: against France twice, Canada, South Africa and Australia. After another week off, the return tests against South Africa and Australia would take place on consecutive weekends. There would then be a month left to the World Cup kick-off – a month that would be used to build a greater understanding of the game-plan, unit skills and individual levels of fitness.

Every coach in world rugby was burning with envy at the preparation road the All Blacks would be travelling. Once the 22 players returned at the end of March they would be playing big games throughout April, most of May, June and July. Henry was assuming the majority of the protected 22 would play at least six Super 14 games and then some role in the seven tests. That would be plenty of football to have them match-sharp and operating at the peak of their craft.

Looking back to 2003, it was apparent the All Blacks had peaked in July and August. The players had started Super 12 in late February that year, which meant that five months into their season was when the majority of individuals felt they had the balance right. That was when match sharpness and physical fitness were at the respective highest points of the graph. By October that year it was obvious the match sharpness had remained but the physical fitness had declined. The two were no longer in alignment, with the long hard toll of the season having dug into the legs and lungs.

In 2007 it would be very different. When the World Cup kicked off on 7 September most of the All Black squad would only have five months rugby in their system. They would, so the coaches had planned, arrive with their match sharpness and physical fitness in perfect alignment and peak throughout September and October. With the selection policy focused on form and results, those fringe players who had got through a full Super 14 shift were going to see reduced active service in the All Black jersey. That would allow those players who missed out on the conditioning window time to supplement their sharpness with some athletic work after the Super 14 ended. If there was one concern in the planning, it was the month-long gap between the end of the Tri Nations and the start of the World Cup. That would put pressure on the All Blacks' match sharpness for their opening game against Italy in Marseilles on 8 September. But again, this was something that had been considered and researched.

Henry and his coaching team reckoned it took about one game for the best players to work off their rustiness after they returned from some time out. It was a conclusion they reached after monitoring the form of all the All Blacks who had been involved in the 2006 Tri Nations. When the squad returned from South Africa, all 30 players were granted a minimum of two weeks off, with Carter allowed three and McCaw, who had taken some serious physical punishment throughout the competition, told to take an entire month off before returning to provincial colours. The coaches reckoned most players were a bit off the pace in their first game back but didn't see any sloppiness emerge the following week. In that month before the World Cup it would be possible to play live training games that carried a serious intensity, and there would also be opportunities to play training matches against invitational sides behind closed doors as Henry had done before the end-of-season tours in both 2005 and 2006.

Physical preparation was not going to be a problem nor were the logistics. The NZRU had set up a dedicated World Cup team in 2005 to map out every detail of the campaign. Everything that could be done to ease the path of the All Blacks would be done. Travel and accommodation would not become issues. All Black manager Darren Shand would see to that. The 2006 tour had helped settle any debate about hotels, training grounds and transport modes.

Shand had also been instrumental in evaluating the team culture and the role of the leadership group before departing for Europe in 2006. Every aspect of the All Black set-up had to be challenged to ensure the wheels would not come flying off as momentum built towards September 2007. 'It is easy for the All Black management team,' said Shand on the eve of the All Blacks' departure to London in 2006. 'We just do our campaigns, but these other guys are exposed to the same sort of stuff in other campaigns. We have got to keep it fresh and interesting. It can quickly go stale. Whether management intervenes is something we constantly assess. Sometimes it might sway more on the management side. We might say we are going to take a more demanding approach here or we might say it is time for you guys to drive the ship now. In the next 12 months the bulk of these players will only be in the All Blacks with seven or eight weeks in Super 14. It is really important that we lay a platform now that will see us through the next 12 months and that we establish expectations with a framework that we know we can use right through that period.'

Every stone had been lifted, checked, put back and checked again, yet Henry still felt uneasy. He was concerned about how some of the players would handle the mental toll of being away from home for such a long period. If the All Blacks were going to win the World Cup, they would be away from home for 53 days. That was plenty of time to get homesick in a country where few All Blacks understood the language. The desire to build better people and broaden the horizons of each individual had been a goal since 2004 and the creation of the leadership group. Progress had been made. But maybe not enough to satisfy Henry, who still felt that while on tour the players could do more to distract themselves from the mental grind of training and playing. 'The mental and emotional toll big test matches have on players is quite significant, just as significant as the physical. I think that is one of our biggest challenges,' he said in November 2006. 'It is not so significant when we are at home because players have got other interests. They might be married, have family and obviously they have got things they do outside of rugby. Richie McCaw and Anton Oliver both fly, for example. People have got interests they have at home but they can't do overseas. We are away for 34 days at the end-of-year tour and 53 days at the World Cup, with language problems on top of that. They are the challenges for the All Blacks over the next 12 months.

'It is something we have got to address as a group and as individuals. You don't often get opportunities to tour like you used to. When Brian Lochore was an All Black in the 1970s, they used to go away for a 20-match tour and they got used to touring. Because of the amateur days, there was a lot more social activity so it wasn't a be-all-and-end-all, although I think All Black teams were always pretty professional. We have to get the best out of ourselves on long tours. The individuals have got to take some responsibility for that. They can't be entertained, they have got to entertain themselves. There has to be a balance, but I think it is mainly individuals taking control of that balance.'

It was Henry's concern on that front which led to the All Blacks opting to use several bases during the World Cup. Some thought had been given to setting up camp in one venue and remaining there for the majority of the competition. But this plan was ultimately rejected, as there were fears the players would become easily bored as they supposedly had when they spent most of the 2003 World Cup in Melbourne.

These concerns also led to the All Blacks taking French lessons on their end-of-season tour. Learning the language would alleviate some of the stress and boredom of being away from home, and it would also have the welcome effect of endearing the All Blacks to the French. The All Blacks also played another smart PR card on their end-of-year tour. Through their relationship with adidas, an arrangement was made for the All Blacks to eat with the French soccer team before the latter's friendly match against Greece in Paris on 15 November. The entire All Black squad was photographed in the stands at the Parc des Princes wearing French jerseys. The Parisians loved it. And they loved it the following day when the All Blacks visited the famous French rugby club Stade Français and returned to their team bus resplendent in the Stade's famous pink shirts. These initiatives provided the players with positive memories that made touring the happy and enlivening experience it had been during the amateur era. They also saw the All Blacks capture the hearts of the French public – a point illustrated by the sporting reaction of the crowds in Lyon and Paris. If everything went to plan, the real strength of that bond between the All Blacks and the people of France was going to be tested. The World Cup draw was set up so that if everything went to form, the All Blacks would be back in Paris on 20 October for a World Cup showdown with Les Bleus.

16 Secret ingredients

IN HIS efforts to entice the Americans to enter the Second World War, British Prime Minister Winston Churchill ended one of his most passionate public broadcasts by saying: 'Give us the tools and we will finish the job.' The best war-time leader of the modern age had the strategies, the belief and sheer bloody-mindedness to carry his people through the most atrocious conflict. What he didn't have was the raw materials. Britain was outnumbered and outgunned.

The polar opposite has been true of New Zealand rugby in the professional age. Everything has been in place except the Churchillian personality. The raw materials have been of stunning quality. Travel across New Zealand on a Saturday morning and the talent on display is phenomenal. In every town and city there are hundreds, if not thousands of schoolboys with genuine hopes of becoming All Blacks. Every winter some of those hopes cease to be genuine. But for every kid who doesn't develop the way he once threatened to, there is another who surprises – who produces a previously unheralded skill-set that leaves his parents glowing with pride and his teachers dreaming that in the not too distant future they will have a live connection with the All Blacks. It's non-stop. New Zealand is a rugby talent factory with a production rate that no other country in the world gets remotely close to matching. Australia produces a good quota of brilliant individuals, as does France, and occasionally world-beaters pop up in South Africa, England, Ireland and even Scotland and Wales. Nowhere, though, produces so many players with an innate understanding of the game and the basic skills to execute any type of game-plan that takes a coach's fancy.

That's why the British Lions will always regard New Zealand as the ultimate challenge. When they were in New Zealand in 2005, it was apparent the touring side developed a sense of awe at the way every provincial team they encountered probably had the edge in basic skills. It didn't matter if it was Bay of Plenty, Taranaki, Wellington, Southland or the All Blacks – whatever the team all 15 players could pass off both hands. All 15 could tackle, run into space, work effectively at the breakdown and all 15 just seemed to know what to do and when to do it.

That situation has not come about by chance. It's the result of more than 100 years of devotion to the basics. It has happened because thousands of parents, teachers and coaches across New Zealand give up hours and hours of their time to teach every boy who picks up a ball how to pass and when to pass it. Perhaps some New Zealanders take that devotion to the next generation for granted. Surely the same scenario of young men being taught their craft is replicated across the globe? In most mature rugby countries it is. But what marks New Zealand out as different is the amount of intellectual capital in the system. The knowledge is carefully passed on so that each new generation is taught the game by people who know it inside out. Almost every schoolboy team will be coached by someone who has played a bit themselves. Players can go home and talk to a father who probably has some insight too. Then they can turn on the TV and learn even more by watching the very best. Knowledge of the game is everywhere, and that's why most players who make it to the professional ranks have an innate understanding of the sport.

It's from that incredible talent base that the All Blacks have created their dynasty. Graham Henry has worked with schoolboys, clubs, provinces, Super 12 and All Blacks, and knows just how much competitive advantage he has gained by sitting atop a finely tuned network that produces so many well-equipped individuals. Days before heading to Europe at the end of 2006 he said: 'I think there are a lot of people who are doing very well at working with young people to bring them through from talented athletes to talented rugby players. The challenge for a lot of these guys is to put the onus on themselves and have a lot of intrinsic motivation. But there is plenty of hard work being done to help these young people fulfil their potential.'

The efficiency of the rugby framework in spotting, then nurturing talent from grassroots to All Blacks has been a critical factor in Henry's success. Unlike other international coaches, he has not had to bang his head wondering how some individuals have managed to win tests caps without being able to beat a man or pass off their left hand. The system in New Zealand has all the cogs working together – something evidently not happening in the other main rugby centres. But New Zealand has not prospered on the strength of its development programmes alone. The raw ingredients being fed into the programmes are the best on the planet.

New Zealand's dominance of world rugby defies statistics. Here's this little outpost in the far-flung reaches of the Pacific Ocean with just four million people, trying to compete against European giants like England and France who have 15 times the population. South Africa has 35 million, Japan 123 million and even Australia has five times the population of New Zealand. Statistically, the All Blacks have no right to be sitting where they do.

But while New Zealand's population is comparatively small, it is rich in ethnic diversity. According to the latest census about 80 percent of the population is New Zealand European. Many of these people trace their heritage back to Great Britain, but every part of Europe has stuck a genetic flag in New Zealand. The gene pool is a crazy concoction from almost everywhere, and as a consequence New Zealand has access to some stunning athletes.

The critical edge, though, has not come from Europe. It has come from Polynesia, which has produced a disproportionate number of world-class players. New Zealand's multiculturalism is often cited, rather uncomfortably, as a critical disadvantage. Perceptions exist in rugby circles that players of Polynesian descent can often be brilliant, instinctive athletes but are incapable of implementing a predetermined game-plan and prone to melting down when put under pressure. The only part of that thinking which has been supported by research is that some Polynesians are genetically predisposed to building muscle mass around the key joints and are, therefore, naturally equipped to become elite players.

In the same manner that athletes of West African descent have come to dominate sprinting, athletes of Polynesian descent are starting to dominate rugby. A predisposition towards building explosive power is an ideal quality as rugby continues to become higher-impact and more confrontational. If an athlete has natural upper body strength and a powerful leg drive, he's going to be a useful asset in any back-row or midfield. There are plenty of players of European descent who are equipped with powerful physiques, but few have materialised into the same explosive package as the likes of Jerry Collins and Ma'a Nonu. Those two, as well as occasional All Blacks Sione Lauaki and Sam Tuitupou, are capable of breaking through the meanest defences in a manner that few, if any, players of European extraction have been able to. That ability to drive through tackles has become more and more valuable in modern rugby and goes some way to explaining why players of Polynesian descent are over-represented in New Zealand's elite rugby teams. It's a power game and there are significant numbers of Polynesians who are power athletes.

There is also a socio-economic element to be considered. When mass migration from the Pacific Islands into New Zealand first began in the 1950s and 1960s, rugby was an integration tool. It was a means of gaining acceptance and breaking through social barriers. Many of the Islanders who first came to New Zealand were employed in unskilled rural jobs or in 'dirty' manufacturing jobs. When the economy turned sour in the early 1970s and the infamous dawn raids began across Auckland to discover Pacific Island overstayers, rugby became one of the few ways in which Polynesians could establish their worth and sense of self.

The sport had been popular in the Islands for most of the twentieth century, and many of the Polynesians who came to New Zealand were able to make an immediate impact on the rugby field. The rugby club became a focal point for Island families and the sport is ingrained in the way of life of many Polynesian communities in New Zealand. That desire to express through rugby remains today and partly explains why so many Polynesians play with such unrestricted, intuitive creativity. It's as if the best Polynesians are guided by their hearts rather than their heads, which, when combined with natural strength and athleticism, can make a devastating combination.

Census figures indicate that about six percent of New Zealand's population is of Pacific Island extraction – principally Fijian, Tongan or Samoan. In 1999 there were six players of Pacific Island descent in the All Blacks' World Cup squad – Jonah Lomu, Tana Umaga, Alama Ieremia, Pita Alatini, Andrew Blowers and Dylan Mika. That figure equates to 20 percent of the squad. By 2003 that figure had increased to eight, with Keven Mealamu, Collins, Rodney So'oialo, Umaga, Nonu, Doug Howlett, Joe Rokocoko and Mils Muliaina. And by 2006 there were 10 players of Pacific Island origin in the 32-man squad that toured Europe at the end of 2006 – Neemia Tialata, John Afoa,

Mealamu, Collins, Chris Masoe, So'oialo, Nonu, Muliaina, Rokocoko and Sitiveni Sivivatu.

The figures for Auckland – the largest Polynesian city in the world – were just as skewed. In 2006 there were close to 22,000 registered players in Auckland. Almost 9000 of these were Polynesian, with about 8000 New Zealanders of European descent and the remainder coming from Asia and other groups. The Pacific Islands featured far more heavily than the six percent of the population they made up. The interesting breakdown within those numbers was that in the 0-12 age range, New Zealand Europeans were the dominant group. But in the 13-20 age range, the Pacific Islands were providing the most players, as they were in the 21-plus age range. And perhaps most interesting of all was that when premier rugby was broken down by ethnicity, there were more than 600 Polynesian players compared with about 200 New Zealand Europeans.

These numbers suggest the Polynesian dominance is only going to get greater. There are increasing numbers of powerful Polynesians who are natural athletes coming through the system. And presumably rugby is going to continue to become more explosive and high-impact.

But the dominance of Polynesian players is not without its problems. In 2004, research by the NZRU found that about half of the 8000 13-year-olds who were playing rugby that year would not be playing by the time they were 18. Part-time work commitments, fear of being injured and actually being injured were cited as the three main factors behind the drop-out. There was a suspicion in Auckland and to a lesser extent in Wellington, which also has a significant Pacific Island population, that the fear of being injured was a bigger factor than the kids dropping out were letting on. It was a suspicion fuelled by the obvious physical differences parents and teachers were witnessing as they stood on the touchline every Saturday.

There is indisputable evidence that Polynesians mature at an earlier age than other ethnic groups. It is not uncommon for leading rugby schools in Auckland to field a front row of 16-year-old Polynesian boys who are collectively heavier than the All Black front row. Faced with the prospect of playing against kids who could be anything up to 40 kg heavier, plenty of European players are choosing to go and do something else.

The high drop-out presents a double whammy: a number of players who could physically mature in their late teens are lost to the game, and high numbers of Polynesian players are able to star in schoolboy rugby without ever having to develop a full range of skills, as they are able to excel on size and athleticism alone. It is an issue that both the Auckland Rugby Union and NZRU are continually trying to address, to ensure that cultural diversity remains a strength. It has also been somethng that Henry and his coaching team have been acutely aware of. The likes of Collins and Nonu have been encouraged to use their power and athleticism, but much work has also been done on other aspects of their game. In 2004 Collins struggled to hold down a place in the All Blacks. The coaching panel felt he was one-dimensional in that he was always looking for confrontation. Time was spent adapting his approach, and by 2006 Collins was a bag of tricks. He could make the big hit, offload early or make the big hit and still offload. His vision improved, his decision-making improved and within two years he was a far more rounded player.

Nonu was labelled by Henry in 2005 as the best line-breaker in world rugby. It was a valid claim. But still, Nonu was only on the periphery of the squad as his game was bash, bash with no creative edge. He remains a work in progress, but every effort has been made to arm him with some softer skills.

Off the field, the All Blacks under Henry have never lost sight of their cultural diversity. Team manager Darren Shand said it was obvious when they were establishing the leadership group that the new team environment had to reflect the fact that almost half the squad were Polynesian or Maori. The environment had to be inclusive and embrace the different backgrounds. Some of the Polynesians in the squad were naturally shy and disinclined to lead. That shyness and natural humility are often mistakenly interpreted as an inability to lead. But there are plenty of superb Polynesian leaders, such as Umaga, Pat Lam and Michael Jones, to categorically smash any notion that there is a genetic impediment preventing Polynesian players from taking senior roles. The All Black panel felt that they couldn't impose a one-method-fits-all mentality. The players came from an array of cultural and socio-economic backgrounds and some would respond well to traditional methods and others wouldn't.

Significant time was spent by all the players getting to know more about European, Pacific Island and Maori cultures. A player like Ali Williams who had grown up in central Auckland, living with reasonably affluent British parents and attending the prestigious King's College, had an upbringing that was entirely alien to someone like Collins. Collins was born in Samoa, came to New Zealand when he was four and was raised by parents who struggled to make ends meet. Before gaining a professional contract, Collins had been a bin man. What made Williams tick was unlikely to work with Collins, so different management approaches had to be applied to get particular players to respond. It was a tricky line to tread, but given the way players such as Collins, So'oialo and Muliaina have grown in stature since 2004, Henry has ensured that the rest of the rugby world has felt the full might of New Zealand's ethnic diversity.

Having a great idea is one thing, but the trick is being able to get the great idea to the market. Arguably Henry's ability to keep harmony in his squad could sit as the greatest achievement of his reign. Probably every international coach in the last five years has sat back after a defeat, popped the cork off the claret and thought how different life would be if he could implement a rotation system that allowed him to rest his established players and blood new ones. Henry's thinking on that front has not been radical. What has been radical is that he's been supported by a visionary board that has been prepared to take short-term risks for long-term rewards. He's also been fortunate that New Zealand adopted a central contracting model that has allowed him to control his players in a manner that makes every past coach of England insanely jealous.

The Poms have been torn apart by a civil war between the Rugby Football Union and the clubs. The England coach can only dictate an arbitrary limit on how many games an individual can play in a season and then hope every club adheres to that limit. An absolute limit, though, is some way short of a working solution. Some players could manage 35 games a season, while others would probably be best not to play more than 15. With central contracts and the backing of the NZRU board, Henry has been able to tailor the workloads of his key players. His vision has not been revolutionary. What does mark him out as a leader of exceptional quality is the way he has implemented his ideas and managed to get the players to buy into them. Change in any regime is never easy to implement. It is especially difficult in institutions that have a proud heritage to maintain and enhance. What Henry proposed with his rotation and reconditioning policies went against everything that had gone before within the All Blacks. He was asking players to accept not playing. He was asking them to hand over their jerseys to the guy behind them in the queue and then cheer them on. He could prattle on about the long-term benefits to the individual and the team, but most of the players subscribed to the old adage of never giving a sucker an even break.

There was rejection of the policy at first. When it was put to Umaga that he and other senior pros take some time off during the 2005 Tri Nations, the players weren't having it. But Henry wasn't budging and by the end of that year the players had no choice – they either bought the strategy lock, stock and barrel or they didn't get picked.

It has been apparent that some players have accepted that stance on sufferance. Throughout 2006 there were some players who would draw a deep breath and sigh when asked how they felt about wholesale rotation. Answers were given along the lines of, 'it's not ideal but that's what the coaches want'. No doubt privately some players expressed their dislike in more direct language – language that became more colourful once details about the conditioning window in 2007 were released. While some players such as Reuben Thorne and Byron Kelleher, who had not had a decent break for years, loved the idea of getting through an extended training window, others were clearly nonplussed at the prospect. Crusaders coach Robbie Deans summed it up eloquently when he said: 'It will be intensely difficult for the players to watch their team-mates from the stands. I don't think you can underestimate the frustration the guys will feel at working so hard all week and then not playing at the end of it. But it is in the best interests of New Zealand rugby.' There were actions, too, that hinted at a frustration bubbling under the surface. In 2006 Collins played for his Wellington club side. Henry was hammering home the need to tailor workloads and here was Collins sneaking in a game with his club. Collins seemed to be reminding the All Black coaches that within every player there burned a passion for playing the game, not watching it.

A similar point was made again in August that year when the All Blacks had a two-week gap between Tri Nations games. When asked by the leadership group how they wanted to handle the mini-break, almost every player took the opportunity to state exactly how much he wanted to play for his province during that window rather than be given more time to rest. Again, it seemed the players wanted to get the message across that they were only buying into the big picture so far. They could see the benefits of rotation, resting and building gradually into the World Cup. But there was a break in the Tri Nations, and this was territory where the All Black panel didn't necessarily have jurisdiction.

And if there was a grey area, the players were going to make sure they took control of the outcome and got what they wanted – which was to play for their provinces. The relief that some players felt to be in an environment where they knew the best team would be picked each week was obvious.

But no matter how much frustration was bubbling under the surface, it never spilled over. Disharmony and rebellion never set in. That was partly because there were enough senior players in the squad who backed Henry's plan and made sure that others who had their doubts released their concerns in non-toxic ways. It was also partly because Henry was big enough to adapt his thinking. When he coached the Lions, disharmony was rife. Henry admits that back then he was too task-orientated. He needed to become more empathetic, more player-orientated. In his job-winning pitch to the NZRU he portrayed himself as older and wiser for all his various experiences. It wasn't an empty election pledge.

Initially he had wanted to remove 22 players from the whole of the 2007 Super 14. When too many investment partners baulked at the idea, he compromised. It proved to be a critical gesture. If he'd remained adamant that the players were to miss the whole competition, the NZRU would probably have lost the support of key sponsors, franchises and Sky TV. Without their support, the NZRU would have been forced to take an enormous financial risk in backing Henry, and might have felt it had no choice but to scrap the conditioning window altogether.

Compromise delivered a satisfactory result, as it did on the eve of the Tri Nations when there was some consternation among the players about the non-involvement of Thorne. The former skipper had been in belting form for the Crusaders, finding a dynamism and aggression that had previously escaped him. He was overlooked, though, for the first three tests of the year and was instead named as captain of the Junior All Blacks. Almost as soon as he was named, he withdrew from the squad, citing the need to rest having started all 15 games for the Crusaders. The situation created some intrigue as there had obviously been a breakdown in communication as Thorne would never have been named if the selectors knew he was going to make himself unavailable. The plot thickened a few days later when Thorne's wife, Kate, took the unusual step of phoning a talkback radio station to have a pop at the selectors. She insisted her husband had only received one cryptic voice message from Henry a few weeks earlier, and that being named in the Junior All Blacks was a major surprise.

Marty Holah, Jerome Kaino and Jerry Collins were all given stints on the blindside while Thorne rejuvenated his weary limbs. Collins was by some way the best No 6 in the country and was a certainty for the Tri Nations. Holah was a natural openside and the experiment of playing him at blindside in the first test against Ireland didn't quite work. Kaino, an athletic player from Auckland, didn't convince either in the second test. The All Blacks were still looking for a back-up blindside and Henry was thinking the versatile Troy Flavell could be the right man.

Assistant coach Steve Hansen had never hidden his desire to unearth a 1.95 m, 110 kg, rangy loose forward who could play both lock and blindside. Flavell at 1.98 m and 118 kg was the ideal specimen. Henry had gone the full nine yards to try to keep Flavell in New Zealand when he first came into the job. He was a big admirer of the raw athleticism and confrontational approach of Flavell, who returned to play for the Blues in February 2006. Flavell had played lock against Ireland, but switching to blindside was a possibility. Or it would have been if the leadership group hadn't made noises about Thorne. His peer group supported his selection, and on 27 June the 31-year-old was the shock inclusion in the 30-man Tri Nations squad. Compromise kept the harmony.

And that harmony is evident every time the All Blacks play. Performances are always the definitive proof of a squad's unity. If a team doesn't like the coach, they can survive for a period despite the man at the helm, but they can't sustain brilliance. If the players are divided by rifts they can't hide it on the field. At some stage an unhappy squad will be exposed, particularly on defence, which is entirely attitudinal. All players can learn the correct technique, but for a screen to be effective the tackles have to be made with conviction. The individuals have to believe in the collective cause if they are to put their bodies on the line. The All Blacks under Henry have had very few defensive lapses and their efforts in Lyon, Paris and Cardiff were about the best ever seen.

If there was no belief in the way Henry was running the show, the players would not have been smashing defenders the way they were. There was an intensity and speed in defence that screamed out just how much pride there was in the jersey. Tackles were made and the next instant the players were back on their feet ready to make another. There is no manual Henry can leave behind for his successor. He's had to judge the right method every step of the way. He's relied on intuition and experience to guide him through what was a potential minefield. He stepped on a few mines along the way but was smart enough to escape with everything intact. New Zealand rugby at last, for the first time in the professional era, had the Churchillian leader it craved.